ONE OCEAN TOUCHING

*Papers from the first Pacific Rim
Conference on Children's Literature*

edited by

SHEILA A. EGOFF

The Scarecrow Press, Inc.

Metuchen, N.J. & London

1979

The title of this volume is taken from a Pete Seeger song, One Ocean Touching.

Library of Congress Cataloging in Publication Data

Pacific Rim Conference on Children's Literature, 1st,
      University of British Columbia, 1976.
      One ocean touching.

      Includes index.
      1. Children's literature--Congresses. 2. Children's
literature, Canadian--Congresses. I. Egoff, Sheila A.
II. Title.
PN1009. A1P28   1976   028. 5   78-31308
ISBN 0-8108-1199-5

CONTENTS

Introduction (Sheila A. Egoff)

PART I: INTERNATIONAL

PART II: CANADIAN COMPOSITE

INTRODUCTION

The first Pacific Rim Conference on Children's Literature was held May 10-15, 1976, at the University of British Columbia under the auspices of its School of Librarianship. It was the largest international conference on children's literature ever held in Canada, presenting speakers from ten countries.

The child and the book--the main idea behind the Conference was as simple as that. Its framework was set up to offer the widest possible variety of speakers and topics within the constraints of time, money and geography. Time: a week. Money: reasonable but not extravagant. Geography: neatly but not exclusively the Pacific Rim. One could argue that Canada's Atlantic Coast is no more Pacific Rim than Great Britain, both of which were represented by speakers, but then what true lover of children's literature would worry about such minor anomalies? A second major purpose of the Conference was thus to share the likes and explore the differences among the countries represented and to provide an international setting for a discussion of Canadian successes and problems.

There was one more aim of the Conference, perhaps the most important. At first glance the world of children's books seems a vast field of purely individual endeavors. The authors, the artists, the editors, the publishers, the translators, the re-tellers, the parents, the librarians, the teachers--even those passionately dispassionate involved observers, the critics--all appear to be following separate and distinct paths. It is all too easy for us to look at only that rather narrow field in which we work on a daily basis. But second thought suggests that single-minded concentration is not enough. For all the specialist endeavors mean little unless they can come together--seamlessly, successfully--in that moment of fruition when somewhere, for some reason, some child sits down with a book. Our adult imagination has to cope with that extraordinary moment--to remember what it was like to turn to a book for the first time, and to come in contact with characters and situations that will remain constant and ever-living companions. As Roy Stokes, the Director of the School of Librarianship, said in his opening address: "All that we do, all that we say, all that we discuss throughout the Pacific Rim Conference is simply that we may better understand the child and the book and that relationship. And if each of us can think of children and books beyond our own country and our own language, then the situation becomes obviously both more complex and more exciting." It was to explore that complex relationship of child and book from every useful approach, it was to bring together all those "individual endeavors" of children's literature that the Conference set itself to accomplish.

Mr. Stokes's remarks recall two features of the Conference that cannot be fully reproduced in these papers but the influence of which is evident in almost every one. This was a conference on children's literature that featured children: in the most direct way, as virtually every speaker and many other special participants went out to talk to children and their parents in public and school libraries of the greater Vancouver area and to other parts of British Columbia. And in continually talking to and about children, and in having to discuss books in a more than local context, people who had been working in isolation found that they "were not alone." There was the release and relief of comradeship in shared struggles and problems.

Most of that emotion--the close relationship to children themselves, the enlargement of horizons--remains in these published papers because they were not submitted before the Conference and so were shaped by it. Indeed, some speakers changed their originally prepared addresses almost entirely; and all the papers were edited from the tape renditions rather than from the preprints. Individually, then, these addresses of the main speakers comprise a group of papers of notable value for their insights into the world of children and books. And these papers do not merely occur, they combine. They add up to a clear and consistent viewpoint although within varied themes.

The greatest unanimity is observable by default, as it were; strikingly absent is any attempt by anyone to define "children's literature." It was just assumed--and the calm assurance of the assumption is in itself striking--that children's literature, like any other kind of literature, was simply good writing. The difference between literature for children and that for adults was in the nature of the audience, not the character or quality of the material. Indeed the authors, some by implication and some quite bluntly, reject any notion that to write for children is any less an art or of lesser importance than to write for adults. "How can anyone," asked Edward Blishen, the noted author and critic, "who cares for literature, let alone anyone concerned in the creating of literature, regard any part of literature as of less importance than any other part?"

As a corollary to this approach, then, no one is particularly concerned with children's literature as a social or teaching vehicle. That there is a link between reading and social ills is movingly expressed by Carlota Carvallo de Núñez in speaking of children and books in South America: "How can you," she asks, "put a book into the hands of a child who is starving?" But note that Señora Carvallo de Núñez wants the amelioration of socio-economic conditions to assist children's literature, rather than have it go the other way round. At this Conference children's books are seen as important in themselves, not as a means of dealing with social problems.

If it is its special audience that gives children's literature its distinctive character, then it is no surprise that childhood itself is a continuing motif throughout these papers. Speaker after speaker emphasizes childhood, and particularly his or her own childhood, as a crucial state of mankind. There is not only excitement and joy in the contemplation of childhood but in the expression of it in writing for children. And, in the Pacific Rim at least, its practitioners do it mostly as a labor of love. In terms of financial rewards, writing and illustrating for the young is depicted by the Conference participants as a "cause," not a livelihood. Indeed children's literature itself is also seen as a cause by those who work on behalf of children and books, which in turn accounts for the strong sense of adult responsibility noticeable in these pages. There is no laissez-faire attitude. This viewpoint is strongly expressed by Margaret Johnston of the Toronto Public Library in speaking of picture-books as the beginning of literature and art:

> Children are not born with likes and dislikes, prejudices and enthusiasms, good taste or poor taste; these are critical developments which they acquire through experience. This experience is directly dependent upon their relations to adults and what is provided for them. These experiences can be deep

or shallow, broad or narrow according to the direction and the influence of the particular adult world.

Above all, these papers are packed with a sense of revelation and enlightenment. Here are enthusiasts who want to explain, inform, discuss a subject that is very near and dear to them. Whether they are Leon Garfield talking about himself or the educational psychologist Dr. David Bain analyzing the five stages of childhood, the keenness is evident. The survey papers--children's literature in various countries --are not written by ivory-tower people but by those who have been actively engaged in working with children and literature on a daily basis. They are thus able, in a frank way, to discuss failures as well as successes.

A word of special comment should be made regarding the Canada Day papers. These are not to be thought of as a nationalistic intrusion in an international conference. Rather they were to be seen as a kind of extended unit which would offer a comprehensive view of the state of children's literature in Canada within an international context. And it worked; Canada's achievements and problems were not only recognizable to people from other countries but appreciated by them.

In all this description of overall conference aims and themes, it must still be admitted that their ultimate import is individual. Each paper offered its own special and even idiosyncratic insights into the human condition as related to literature. And the effects of these papers will be just as individual, for no one can tell a reader what to think. As Ivan Southall reminds us, "we make our own reality out of things that only we can see, writer and reader together, though we may never have met face to face." Yet, believing in that traditional point of view which can never be abandoned, unless literature itself is to be abandoned, these papers show that children's literature is a part of the modern world and so a part of its delights, its potentials, as well as its problems.

Sheila A. Egoff,
Conference Co-ordinator
and Editor

viii

PART I

INTERNATIONAL

Chapter 1

TRANSTEMPORAL COMMUNICATION

by David A. Bain

> Alice was beginning to get very tired of
> sitting by her sister on the bank, and of
> having nothing to do; once or twice she
> had peeped into the book her sister was
> reading, but it had no pictures or con-
> versations in it, 'and what is the use of
> a book, ' thought Alice, 'without pictures
> or conversations?'

The world of a child is much like that of a book. Its
pictures are perceived through one's many senses. Its con-
versations are carried on through our five basic languages
of communication. It has a beginning, a part at which we
are currently reading, and an ending. We are able to use
our memory to recall what we have already read, and our
imaginations to anticipate what we still have to read.

We first hear the story within a book by having it
read to us within the warm intimate contact with a parent.
We all grow up within our many different environments but,
eventually, many of us take the time to tell or read our own
favorite stories to our own children.

Through books, we can span space and time. We
learn about the worlds and lives of other peoples and of our
own culture. We begin to see temporal patterns of events.
Sometimes, we are able to anticipate the futures likely to
happen to us, and make plans to alter such futures so that
the most preferable future will occur. But, let us begin at
the beginning, and perceive some of the many ways by which
a developing child senses his world:

In the morning of my time, before I was born, where was I?
Did an empty playground pause, between children, awaiting
     me?
Did my future brother push the empty carriage which would
     --oh so soon now--carry the intricate human form my
     parents would call their child?

I COME! and full of glee
and awe pursue, through many senses,
the universe aboue me; My eyes
and feet and fingers feel the multi-surfaces of things;
I walk on boulders that reflect the morning-shine of my
     existence,
on wood of ages past
now sharing with the barnacle shells
the sandy soil of eternal ocean-sides.

I open wide my eyes
to see
the light
and shadow
of
my world.

Wet motion comes
in waterfalls
and splashing waves
of inland seas;
and metal mermaid dipping finned feet in waterside.
The waves recede,
The sands are dry.
The sea discards,
and man
and bird;
And so does God. But what He scatters feeds upon the moist
     sea-sand--and grows!
I stand amazed at all the colours from this growth:
Green on green
White on green
Mauve on green
Red on green and grey;

Yellow on brown,
Yellow on green,
Red on green and brown.

I test the hardness of the chain that binds the ship to post;
A firm-clutched stick--the thud of boots on wooden walk.

I open now my ears and listen--
To cries of glaucous gulls
Screaming overhead
Or chuckling as they rest in upstream pattern--
Each one is alone as I.

I feel the softness of the snuffling rabbit;
It multiplies my senses.
Impish kids which pull upon my hair,
And jump upon my woollen sweater--
But how much better to feel the shaggy wool upon the ewe
    and lamb!--they smell of pungent lanolin
I catch, beside, the sharp sweet tang of new-sawn log,
And cedar sawdust strewn upon the ground,
Then husky scent of pfitzer juniper
and new-born buds of mountain pine warmed by sun's gentle
    rays.
Warm, also, am I amidst the woods where young trees grow
    from old; a faller's fire removes the traces of man's
    cutting.
I move aside. Its heat has made me shiver!
I look upon the ice which blocks my path.
I stamp! and feel the power of destruction which my feet
    can wreak upon this frosty masterpiece.
But ice is elsewhere too. In hoary rime, it coats a fallen
    giant,
Or trickles frigidly from rocky ledge. But frozen motion
    is not enough.
I must follow upon the trail of things that move
To and fro in harmony with heaven's heartbeat. In swinging,
    I discover up-ness
In planes that fly,
In steam that rises to the sky,
And moons that never fall.

I discover down-ness
In a robin, hunter-hungry, rustling through the leaves;
A preening mallard just beneath my toes,
And white ducks searching for their lunch below in murky
     waters;
A floral partnership of man and Nature;
A covert cove where sailing vessels wait the morning tide.
As I look down upon my world, I feel as huge as
Strutting turkey in the yard.
But then it's hard to understand, as I lean against a tower-
     ing wall,
Why some things are so large and I'm so small.

With nose and tongue, I sense the wealth of taste around,
     as chickens search the fertile soil for food,
As yearling chews upon the leaves of grass, through all my
     senses I ingest
The world, and find it good!

Ship ahoy! The solitary searcher seeks the new found land
     of friends.
I share with mother on a swing,
And with another's daughter on a teeter-totter.
Because of warmth of family all around, I dare to venture
     forth
To span the gulf from mine own immaturity.
I stretch my wings and go
Beyond the pond, that ripples in the light of day.
And I discover--art and imagery,
A sacred past in architecture
And shining totem of my heritage.
I venture forth through books which line my shelf
To discover times and people other than myself.
My pointing finger moves.
I take delight, in my imagination,
As I recall from all my senses
The basis for communication.

     There are at least a dozen of these senses by which
the young child develops a growing awareness of his world.
How he uses them forms the basis of a continuing two-way
communication.

The young batter tensed his muscles, face set,
teeth bared and cheeks taut. His bat rested on
his shoulder, then swung testingly forward and
backward. The pitcher scrawled designs in the
sand with the cleated toe of one boot. He glanced
at the catcher, grimaced, raised an eyebrow,
then apparently satisfied with the message he received, in turn, from the catcher's right hand,
spat in the soil, gyrated like an abruptly unwind-
ing spring, and hurled the ball unerringly at the
plate. A mighty swing. A resounding plop of
baseball in pitcher's glove. With studied indif-
ference, the umpire roared, "Strike one!" The
batter groaned in effort and dismay.

In this short description, we have examples of the five
basic languages by which we communicate with our world.

Physical Language

As children grow and develop their physical and
mental capabilities, they are acted upon by their world and
in turn impose an order upon their environments. Such an
order will vary from child to child and from culture to culture. Also, it will undergo change as the child grows up.
All children begin their development by exploring their
physical surroundings with mouth, fingers, body and feet.
They find that certain things happen to them, and that they,
in turn, are able to manipulate things to change their position and sometimes their form. They discover, moreover,
the natural order of events. Certain things seem to happen
at regular times.

All people need, and use, such ordered regularity as
a basis of security (a home base, a set of guidelines, social mores, traditions, call it what you will). Upon such
security, they build their own personalities, and form their
relationships with their environment. This security is a
mental, physical and emotional haven to which they can return should their voyaging upon the sea of life become too
rough. It can also be a set of references by which one can
ask, "How am I doing so far?"

Emotional Language

In every physical conversation with his world, a child tends to develop an emotional attitude which is either positive or negative. If the situation is uncomfortable or painful, then it is seen as negative. The child tends to avoid it in the future. If it brings happiness, satisfaction or comfort, then it is perceived as positive. The child tends to anticipate its recurrence with pleasure. From such positive and negative attitudes, the whole gamut of emotions, of which fear, anger and love are the extremes, emerges.

Gestural Language

From physical and emotional encounters with reality, the child learns to remember and to anticipate the future. He begins to coordinate past with present and future. There come times when he would like to try out physical events whose elements he may have experienced, but the unique combination of which he has conceived only in his imagination.

The game of "Let's Pretend" is a vital one to the growing child. It is the basis of all play, of testing the world of reality in imagination. He tries out events as-if-they-were-real. He struts, threatens, smiles, frowns, pounds imaginary enemies and dances with imaginary sweethearts. There are no real consequences to these gestural activities; therefore they can be tried out, safely, in one or several experimental versions. The world of play is truly a serious business of childhood!

Representational Language

If gestural language is an abstraction from the physical/emotional world of reality, then representational language is an abstraction from the rules by which physical and social relationships are governed. Usually we think of representational language as consisting of visual signs and symbols. It may be a circular drawing, or rolled lump of clay, which is meant as a human head. It may be a mathematical number, or directional arrow, or the particular size of a rug on the floor of an executive's office. Whatever it is, it stimulates some expected response in people. From early times of mankind, cave walls have been covered with drawings of animals and people. In modern times, the very form of an entire city may be a single representational symbol.

Verbal Language

The full impact of verbal language emerges rather late in a child's development. True, he enjoys being read to from about ten months of age on, but this is probably because he is listening to the emotional language, and sensing the physical presence of his parents far more than understanding what the words may convey.

He speaks words in short sentences from about age two on. But much of this is merely another tool by which he can manipulate those physical things in his world, which are such wonderful means of satisfying his own needs, namely, his friends and parents!

The use of words in true social communication to relate to others in a group, and to choose to abide by group rules, probably is in full swing following age six. The stories he chooses to have read to him prior to this age are largely imaginary gestural language--the "Let's Pretend" type, where animals and people interact as equals, and animals can carry on human language, too. Imaginary lands and fantastic situations create emotions of humour and awe.

Let me pause at this moment to share with you a summary of the world of senses and the five languages of communication:

There was a tension in the air which prickled his skin. The very atmosphere crackled with exciting things to come. Heavy clouds sat with their dark bottoms on a layer almost right above his head.

He bent down suddenly, feeling a rushing sound and a full feeling around his eyes and ears. His nose tickled as he brushed it against the kitten-soft blooms of some of the grasses. He pressed them against his cheek and purred with the silky smoothness of them.

He felt the hard bumpiness of the earth crunching

slightly as he put the top of his head on the ground and looked at the sky upside-down. He laughed as the clouds seemed now so far beneath him and he had the power to change his world so completely in reverse.

He became a steam-roller and, head-over-heels, tumbled down the hill, spinning his world around him. He became a giant now as he slowly rose to his feet and looked down upon the grass-trees from his immense height. One toe stretched forth heavily and crushed an apartment house. His other foot reached forward three miles to cross completely over a forest.

A butterfly-pterodactyl flew by. One mighty swing of his arm reduced this monster to helplessness. He turned around and around to survey all his kingdom. Turning faster and faster, he made his world start to dissolve in blurry circles about him. How strong he was! How big and powerful!

Boom! Rumble! Rumble! --distant thunder rolled across the hills and bounced around inside of him. "The hunters are coming. The hunters are coming!"

Stretching his arms skyward and flaring his fingers into stony antlers, he became a mighty stag striding forth to meet his pursuers. His walk became a lope, then a full bounding gallop as he became airborne, leaping mighty distances from one hillock to the next.

"Boom! Boom!" he re-echoed as the thunder rolled once more in the distance. In the close-ness of the air and the space around him, he re-membered the closeness of the other times when, "centuries" ago, he had snuggled soft, warm, and protected in the fold of his father. His father's voice boomed gently to him from the distance and he boomed back gently once more. He glanced around. His mighty leaps had carried him com-pletely around the world now.

"I am a mighty father deer," he felt within his breast and mind. "I can do anything."

Flash! Crash! --lightning split the air above
his head, under his feet, inside his mind!

His insides were filled with red fear, stretching
and stretching as he tried to move. The stag became a frightened little grey rabbit that skittered
and bounced across the prairies as he tried to
reach home before his hunters reached down to
destroy him.

Flash! Crash! --once again lightning split the
sky around him like a fiery angry mouth, and the
thunder roared at him as he fled.

Faster and faster he ran. The white house. The
shape of home. The green door. Opening. Open.
His mother. Then his mother's arms. His
mother's protection....

"Oh, Mommy! Mommy! I'm scared. God was
chasing me!"

Many times, for the pre-six child, the world of
imagination can suddenly turn into a place of reality and
terror. But the world of the post-six can now be increasingly controlled through verbal language. He does learn
the social rules; he sacrifices a bit of his feeling of omni-
potent control over his real and imaginary worlds in order
to gain greater security through the peer group protections.

Then, something almost magical happens to children
between the ages of eight and ten. They move from merely
having control and understanding of their physical world of
here and beyond here, to a transtemporal control and understanding of times from prehistoric past to far distant futures. With a control of physical events, fears of being
physically damaged by the real world diminish, but with
control over time, fears of being controlled forever by
forces outside oneself also begin to fade. One day, the
child awakes knowing that he has the power to control his
own future!

The development of a sense of time, in children, is
at least as important as their development of a cognition of
space. A very young child, like any young animal, lives
almost entirely in the world of the present. He experiences
it in many ways, experiments with its various aspects,

feels the imminent needs of his own body, and demands immediate satisfactions of those needs.

As he experiences regularity in his world, awarenesses perhaps that his needs are satisfied on a regular basis, he comes to anticipate their satisfactions when those first few pangs of need arise. He learns patience, and he learns that he has the power to go to the sources of satisfaction of his needs should they fail to come to him. Thus, his first temporal change away from the immediate present is actually toward the future. In his spoken language, he tends to develop the future tense long before the past tense. It is maybe two years later that he comes to his mother or father, and asks, "What was it like when you were young, Daddy?"

But for the first half dozen years of his life, the past and future are really only an extension of his own immediately sensed present. He can not really identify with the times of other people as they sense them. He asks about their past times, essentially as a means of comparing his own remembered earlier experiences.

However, about the equivalent of grade three, in elementary school, there comes that incredible temporal conservation period, when he is able to identify with other people's times, and with his own long-range future, and even with the heritage of his own people. Truly, we can call these early gropings for communicating with other times--TRANSTEMPORAL COMMUNICATION. When the young child is able to communicate only with the present time, he is immaturely dependent upon those adults around him who have a long-range future, and so can provide the necessities of life for him.

As he becomes aware of immediate past and short-range futures, he begins to gain control over his world of space and time. He finds it satisfying to share his control with others who can handle other aspects of this developing world, and who together can use a maturely dependent means of control and responsibility.

But when he achieves long-range or transtemporal conservation of past and future with present, then he is able to anticipate long-range outcomes of his present activities. He becomes able to choose from among his present efforts those which will bring both to himself and to others the

greatest satisfaction in the long run. He has reached a level of
independent responsibility where he may rely upon adults and
upon members of his peer group, but he no longer needs to.

Life, to many a young child and adolescent, is much
like a circle. The routines of the day roll around cease-
lessly. The major events of the year likewise are repeated
annually. One sees that the present, the past and the future
occur over and over again. Thus, there comes a great
deal of satisfaction in this routine ordering of time. The
youngster, now, need pay less attention to such routines,
knowing that they, like the warmth of the family, form a
haven to which he can return should life's experimentation
prove too threatening. It can be said that routinizing one's
habitual activities really releases the individual to become
freer and more creative.

There is a real need for us, as adults, to recognize
this developmental transtemporal process in children and to
provide the opportunities and the gradual release to our
children to grow up within their own time awareness. Thus,
we provide a transtemporal bridge between adult and child.

If a child has reached the level of recognizing and
using short-range time, then there should be opportunities
for him to carry out routine activities (to develop his sense
of circularity of time), but also to share with his friends
in planning, carrying out, and experiencing the mutual consequences of such shared activities.

And when he reaches the stage of temporal conservation, somewhere between ages 8 and 10, then he needs
time by himself to think, plan, work at solitary projects;
and to share with others those ideas, imaginings and results
which he has achieved.

Later, possibly in early adolescence, one's awareness of time takes a further jump. One becomes curious
about the future society into which one will later take an
adult position. The youth anticipates himself in a variety
of roles. He imagines the effect that he will have upon that
future world and, also, the effect that that world of time
and events will have upon him. A broader value system
begins to develop. Decisions, often shared with friends,
occur regarding the worth of that future world. Possibly
there is need to change that world, or possibly it is one's
own perspective that needs changing. Whatever--because

of his ability to cross large gaps of time, and because of
his ability to communicate with his world in his five basic
languages, the child or youth is well on his way to becoming a responsible adult citizen. In the meantime, he is
more capable of living as a mature child and youth.

In a way living is a little like investing in the stock
market of time: some of us bet all of our earnings upon
the past, confident that the wheel of time will return to
yesteryear once more; some plunge heavily on the present,
certain that only by experiencing "now" to the fullest they
are not bound by the traditions and morals of the past,
and that somehow the future will take care of itself; some
of us gamble only on the future, rejecting the social order
of the past, and tolerating less-than-optimum conditions
now, in order that our future, or possibly the future of our
children, will be the Golden Age of mankind. However,
from the little that I know of the stock market, I understand
that the wisest way to invest is to develop a portfolio, to
select a variety of options, and to choose what percentage
of our assets will go into each. So, possibly, it is with
life. We need to invest a little something in the past, in
the present, and in the future.

One vitally important aspect of transtemporal communication is to look across time in terms of decades or
even centuries. In North America, I have watched the
movement of events from the circular small communities of
the past where individuals grew up very dependent upon
their parents and upon other adults of the community. They
also learned quickly their roles as sharers in the tasks of
the community, and were seen as essential participants in
the annual cycle of events. From time to time, the more
independent of the youth would move away from the core of
the community to form the nucleus of a new community
where the circular time process was repeated.

However, when industrialization hit us in full force
at the turn of the 20th century, not merely the occasional
adventurous youth but entire families moved away from the
rural communities toward the bigger cities, where they
immediately took on an immaturely dependent role within
the factory system. Their awareness of the total community and the necessary role they were performing for that community ceased. Family breakdown, emotional breakdown, juvenile delinquency, moral breakdown and religious breakdown
occurred. It took a world war to unite many people

together once again in an expanded community, seeing their task as fighting against an external aggressor.

During the 1930s and '40s, an internal development occurred as people within their nations underwent the process of working together to build a new society for themselves, one which incorporated industrialism and the processing system as essential ways of living. A feeling of fraternity and mutual dependency arose and democracy reached its highest peak.

The 1940s brought the Second World War, and the United Nations organization. People here gained the feeling that the individual was important. And strong individuals arose. Small nations split away from old dependencies, and for their brief moments in history stood alone, proudly.

However, mighty international forces, many of which were destructive to man's independence and to ecological harmony, began to dominate the entire world. In the face of these forces, there was rebellion. The anti-institutional groups rose up to demand their continuing freedom and recognition of their rights, also. During the 1960s and '70s there were brief confrontations, and momentary recognition of race, color, sex, and even human age groups, as valuable. The multi-communication media had tremendous potential to help the world become a true global village. But most of these media agencies sold out to the very international agencies they were helping to hold in balance. There came the recognition by individuals (both persons and small countries) that their worth was not very highly esteemed by the powers which held them in growing immature dependency.

We have now reached that vital period in our global history when, possibly for the last time, we have the opportunity to communicate in a positive manner with all peoples. The communicators of radio and television are no longer believed by many of their audience. There is an accountability and a credibility gap which may never heal. The authors of literature for adults are writing for a generation that largely has become apathetic and feels powerless about changing its own destiny. It is the writers of children's literature who now have the potentially most powerful voice for the future.

Books by children's writers are being read by the

children of that generation of minority protestors. These young adults are the only generation in the entire history of mankind who have been pampered from birth. When they were little, there was still in sway the developmental psychology which held the importance of the young child, and of early childhood education. (Then we became aware of the skyrocketing population explosion.) As these children were growing up, there was welfare, with the movements for universal, and in most cases free, education and economic support for the children and young. (Now, we realize the escalating economic problems which so far have remained largely unsolved.) As youth and young adults, they entered "The Pepsi generation--for those who think Young." They entered the age of the pill, where they could easily avoid the responsibilities of embarking upon parenthood, and where the promise of the future lay in apparently eternal childhood. However, the energy sources which promised to provide the Golden Age of Materialism for them forever, are drying up.

In the 1930s, just as a similar but more limited period was under way, there arose a generation known as the Angry Young Men. The children of these young people whose thoughts, experiences, emotions, morals and motives over which writers have such a powerful influence, are well on their way to being either the most furious generation that ever lived, or the most terrified!

Children need to develop from an immaturely dependent control by a powerful, hopefully wise and far-seeing parent. So do nationalities, ethnic groups, races, and religions. Children need to join as equals in a fraternity of group sharing, planning, common activity and common pride in achievement. So do nations, ethnic groups, races and religions. Children need to become independent; to take responsibility for their own futures, and progress for the common good of the whole group. And so do nations, ethnic groups, races and religions.

Children need to have the freedom to explore all five languages of communication with their worlds of space and time. They need to have the freedom to select from such languages their own peculiar combination by which they can best communicate with their world. This right to do so needs to be respected. (Similarly, each one of us adults needs this same right to communicate through whatever combination of languages best suits us.)

For just as children develop from immaturity to mature responsibility, so they, by the time they reach adulthood, have had the experiences which help them to be wise in raising their own children. An immature adult can do nothing but raise immature children. An adult who has communicated fully with his world of space and time becomes an excellent model for his child to do likewise. If we can share in our time-space worlds physically, gesturally, emotionally, representationally, and verbally, in full understanding of and responsibility for the best possible futures for each one of us, and for all of our various religious, racial, ethnic, and national groups, then we will have taken a major step forward to a true brotherhood of mankind.

In closing, I challenge the writers, librarians, teachers, and parents of today's children to do the following:

Write and read literature that explores the world of space with all of the various senses which we possess, not merely the traditional five.

Select literature that utilizes all five basic languages of communication, and which teaches respect for others who communicate in combinations of languages which we may have not selected for ourselves.

Write and choose literature which is transtemporal. This is literature which is not merely for the moment, but which selects from the best of our various cultures, and through which we can come to understand the best in other people's heritages. It is literature which explores the different ways in which the people of the world handle their environments in the present. For too long we have maintained an ironic curtain between nations, which has said, "If it is not my way, then it must be inferior!" Transtemporal literature, especially, is that which helps children gain the understanding and the skills by which they can anticipate, select, and work toward the best of possible futures.

And finally, remember that there are human beings out there on the other end of that book, who hold the destiny of mankind in their hands and minds.

Chapter 2

ONE MAN'S AUSTRALIA

by Ivan Southall

"The general store was at the end of a long, long, long road. It wasn't really at the end of the road, although it was. And the road wasn't all that long either. It depends entirely upon your point of view; upon what the weather's like and how comfortable your boots are and whether you're riding a bike or flying an aeroplane or running away from a mad dog. On the window it said in fancy script: Home-Baked pies fresh daily. So Sam walked in. I mean, coming upon a sign like that away out here! It was like finding a fresh-water island in the middle of a salt-water sea.

"Inside it was a wonderful place, oh, a wonderful sight to behold; like an Eastern Bazaar where travelers on camels might step down to spend an hour, or explorers might buy supplies, or exotic people in exotic clothes might speak exotic languages around the door, or exotic creatures like Afghan hounds might lie and growl. Oh, to step inside and come upon it by surprise. Things must have been there undisturbed for years and years and years, as if arranged for a special occasion and no one had arrived. Nothing was meant to be disturbed; oh, nothing was ever meant to be sold. It would be awful for those things to be wrapped up and taken away, no matter how much money people left behind in exchange.

"Oh, what a place to find at the end of a long, long road. And oh, the smell of it: cinnamon and salt and bread and apples and vinegar and cedar and linseed oil and cloth and cane and flour and honey and clean back iron and, who knows, maybe even gold.

"Someone moved, but no one came.

18

"Life was there, but not to be seen. <u>Mysterious</u> life; you know? Like life underground or inside the kitchen wall or just over the edge of your midday dream. There were clankings as of weights going on to scales or coming off them, and rustlings as of brown paper bags being opened for things to go inside. There were scufflings and scrapings and shufflings and slappings as of butter being patted or sugar in packets being thumped down to make room for more. Or were they animals out of Beatrix Potter heard when you were very small? Animals living half-human lives? Oh, great imaginings.

"Who would come? Hey? If he dared to call?

"A Turk with a flat curved knife tucked in his cummerbund? An Indian in a turban? A Chinese in a dragon gown? A little old man with rimless glasses like Mr. Vale and white calico apron and stooped shoulders and droopy moustache stained yellow-brown from half a million cigarettes in fifty years? Who could say when you couldn't see? A little old lady with a sweet smile or a large middle-aged lady with a jolly bosom bounce, or a sinister kind of man with a big belly and a red neck and no hair? Or a Tibetan? Or a Russian? Or a Kurd? Oh, Sam had always longed to see a Kurd. (He should have been born one, I suppose.)

"He said. 'Is anyone there?'

"A head appeared around a tea-chest--like a Punch and Judy show on its side. Oh my goodness. Oh my goodness. It was a girl."[1]

One Man's Australia, my Australia, entirely mine, a world of images originating somewhere inside my heart and my head. Seen only by me, filtered out of a life's experience only by me. In reality none of it may exist at all, yet my Australia may well be the Australian that children reading in some distant part of the world may come to believe is the real Australia. Does one call that an honor or a responsibility or a terrifying thought indeed? Well, I guess one's reaction depends upon mood.

My Australia lies undiscovered and unexplored even by me, unless I catch a glimpse of some part of it I haven't seen before and can make enough sense of the

glimpse to turn it into words, and the sharing of it with
other people is able to begin. Seeing anything clearly
enough to make words of it: this I find to be the adventure
of the writer's life. The adventure when all goes well--
but the despair when nothing is there--because communicating is what my kind of writing is about. Once I can see,
I can communicate. Once I communicate, I can see more.
The chicken or the egg? I'm not sure.

I don't consider myself any longer to be a story-
teller as such. I did once, and made everything fit the
story I had in mind. One could call that a form of absolute control, and you can live with it until your patience
runs out. Mine ran out a number of years ago. Since
then I have found life to be more fascinating than story,
and character to be more engrossing than plot, although I
must say I greatly enjoyed the writing of the three adventure stories a decade or so ago that were to establish me
as a serious writer for children and I am not unaware of
the continuing readership they enjoy; but they are written,
they exist, they do not need to be written again.

All serious writers change, because to them the
work itself is more important than expectations imposed
from the outside by fashions of taste or literary criticism
or the readership one attracts. You cannot write the same
type of book over and over again if you are to grow as a
writer, any more than you should read the same type of
book over and over again if you are to grow as a reader.
Growth, I feel, is an obligation demanded of both of us--
writer and reader. This is not to deny the need of pauses
in our developments. Life is a climb, but it need not be
continuous.

I came to my Australia over a fairly long period.
It was a destination I arrived at although I didn't set out to
reach it. These things happen. Through the accident of
my profession, it has turned out to be an enchanted place.
Not necessarily for these people with whom I communicate,
but certainly for me. I now find I can make it real and
solid out of the flimsiest of vapors and can add to it or
draw from it just as I need, and I have a pile of books feet
thick to prove it, yet cannot issue to anyone else the passport
or the ticket to enter this country. Others may go along
on the journey once I have undertaken it, but no one can
get there before me, and no one can go without me. Have
you stopped to consider that this might bring pressures to

bear upon a writer, unexpected pressures? A point.
Twelve years ago I wrote a book about a bushfire, Ash
Road. I suppose this book has sold more copies than any
other I have written; possibly it has influenced more people
than any other I have written--in it I have projected my
Australia in its most terrifying aspect. From all over the
world people have written to me asking me about heat,
about fires, about survival, and the Education Departments
in two Australian States asked me to write a textbook on
the steps one should take for survival in the event of a
major bushfire--because, as they said, I had researched
the matter thoroughly to produce Ash Road.

Researched? To write Ash Road? This is the gulf
that exists between two minds, between two types of mind.
I have stood in the path of a great and horrifying conflagra-
tion but never seriously studied a word relating to that kind
of experience. So I wrote the textbook, of course. And
national fire authorities endorsed it with not a sentence
changed. So one need not necessarily produce an unreal
world out of abstracts. One does not necessarily mislead
people factually by giving shape to one's imaginings. The
creative writer can produce reality, a reality that stands
up and works in a real world, out of projections, out of
identifying with people or situations, out of imaginings. I
state this simply as a fact. It is not meant to impress
you.

This personal, one-man country--the rhyme and reason for so much of my life--is peopled largely by children,
particularly by children who are themselves beginning the
most exciting journey in the world, the journey into growing self-awareness and deepening self-discovery. Is there
a more breathtaking point of departure in all the drama and
panorama of life? And people ask me why I write for children when there is so much else in the world. One needs
to have forgotten a lot, I think, to be guilty of a question
of that kind. And one needs to be dead, I imagine, to have
the gift of seeing into the consciousness of children, and
the heart to feel the daily wonder of their emerging world,
and have no wish or compulsion to share the experience if
the capacity happens to be within you.

A person will take a journey on horseback into Central Asia and write a tale of the great adventure. Another
will ride Apollo to the moon and write of that. Another
will fight in the jungle and the laboratory to save a

threatened species and write stirringly. And all three are
heroes and in demand for Rotary dinners, Secondary School
speech nights, and lecture tours from here to Kingdom
Come. "What lives they live," people say, "what grand
adventures. How colorless are our own lives by compari-
son." Do you think so?

If one writes for children in the way that I do, it is
childhood itself that draws you in, not the lure of story or
a desire to beguile the adult librarian or critic. Once it
was the story that drew me in, as I have said, but not now.
Not for years past. My interest now is to explore what I
believe to be the most glorious and challenging of all human
adventures: Growing up. And indirectly this has led me on
to a further feeling--that the writer who writes for children
must himself go on growing up. Just as the person who
works successfully with children must go on growing up,
must go on living the process. On and on and on, always
growing up. Once you accept that you are a man or a
woman of adult estate and growing up at last is over--it is
over, the magic has gone. And I have come close to it, very
close to it, through the pressures of life, a few times. And people who have my interests as a writer genuinely at heart tell
me I have written enough for children, that I have said all
I should say to children, that I should begin now to write
my novels of adult experience because I appear to live a
life removed by cosmic distances from the lives I write
about. I think this happens to most serious writers for
children--people tell them they have outgrown their audience, as if writing for children were a stage or a phase or
a step.

Novels for children have origins and those origins
are in the minds of writers who are constantly being asked
to justify themselves, virtually to defend themselves, to
explain their creative processes in a way rarely expected
of others. I used to get very up-tight about it, and defen-
sive, but you grow through it and learn to shrug. "Why
do you write for children?" people say. "Don't rationalize,"
they say. "Honestly--why do you do it?"

These people are not inventions for the purpose of
this essay--like the anonymous bystanders who so often
confirm for the journalist his own view of an event. These
people are real, one or two of them excruciatingly so, and
there are times when the question gets under your skin.
Well, what about it? Why? Is there a committed writer

for children who has not asked the question very seriously
and profoundly of himself or of herself? Why? Why begin
at all? Why go on? As distinct from the reasons of now,
which are easy enough to find, because so much about writing real novels for children is its own reward, but then,
you know, back a bit in time, when decisions were to be
made as to which way one would go as a writer?

I have sometimes said in private, across dinner
tables, though never before in public, that traditional family
pressures, traditional family mores--and my background in
the puritanical Protestant ethic--virtually put the fear of
God into me and denied entry for me as a creative writer
into explorations of the kind of adult experience that would
be most likely to interest me--and I believe there is truth
in this. I am a product of an extremely strict religious
upbringing of narrow focus, that regarded sexuality as im-
pure or evil and effectively indoctrinated me in its dogma
and tradition. So it is that many of the crises of my life
have originated from that background, from the struggle to
be myself without the compulsion to look back in guilt, yet
I neither despise nor regret my origins. They have made
life difficult and I have had to fight dourly sometimes for
freedom--yet the restrictions of my background have oper-
ated constructively, even if obliquely, upon the end result
of what has become my life's work--the writing of novels
for children about the breathtaking physical and emotional
experience we call adolescence.

I have heard the observation that all writers for
children suffer from some form of arrested development.
Well, I'm still thinking about it. At the start it did seem
easier to me to go that way, that I'd run into less trouble,
that I'd offend my family less and trouble less all the people who had overseen or influenced my upbringing. I know
now I was far too sensitive to this--they'd have grown used
to the idea soon enough and if they had been unable to do
so it would have been their problem, not mine--but my upbringing also denied me the consolation of knowing that.
The realization that I don't have to justify or explain or defend my every action had come very late--in these last
five years, which have been, by far, the most intense and
the most illuminating of my life. Their problem, not mine.
A shattering realization.

It seems to me that in every institution of childhood
I was taught to put myself absolutely last. This happened

to me and to others like me in the context of a uniquely
restrictive, yet not oppressive environment. The distinction may seem fine to some, but the few incidents of active
or felt oppression were rare enough to remain vivid until
now. After all, if it's what you're used to, you don't
notice it. Yet I think ours was the only family round about
to continue rigorously the Victorian tradition of Bible reading and prayers after the evening meal every night--unless
the adults were about to leave the house for some function
or other, which would have been at the church, anyway.

Once, on bonfire night, I was kept at table to finish
prayers until way past seven o'clock, although the bonfire
was to be lit at seven and the local boys, I among them,
had taken weeks to construct it, clearing up the neighborhood of rubbish and dragging parts of fallen trees by hand
or behind our bicycles from open country more than a
mile away. "Let me go," I said, "please. It's our bonfire night." But God comes before bonfires even when bonfires come once a year. Would God have minded? Not the
God I know now. When at last I rushed out into the night
the glow was in the sky. All the way I ran, wailing inside.
It was a heap of glowing ash; that's all that was there.
Well, it was not like being put in the workhouse or sent to
a home--another brooding insecurity of my childhood.

I was taught that personal martyrdom was a virtue,
that stoicism and self-denial and inflexible dedication to
principle and unthinkingly turning the other cheek in all circumstances were the keys to wisdom and the keys to Heaven.
They're not, you know. They are the keys to Hell. But
on the credit side they once led me to think that writing for
children would be less likely to expose me to the disap-
proval of my peers, specifically those among whom I lived
and had grown up. These people had expectations of me
never to bring a shadow upon family, school, or church.
Anything remotely connected with sexual experience of any
kind was the supreme and ultimate disgrace.

I remember the headmaster raging one day before
the middle school assembly, shaking his fist at the sky,
his voice shrill. "I will not have it," he shouted, because
a few boys and girls had been up to it, it seems--though I
had no idea at the time what they could have been up to.
"I will not have people playing popsy-wopsies, in my
school."

I didn't know how you played popsy-wopsies, though it sounded pretty good. And I didn't ask anybody to tell me in case it was something I should have known. When you're ignorant, you don't let on. You keep it inside.

Another time--oh, I must have been thirteen--I was caught comparing notes with a little girl. First time ever, first time, simply comparing notes--I wouldn't have had the vaguest idea what else to do. One should explain that I had been at work more than a year and was fifteen years of age before the facts of life seeped through with understanding. So at thirteen I was caught simply comparing notes-- I was goggle-eyed, as was the little girl if I remember correctly--but my mother was at a loss. I don't judge her --I love her--but, oh, the disgrace upon the whole family! So she said. "If I had known you would do a thing like this I would never have brought you into the world." That mysterious remark, that dire comment, filled me with awful shame. It represented the sum total of my sexual education. From no other adult did I hear another word about sex, except that I should always be on the alert in case "I lost my head." Shame--loads of it by innuendo--and fear. Don't lose your head. Don't lose your head. What on earth did it mean? How do you fight a force about which deeply religious people warn you--but can not bring themselves to utter a word of explanation?

So my vision as a writer and my motivations spread from my own experience, a personal experience of living followed by contemplation, as distinct from reading followed by contemplation--a life-story and a life's work given largely to making books for kids out of the tensions that have turned me into the kind of person that I am.

I think the fundamental reason why I got into writing for children goes back to the things I have been talking about--and I don't mind revealing them; it doesn't upset me. It's one of the major accidents of my life that I bless. I thank God that it happened. I know the reasons may not be seen as elegant or possibly even as desirable, but they guided me to my proper place and I have no ultimate complaint ... none about what has passed; none about the commitment to what may still be to come.

I do not believe that growth in a writer should drive him away from his proper place. His growth may be used by himself to build better and better structures within the

environs of his past achievement. I do not accept that he
should readily abandon the wonder of translating into words
the most marvelous and mysterious and profound of all
human experiences that so many adults appear to have forgotten ever happened, if their lack of sympathy for the
youngsters of now is to be taken as a guide. What is it,
what is it, that turns grown-up people into kid-haters?

One of the simplest truths of any human experience
is that we have to share it, that we need to share it, that
we must share it, or remain blind to much of its grandeur
and mystery. The sharing of a human experience sharpens
our appreciation of it, and makes the experience itself
larger and richer and electric. Until we share what we
have, we often cannot even see what we have. Until we
make the effort to share we will not know how much of life
we are missing. Until we deeply love another person we
cannot know what love we have within us--nor do we learn
how bleak it is to be without it, to be alone.

But nothing ever happens by chance. Have you noticed that? That everything in life has faces--once you
look closely enough. That there are no boredoms in life
and no vacuums--nothing is without meaning if we hold it
up to the light. So when I hold my act of expediency up to
the light, surprises await me. My Australia turns out to
be an enchanted place, peopled by children growing up, by
children discovering their minds and spirits and bodies and
the living world around them, but enchanted in another way
also--by the closeness of its relationship to your Canada,
to the Canada in your heart and mind, or to your Britain,
or your U.S.A., or your Japan, or your China, or your
New Zealand, or your island of the great Pacific, or wherever it is that you first came upon the world, wherever it
is that your own journey of discovery began.

Each of us is the product of a hundred thousand
causes, each of us is as different as East and West, yet
my enchanted place, all mixed up, as it is, with a childhood once lived eight thousand miles from here at the bot-
tom of the world, is part of your enchanted place, and so
we speak a common language about wonderful experiences
we have shared. This is the nature of our bond--the bond
between you and me--and it is the nature of our bond with
the children of now. Kids are the same, kids haven't
changed, not in the heart and the spirit. The environment
is different, the trappings are different, the idiom is

different, the snares and the tensions are different, but the business of growing-up, of watching the changes in your self, of feeling the changes in yourself--however fearful or mysterious or exciting they may be--and of watching the kid next door, the boy or the girl next door or down the street, the one you've grown up with, slowly turning into another kind of creature--the same person, yet not the same person--this fascinating creature arousing in you curiosities and perplexities and questions.   These things have not changed and probably never shall.   Only the chronology of it, the timing of it, varies a little from generation to generation, sometimes earlier, sometimes later. And isn't that marvelous.

How strange it is that serious books written about children growing up are so often considered as unsuitable reading material for children.   How many times people have said to me, and to writers like me: "But you're not writing for children; you're indulging yourself; you're writing about children!"   And isn't _that_ marvelous.   What kind of gymnastics do you have to perform to arrive upon _that_ pinnacle of perception?

One of the most disturbing things I have heard from a public platform happened during a visit of mine to this continent.   A writer for children, whose name I am led to believe is a household word, though I swear I have forgotten it, expressed her life-long devotion to the proposition that all parents in books for children should be depicted as beyond reproach, that the children themselves should be universally good, loyal, and obedient, that every story should have a moral, that every virtue should be rewarded materially, that in every book there should be a kitten, a puppy, and a kind old lady, that every ending should be happy, that nothing in society should be questioned and that reality should never be written about at all.   Writers, she said, who put reality in their books, knew nothing about children and cared nothing about children and deserved the strongest censure.   Do I remember her saying that she regarded the propagation and promotion of purity and light and sweetness above all things?   I believe so.   Do I remember her saying that she would never write about a disadvantaged child or a handicapped child or any other ugliness?   Yes, I think she said so.   And said more.   Very much more.   Except that I became too upset to retain what I heard.   Not by the expression of her view--she was entitled to that--but by her dismissal of all opposing viewpoints as anti-child and

anti-God, and by her disregard or ignorance of what should
be the most obvious fact about children's literature: that it
is inherently diverse, by simple basic necessity. Do you
write for a child of three, or a child of seven, the same
book that you write for a person who is adult in all but
name only?

Have you noticed how frequently films and television
programs of some sensitivity about children simply being
children become "Adult Only" entertainment, "Not suitable
for Children." As if truth about childhood is not for children to know. Once children in picture or story cease to
be sentimentalized--and sentimentalizing is simply the process of dehumanizing--once they become recognizable as
real children in a real world, significant numbers of
grown-up people start getting the prickles. If a novel for
children deals with sexuality in children, which is the most
natural thing in the whole wide world, even stranger things
start happening. One of my books is banned in some areas
of my country--in libraries and schools. A librarian said,
though not to me face to face, "I got to the masturbation
scene and as far as I was concerned that was the end of it.
No child I'm responsible for will get that book from any
library of mine." What am I supposed to say to that?
That masturbation is natural; that masturbation is human;
that it is probably part of the life of every human being on
the planet? I could say that, couldn't I? But why should
I? There is no masturbation scene in the book. And I
know, because I wrote the thing. It happens only in the
mind of that particular reader who banned my book because
of her own interpretation. Again, I do not dispute her
right to her interpretation--the function of individual interpretation is one of the exciting mysteries of the author/read-
er relationship. I dispute the arbitrary reaction of with-
holding the book from others. About the same novel a
school principal wrote to Penguin Books threatening to institute Court proceedings against them and against me for
publishing an obscene work, on the grounds that my account
of a twelve-year-old boy rolling in the rain in the wet
grass without his clothes on would pervert innocent children.
This person enclosed a copy of the book with offending passages marked in red ink. Every innocent thing, every living and vital thing, every poetic image in the mind of my
boy, in the mind of the boy I used to be--in red.

There are two conspiracies, I believe, running par-
allel. The first is in the grown-up world where certain

adults conspire to conceal from children creative works of
any kind that speak the truth with clarity or beauty about
childhood. The second conspiracy is in the world of childhood itself, that closed society where children conspire to
pull the wool over the eyes of their elders. The gap between Earth and Moon is less, I think, than the gap between
child and adult man or woman. Where does the child go?
A recurring theme of mine in lectures and talks is that we
misread First Corinthians 13:11 at our great loss and great
peril, yet few of the basic truths of Scripture are more often taken out of context or more often used by ourselves
against ourselves. "When I was a child, I spake as a
child, I understood as a child, I thought as a child; but
when I became a man--or a woman--I put away childish
things." This theme recurs because upon it stands my philosophy as a writer. The child is not my inferior, he is
my equal, we are contemporaries. Not only does my philosophy as a writer stand upon it, but my philosophy as an
adult also. I am all ages together. I do not perform as a
child, but the heart of the child remains within me, and I
will not accept that this is anything other than man or woman
should be.

When the writer who writes for children as I do
raises his eyes, he sees a world without frontiers and people everywhere sharing with him the world he has discovered within himself. Grown-ups discover my world with
surprise. They hold onto my hand and say, "I had no idea
that books for children were like this." Well, their surprise is no greater than mine. I had no idea myself, that
books for children were like it until I wrote them, just as
other writers around the world who have charted the courses
and done the pathfinding had no idea either. We, too, hang
onto each other's hands and say, "I had no idea. It's such
a surprise."

My first foreign edition was published in Norway
twenty-five years ago. Compared with what I write now it
was a crummy book; but oh, the excitement, the thrill of it
at the time. Norway. So far away. Could there be a
country less like my own? I must have grown an inch from
the sheer elation of it. I have lost count of my foreign editions now--it's a great number and it's not decent to be
precise about it any more, but I receive with delight each
new parcel as it arrives in my very large letter box (large,
because it needs to be, to receive these parcels), and with
delight I unpack it and handle the book and open it and smile

over the art work, because it is fascinating how artists who
live at great distances from Australia are inspired to see
it--because in many ways the Australian landscape is funda-
mentally different from the rest of the world.   I'm sure
the most beautiful interpretation of all--don't misunderstand
me, not by any means the best production, but by far the
most charming--is the cover drawing for The Fox Hole as
published by Astrid Lindgren's house in Stockholm; a most
exquisite fantasy, but nothing like my Australia.   An artist's
projection, 13,000 miles removed, of an Australian country
house.   A towering hill all green and thickly vegetated,
surmounted by a towering house rising level above level like
the Mad Hatter's hat.   And this is the universality, for
lack of a better word, of what writers for children are
saying.   Provided the core is not false, we will read it,
and see it, and enjoy it and project it, through our own
eyes or our own traditions.

Yet surprises happen.   Some months ago, I walked
with friends along a steep road on the central coast of New
South Wales.   "You've got to see the tree house ... It's
beautiful," said my friend.   "It's not like anything you've
ever seen."   So we climbed and climbed and the road became engulfed by ferns, and high up, high above the road,
at the head of a winding track like Jacob's climb to Heaven,
stood a house against the sky, sprouting from a tree, level
mounting upon level like the Mad Hatter's hat.   There it
was--part of the real Australia.

I remain an Australian writer, though it is presently
fashionable to disclaim nationality and plug for international-
ity--but I see a writer's origins as critical.   His origins
determine what he is, and what he sees, and what he says
and how he says it.   If he achieves internationality--a descriptive word, even if I am uneasy about it--I don't believe
it is because he sets out to achieve it.   Universality is a
by-product of honesty and genuine emotion.   And you can't
buy these things, and you can't manufacture them.

None of us can stand a phony, though a few practitioners get away with it for a while, in innocent or gullible
company.   They worry you--once you wake up to them--
these glib characters, whether you meet them in daily life,
or, God help us, in the pulpit of a church, or on the title
page of a book.   They have a kind of patter, a kind of
roundness or fullness, yet you get the feeling that it isn't
meant for you, that it's not addressed to you, that you're

being treated as a machine, as a kind of listening device
or reading device, that you're in the presence of a calculated cynicism. When you get this feeling, trust your
feeling, rather than what you hear or read.

It is not too trite to say that readers respect writers
who are true to themselves, who are true to their origins.
The reader may not be able to say exactly where this shows,
but he will be aware that the book has authority. I hope I
am not asked to define what authority is, because I am unable to do so. A book has it or doesn't have it and although history proves that the world is full of people ready
to be deceived, if not actually proving that the world is full
of fools, there's no real reason why we should join the
club ourselves. Perhaps instinct is all we have left; all we
can rely on any more. The earth is full of vested interests, of hidden persuaders, of manufacturers, and our children are exposed to their full assault. I would like to say
that if a book lacks authority it will die, but too much depends upon the budget set aside for advertising and promotion. There are books that go on selling because publishers
go on printing them, because they are business propositions,
because they are offered for sale at the right price in the
right market place. And very peculiar commodities they
are. They kill time, and leave no wound or trace. Therein lies a sermon. How much of life do we allow to be
killed--without wound or trace?

I started this essay by quoting from a novel called
What About Tomorrow--the first novel I have completed in
four years. Completed joyfully, I would like to add, because when a writer goes into a dry period his whole life
is set about with insecurity and anxiety, and it is marvelous to leave such a period behind. I cannot remember having read before from an unpublished book. I have no re-
collection of having read before in public from any of my
books, but that scene set forty-five years ago, eight thousand miles south-west of here, all that ocean in between,
seemed to say more about my theme than the several other
introductions I threw away--and I suppose it is legitimate
to quote from oneself.

The scene is imaginary, of course. Well, for the
writer, I think the scenes he loves best usually are.
There's a scene in Let the Balloon Go where John, the
spastic boy, sings his victory song high in the tree. And
in Finn's Folly, where Max and Alison touch hands--though,

strangely, in Josh, the book I love most, there is no special scene. Perhaps the whole thing was special. But I do
like those few hundred words I quoted at the beginning, and
anybody who's ever written a book that reaches down into
origins will know what I mean. I think the origins of that
country store come from practically every year of life I
have lived; they speak loud and clear of my enchanted place;
though notably from the lean years before the Second World
War when affluence was a word we had never heard. It's
a good word, affluence. An effective word. First time I
came across it, I knew at once what it meant--there was
nothing else on earth it could have meant--although it felt
utterly foreign and alien and defined a world of which I knew
nothing. The origins of my scene are undoubtedly in the
Great Depression, when depression was a reality rather than
a concept. I have heard people calling the present economic recession a depression comparable with that of the
Thirties. Despite the hardships of the Seventies for many
people, I doubt profoundly if anyone who felt the rough edge
of the Great Depression would admit a reasonable relationship. Yet, for me, in the midst of it, it was glimpsed
only occasionally. It is not that I was an exceptionally un-
observant boy, although I was fifteen before I actually saw
a pregnant woman. You might think that strange in a world
with so many people in it. I feared she had a terrible
disease and had to be reassured by my mother that Auntie
Clarrie was not about to die. I remember sitting there, in
that room, trying not to look at her but drawn repeatedly
wide-eyed to the sad and awful reality that Auntie Clarrie
had been stricken by something unimaginable. "No, no;
no, no," my mother said afterwards, nervously. "She's
quite well." I found that difficult to believe, but accepted
the reassurance and hoped that I would never look like it
myself when "Quite Well."

We were discussing the depression, about my being
not acutely aware of it, but if depression is what you're
used to, what else is there? The same as going to church
four times each Sabbath Day and not being able to bounce a
ball in between services, or buy anything, or do anything,
or play anything, no matter what. If everybody else in the
house conforms to the same rules, you don't notice. You
accept it, because it is expected of you. The same as not
getting from Father Christmas what you most reasonably
ask for. Never did I place more than eight items on the
list, not even in the depths of the Depression, and they were
always undemanding ones like Hornby Train Set and Donkey

Steam Engine and Number Three Meccano Set and two-wheeled bicycle with racing rims and cricket bat and Daisy Air Gun and simple things like that. Crawling down the bed in the pitch black middle of the night, groping with your hands out in front, wondering, you know.... "Has he been? Has he been? Has he been?" Yeh.... But the shapes are all wrong. Nothing there feeling right. Easing off the bed onto the floor, crawling off round the room wondering whether the main things had been put somewhere else. Nothing there but the boots you took off before going to bed EARLY. Oh, that fatalistic pit of acceptance growing inside. Nothing but boots and chair legs and cold bare linoleum. What was wrong with that Father Christmas fellow? Couldn't he read? How come his distribution of the basic essentials of childhood was so inequitable, when everything was free, when kids like Jack Donelly had everything already and got loads more. By eleven o'clock in the morning the spring in the clockwork racing car had snapped and the batteries in the flashlight were flat and you accepted that, too, and started counting up the months to your birthday.

But for all that, the fog used to lift occasionally, and you'd see through--and you'd wonder. Seriously, you'd wonder. Where am I? What am I doing here? It was not only on the day that you started school, or changed schools, that you were lost. Yet when you saw through the fog, it was not really on to the economic realities around you--it was onto the landscape.

Oh, landscape is critical.

You'd see through--or I used to--onto a vast, hard, and frightening land, to which people seemed to cling as if the planet were about to topple and tip them off. Australia. My Australia--not taken by choice, taken because it was there. And I lived in the smallest and most lush mainland State of all, but I didn't see it that way. I saw it as vast, as hard, as dry. Except on Sunday School Picnic Day once a year, when inevitably it rained. It was obvious to me why it rained; because it was Melbourne Cup Day. And if Methodists decided to hold a picnic for children on such an iniquitous day, did they not get their just desserts? I never used to say anything about it, not out loud, but couldn't they see? It was a gambling day--shot through with sin. So God showed his displeasure and rained on it. And almost fifty years later on Melbourne Cup Day He still rains on

it--which only goes to show how dull Methodists can be.
Generation after generation of bright-eyed young Australian
Methodists go on paddling through puddles on the first
Tuesday of each November.

I saw the landscape as vast, as hard, as frightening.
Only the old and weathered and worn places seemed to be
right, and it's still true that the most natural landscapes in
Australia--to my eyes--are the old and weathered and worn,
where termites gnaw through timbers and sun blisters the
paint and old grey shrunken wood shows through, where
verandahs are long and low and leaning, and fences and
tracks and roads are overgrown. Australia is allegedly the
land of opportunity, the land of tomorrow, the land of the
new and the brash and the tall and the stark, but it's not
like that in my enchanted place. Spic and span are wrong
in my Australia. New brick and tile sticks out like a
broken limb. I know those things are everywhere you look,
but there is no need to see them if you do not wish to see
them. I see beyond them to origins, to beginnings, to the
simple dignity of what man and woman together make with
their own hands. Lose your vision and you lose yourself.

I was born in Australia of third generation Anglo-
French stock. Both sides of my family arrived in the Gold
Rush--my father's side in 1858, my mother's side in 1861.
That's a long way back. Out of the Channel Islands and out
of English counties they sailed twelve thousand miles in
windjammers and trekked overland, on foot, carrying all
they owned in the world on their backs and in wheelbarrows.
They lived and worked in the bush; they built their own
houses and grew their own food and raised their children
and worshipped God--one side without the loss of a child,
the other side most disastrously. Oh, the characters that
arose: people like Aunt Clara of <u>Josh</u>. Yet, with that behind me, with that heritage of pioneer endeavor, my country
still used to frighten me.

I remember as a boy walking bush roads so nervously that I literally feared to put my feet to the ground.
I don't know that I can convey in words what it was like.
I used to walk like a cat, used to wish myself miles away,
used to wish myself in the air, apart from it, away from
the heat of it and the harshness of it, the aridity of it,
away from the biting ants and the snakes and the sharp
sticks and the sword grass and the hostility of it. I used
to hate it and never felt safe unless my hand was in the

hand of a grown-up. My eyes were never still, darting
constantly, watching everything that could move. There
were no mists of consciousness when I was out in the bush.
Oh no; yet I never saw a snake as a child; nothing ever
hurt me. The first snake--well, there were two--they
paid, poor creatures, for my lifetime of fear.

I have often relived the Australian origins of my
family a century after they began. On that poor farm, in
the blistering summer of 1951, I hoed by hand through a
crop of green peas, while my son, then aged four, sat on
a sheet of bituminized felt that had been blown from the
roof of the house in a storm; there he sat watching me, for
how long I have no idea. But for a time; a very reasonable
time. He moved when I came up to him and with my left
hand I lifted the felt to throw it aside. Underneath it--my
God--two deadly copperheads, coiled. In a fevered flush of
violence, I chopped them to pieces with the hoe, and went
on chopping, and chopping. I leant there then, on the hoe,
dazed and cold. There's an American expression--cashing
in your savings stamps. I cashed in mine that day, for
those years of fear when I felt myself to be a stranger in
a strange land.

I have no idea why that should have been; I have no
such feeling now, and love the Australian landscape, either
arid or lush. But the fear of it then was part of the making of me, part of the awareness of being alive, of having
arrived from somewhere else.

First time I ever felt properly at home was on a
gloomy autumn morning in 1943; I had traveled all night,
with two hundred and fifty others, in a train with blinds
drawn, all night long traveling south from the Clyde, at
the end of a ten-weeks' journey across the world. I pulled
up the blinds onto early morning light as our train crossed
the River Thames and for the first time in my life saw the
Tower of London downstream. I was twenty-two, a pilot
in the Royal Australian Air Force, twelve thousand miles
from Melbourne where I was born, and, I was sure, very
soon to die, but I cried inside because I was home. The
landscape was right at last. Do you know what that
means? I don't. Because I don't feel at home, that way,
in London, any more.

So what happens with the next generation? My son--
now that I think of it--used to shut his eyes and run in

fright along bush roads, shielding his face with his hands.
He said he was afraid of seeing the rabbits. He'd have
been four or five, I suppose. But it didn't last. Later he
borrowed a gun and stalked and shot and skinned a fox--
he wasn't afraid of seeing that! Oh, the smell.... But
my eldest daughter was the one. Even when very small,
off she'd go, down the hill into the bush for hours, on her
own. Once, down there, she was attacked by a domestic
cat gone wild, but after we'd patched her up and had her
inoculated against everything on earth, back she went again
on her own, to turn over stones and climb trees, or sit in
the pea paddock, immersed in tall green peas, endlessly
splitting pods, a one-child crop destroyer.

That boy again--how old? In his teens. Certainly
old enough to ride a bicycle for miles, perhaps old enough
to drive a car illegally. Well, I don't know. I don't know
how he got there. But off he went, miles beyond our bush
home, miles farther on and out to where I had never been--
and still haven't been--and there found a deserted village,
not a ghost town but something like that, a kind of dream
place, an enchanted place, with empty houses here and
there, with a blacksmith's shop thick with spider webs and
artifacts hanging from nails, and an abandoned general
store.

"Dad," he said, "it's as if everyone had gone away
fifty years ago and forgot to go back. There are things in
that store. There are things on the shelves." There was
excitement in his eyes and excitement in his voice. He
gave me a corkscrew, a black iron corkscrew with a goat
horn handle. I have it still. I use it still. I don't know
whether that store was there, but something was there.
The excitement in his eyes. He paints pictures now. So
Drew's store became part of my enchanted place, part of
my imagined Australia, as it must surely be part of his.

So Sam, 14 years of age in 1931, years before
Drew was born, thirty years at least before Drew found
that place, walks the length of a long road and finds at its
end the girl who is to play a major part in his life--just
as Mary, the girl, meets Sam. There stand two kids created out of ghosts; flesh out of ghosts, landscape out of
ghosts, thoughts and emotions out of ghosts, even the day
and the year created out of ghosts. Well, what is memory
but a ghost of incredible complexity? Stir up your ghosts
and who can tell what's going to walk out of there?

That's my story of my Australia--well, the edges of it sketched for you. The detail I leave to you to fill in, because the reader brings to each book his own enchanted place and if the book speaks of human things, we lay our own interpretation and experience over what we read. The reader adds himself to the writer's vision, and the truth either one of us distills out of the same words may be utterly different from the other. We make our own reality out of things that only we can see, writer and reader together, though we may never have met face to face.

Note

1. Ivan Southall. What About Tomorrow? New York, Macmillan, 1977.

Chapter 3

YOUNG SOVIET READERS AND THEIR LITERATURE

by Miriam Morton

Without doubt, reading is the favorite leisure-time activity of the Soviet people--children as well as adults. It is hard to know exactly why this nation reads so much and why it so adores its writers and poets. Perhaps these people are booklovers because it has not been long--hardly more than half a century--since they became a literate nation. Before the Revolution of 1917, three-quarters of the population could not read or write, or even sign their name. Then, having finally become readers, they came to regard books as a special blessing.

Very likely, however, the main reason why the Soviet people are such lovers of literature is that the works of their many good authors have always expressed a deep sympathy with the sufferings and struggles of the common man. The best Russian novelists and poets dedicated their talents to the cause of the people, many of them going to prison or into exile when they defied the authorities and their censors. In return, their countrymen have given them admiration and love--and have read and treasured their books. And so have the children.

Perhaps you can already sense that I am enthusiastic about this vital offshoot of literary culture in the Soviet Union--this country's literature for children and youth.

In the light--or rather the mists--of the nearly constant and indiscriminate attacks on Soviet letters in the Western press and other mass media, and in schools, partially because of the treatment in the USSR of markedly dissident Russian authors, my enthusiasm may seem an affront.

It is indeed a painful paradox that a modern advanced

socialist society with notable literary traditions and achievements tolerates such excessive controls. It is a dismal contradiction. But, alas, paradoxes of this sort, as we know, existed and exist in other powerful lands which are politically and ideologically in conflict with countries of opposing political systems. The United States, for instance, in its panic fear of the communist threat, has had its Palmer Raids, its Joe McCarthy, and its Un-American Activities Committee--inquisitors all they were, victimizing American intellectuals.

Fortunately, discouraging and baffling as such contradictions are, they do not necessarily preclude or negate the existence of positive, or even admirable, cultural manifestations on either side. And Soviet children's literature is a shining example.

I have by now devoted a dozen years or so to the study of Soviet child culture, and especially to the study of the highly civilizing power of its prose and poetry for the young. My findings are based on much reading, close observations, meetings with authors, discussions with educators and librarians, as well as with groups of children. These explorations were made in the course of eight visits to the USSR. As I speak Russian, the effort has been that much more fruitful.

My conclusions have been that Soviet school children, that is young people from three to seventeen years of age, are supplied for their voluntary reading with one of the world's finest and most varied juvenile literatures. In its great diversity, it offers folklore, classical, and modern works in numerous genres. In each of these categories, there is a wealth of not only Russian but also non-Russian Soviet national and ethnic folklore and writing, and prose and poetry from foreign lands on all continents. The latter are made available in Russian translation.

This literature is especially rich in biography, poetry, the short story, the novel, science fiction, historical fiction, fantasy, humor, nature writing, and the greatest diversity of folktales and folk poetry, encompassing that of the many Soviet nationalities and small ethnic groups.

The dissemination of the work of some 1,500 authors who devote themselves almost entirely to writing for young readers, the 3,000 new books published each year in editions totaling many millions of copies, is accomplished within the framework of several central and a number of regional state publishing establishments, numerous bookstores and book stalls, and 250,000 libraries serving children and teenagers, including the 180,000 schools with their libraries and the libraries in the thousand of recreation centers for children and youth.

To make this literature not only available but also emotionally, intellectually, and aesthetically accessible to the young reader, a concerted effort is made by parents, the schools, the libraries and the thousands of literary clubs (called circles) to develop the perceptive and dis- criminating reader--the "talented" reader is the term most often used.

The principle which energizes and guides this highly integrated, coherent, and ambitious program of supplying a rich literature for a uniquely perceptive young reader is that the cognitive, aesthetic, and moral elements in creative literature are indispensable for the lasting humanistic ac- culturation of the young, for their personality development, and for their discovering early what is the good life and good citizenship, in the deepest sense of these two concepts. Aesthetics and ethics, according to this principle, have a symbiotic relationship--for there is believed to be an in- herent affinity between the arts--especially the literary arts--and humanistic values. These values are held to be: love of one's fellowman, and trust in his perfectibility; love of beauty, of justice, of truth, of work well-done, of peace, of creativity, of discovery.

Historically, the aesthetic standards and humanistic objectives generally adopted by Soviet children's authors and editors were determined by a remarkable group of Russian literary greats of the 19th and early 20th centuries. A surprising number of them not only wrote for the young but worked devotedly to crystallize criteria and goals for chil- dren's books. For instance, Leo Tolstoy, the author of the epic War and Peace and other major works for adults, wrote some 620 short and longer stories for young readers, and was the author of four graded readers that were used, prior to the Revolution, in all schools for several genera- tions of school children. Most of Tolstoy's tales and stories in the readers and most of the longer works continue to be published today for young Soviet readers.

The national poet Nikolai Nekrasov, Leo Tolstoy, Anton Chekhov, and especially Maxim Gorky, together with other noted writers, as well as with the help of the leading 19th century critic, Valerion Belinsky, fostered a remarkable children's literature. The movement took on great momentum after the Revolution with the additional help given to Maxim Gorky by dynamic spirits such as Kornei Chukovsky, Samuel Marshak, Sergei Mikhalkov and Agnya Barto, who produced outstanding literature in an uncommon social and cultural ferment.

Let me refer you for part of the story to the five chapters on literature in my book, The Arts and the Soviet Child, [1] to the introduction in my A Harvest of Russian Children's Literature, [2] and to Kornei Chukovsky's From Two to Five, [3] a remarkable work on pre-school children and their reading fare.

To return to the matter of the talented: the concept entered the terminology of Soviet pedagogy, criticism, librarianship, and authorship some forty years ago, when Samuel Marshak, poet and humorist and for forty-five years a moving spirit in the advancement of the literary arts for the young, formulated it. Quite recently I noticed on a wall display at the Moscow Central Children's Library, under the heading, "The Talented Reader--What Does It Mean?" Marshak's explanation, in part:

> ... the reader, too, should be and wants to be creative. He's also an artist--otherwise we writers would not be able to communicate with him in the language of images and nuances.... Literature needs talented readers for its talented writers.

Marshak was convinced that if the best qualities of creative writing are to benefit young readers, they must develop into highly discerning, talented readers. Specifically, they have to develop a sensitivity to the best elements in prose and poetry, a love of books, a respect and even admiration for the special talent and labor of the author, an inquisitiveness about the craft of writing. Furthermore, such young readers should even be quickened by the desire to try their own hand at authorship, or at least want to join a literary circle where some of the children write, where good poetry and stories are read and discussed, where meetings with authors are a frequent event. In other words, children do not become perceptive readers merely by reading a great many books and by enjoying what they read.

How, then, do Soviet teachers, librarians, and literary club leaders go about developing such a sensitive reader, and on what scale? First of all, there is a commitment on the part of the state to provide children with a
plenitude of inexpensive books--most books cost less than a
ruble, and many less than twenty kopecks. The numerous
neighborhood libraries, well staffed with professional per-
sonnel, as well as the school and classroom libraries, make
books and guidance easily available. The virtual glorifica-
tion of the author, his frequent personal appearances before
groups of children and voluminous correspondence with them
make books more enticing and meaningful to the young person.

Then there is the systematic effort to provide the
child in his school curriculum with a wealth of good writing
--with real literature. This begins with the pre-schooler,
and continues with the school readers in the primary grades
and the literature textbooks and anthologies in the remaining
grades of the ten-year school. (There are eleven million
pre-schoolers in the kindergartens and forty-five million
school children.)

Books for pre-schoolers are generally of considerable
merit--in text and illustrations. Moreover, there is a
methodology guiding the manner of reading by the very
young children which helps them derive great benefit from
the expressiveness of the language of the poetry, of the
story, the fable, or fairy tale read to them. Most of the
pre-schoolers' books are in verse, even informational ones.

The six-year-old is taught to read in the last year
of kindergarten. His primer is not a casual affair. It offers selections from some of the classical Russian authors
and from folklore. The first four graded readers (for children from seven to eleven years of age) contain the following: the first reader has some 130 selections and a vocabulary of some 3,000 words; the second-grade reader has
165 selections and a vocabulary of about 4,000 words. The
number of selections and size of vocabulary increase rapidly
in the ensuing grades. The selections are almost invariably
taken from the works of celebrated classical and outstanding
modern authors. There is practically no adaptation or cutting of folklore or classical literature.

Class instruction in literature is departmentalized
from the fifth grade, and will soon be taught in this manner

from the fourth. This means that a specially trained teacher in literature teaches the subject, and not the "homeroom" instructor who teaches non-departmentalized subjects.

Most important, the readers and textbooks are uniform throughout the vast country, for schools in cities, towns, villages and hamlets. In the national republics and national areas, study books of native literatures in the local languages are of equal merit. The Russian language and Russian literature are also taught in all national and ethnic schools.

The school children who are acquiring such a thorough knowledge of their past and present Russian, or native and ethnic, literature in the classroom also participate in an extensive program of voluntary reading encouraged by their teachers, by librarians, and by the leaders of literary clubs. The latter, in most cases, are trained in the teaching of literature or are published authors. (Generally, instructors of literature hold degrees in this field, and those teaching the upper grades--8th through 10th--normally have the equivalent of a Master's degree in literature.) The methodology of teaching is held to be important, but it does not overshadow the teacher's required substantial academic training in letters.

The ready availability of low-cost, good books is practically universal. Even for the youngsters who live near the Arctic Circle, there is at least a reindeer-drawn bookmobile. There is very likely a literary circle for the children to join, or they may start one with the help of a teacher. The widely circulated children's magazines also conduct literary activities with their readers--publishing contributions by the children, conducting contests and printing comments related to books.

These literary circles exist for those youngsters-- and there are many thousands of them--whose experience with books in school and at home has given them a keen appetite for literature. They voluntarily attend these clubs, once or twice a week, for two hours each time. Here their interest is further nourished. They write their own stories or poems, draw pictures to illustrate them, invite authors to address them, take trips to the birthplaces of famous writers, read their own creations over radio and television, read and discuss new books, publish reviews and comments in the club's magazine or "wall newspaper." (The wall newspaper is tacked on a bulletin board in the club's meeting place.)

The literary circles function in schools, in Pioneer recreation centers, of which there are some 3,500 in the country, in children's neighborhood and central libraries, in the urban and rural Houses of Culture and Rest usually sponsored by trade unions, as well as (and this is a more recent development) in the recreation quarters of the large city housing complexes consisting of many-storied apartment buildings. There are a variety of such clubs: Young Journalists, Folklorist Circles, Young Reviewers, Young Poets.

It is the literary circles that lead in the participation in yearly city-wide or regional contests, called Literary Olympiads--in reality literary tournaments. The contests are well publicized in the schools and in the mass media, both print and electronic, and they generate much excitement and anticipation. Award-winning poems, stories, or essays are read over television and radio. In Leningrad, recently, twenty-four thousand children from thirteen to seventeen years of age took part in a literary essay contest. They wrote on one hundred and thirty-four suggested themes dealing with literary history and criticism and literary figures, including foreign ones.

At this point a few words on the question of indoctrination and moralizing may be in order. Tendentiousness is held to a minimum despite the fervor with which writers approach their role as enlighteners and educators. The reason for this is twofold: first, Soviet children, like children everywhere, dislike being preached to, and, second, it is truly believed that standards of excellence in juvenile literature preclude crude tendentiousness. These standards, as we saw, began to evolve more than a century ago with the crusading Russian literary intelligentsia--crusading for a democratic or socialistic enlightenment. They have on the whole held firm in children's books in the Soviet period as well. The simplistic form of "socialist realism" imposed by Stalin has, fortunately, influenced children's books far less than adult ones.

It is held that the young reader is best convinced through books when they are written with genuine artistic merit, in good literary style, and with a profound conviction on the part of the author, rather than with didacticism. Thus, in an authoritative little book for teenagers on perceptive reading its author comments as follows:

> A good book is above all else a source of joy.
> And it teaches the reader about what is good in
> mankind and in life independently of his intention
> to derive, or not to derive, any other benefit
> from it than that of joy. I would say even that a
> well written book teaches and ennobles the reader
> without his noticing it at all. [4]

The socialist value system is indeed reflected in Soviet literature for the young, but not at the price of sacrificing
the subtler and more lasting influence of literary excellence.
In a doctoral dissertation on Humaneness in Soviet Children's
Literature, Professor Margaret Robinson Preska wrote that
in her explorations she found that:

> ... one cannot gain clear ideas about the nature
> of socialism or communism in books for young
> children; didacticism is missing. Individuality and
> uniqueness generally are praised.... [5]

I found that although ideas and ideals of socialism and com-
munism become clearer in the literature for the older child
and the teen-ager, didacticism is, on the whole, intention-
ally and successfully avoided. The writing is sincere, professional, often brilliant.

Soviet writing for the young has a number of features
that all good literatures have in common. Nevertheless, it
is in the main a socialist literature. It is therefore relevant to outline here both its similarities and its differences
in relation to American (and generally, Western) books for
young readers.

In his introduction to A Critical History of Children's
Literature[6] the historian Henry Steele Commager lists what
he considers the basic attitudes to society and the individual
displayed in the children's books of Britain and the United
States over the years. It is in relation to his observations
that I shall discuss the traits most apparent in Soviet socialist juvenile literature.

Commager describes American children's books as
showing a picture of equalitarianism for all classes of society. Until recently, however, there is a noticeable absence
of the subject of a better break for minorities and the poor.
Soviet literature stresses the greater importance of advancing
the well-being of people of humble origin who as a class

were victims of social injustice, neglect and oppression in former times--or still are in parts of the world outside the USSR.

Soviet books extend the American picture of contempt for the bully to include contempt for the oppressors and victimizers of whole classes who find themselves in a weaker societal position--of ethnic minorities and colonial peoples. This includes contempt for the autocrat, the tyrannical army officer, the corrupt judge, the cruel serf-owner, and, more recently, the self-seeking bureaucrat or the small-minded and authoritarian teacher or parent.

Championing fair play is extended in Soviet children's books to the larger concept of social justice and of raising the oppressed permanently through social change, or revolution if necessary, to a status of dignity and equality of opportunity in their society.

The American love for nature in the raw contrasts with the Soviet writer's love of nature in its benevolence to man, and of the solace it brings to his spirit--its varied moods being akin to those experienced by human beings. In an appeal to the world's writers for children this view of nature is expressed as follows:

> A child's communion with nature, and his interest
> in books that teach him to love it, will sow in
> him the seeds of humaneness. May there be
> more and more books infused with the warm
> breath of living nature![7]

The stress on work and the gospel of work, and on ingenuity in mechanical skills, is the same in both literatures, except that work, in the Soviet concept, more clearly includes creative and intellectual effort, along with the manual and the technical--especially work that will benefit or elevate the group, the community, the nation, and humanity at large.

The Soviet writer's demonstration of humanism is based on trust in and love of the human being, as the only one of earth's creatures capable of great beauty of thought, of action, and of creativity. This transcends a mere concern with humanitarianism, the generosity, charity, or kindness which follows on a recognition of the essential nature of the human being.

The ethical values stressed in socialist juvenile literature are largely the same as in the classical and most of the contemporary Western books for the young. (Interestingly, the chief editor of a youth magazine, Yunost, was indeed eager to call my attention to the fact that Soviet morality subscribes to at least six of the Ten Commandments--those relating to behavior toward one's fellow men.) But there is much greater emphasis in all Soviet literature on the principle of "all for one and one for all"--that is, the collective good.

The selection, and rejection, of proposed books for young readers, indigenous or foreign, is based on the criterion that literature, as all culture, is a principal means for rearing the child to become "the new socialist man." Therefore the choice must be carefully made. It is a choice between the instilling of the socialist ethic with all the humane benefits it assures, and the random dissemination of irresponsible, chaotic works destructive of morale and dubious in artistic value. In the all-embracing effort to "build a new world" such choices are held to be crucial.

There is a much greater preoccupation in Soviet juvenile literature with war and peace than in most other literatures. But it does not glorify the adventure and excitement of war, nor does it underplay its horrors, cruelty, wanton destruction, grief, bereavement, anguish. Peace, in all its forms, is glorified. To cite but one example: on the last page of the Soviet primer is a little poem recited daily by all of the country's first-graders. The words are:

> We've made a wish this day:
> May the whole world with us say,
> "Peace, forever!
> War--never!"

> To learn to read and count we try;
> Up to the moon we'd like to fly!
> We're good friends and true to all;
> We serve our country though we're small.

> May there be peace!

There are several other approaches, in addition to those already mentioned, which help develop avid and

discriminating young readers, and thereby make accessible
to them the rich and varied literature created for them.
Some of these are: fostering cultural patriotism; arriving
at a clear view of the function of literature in education and
in moral guidance; the high esteem in which authors and
their calling are held; the absence of counter-productive,
sensibility-blunting programs for children in the Soviet mass
media.

These factors are somewhat exceptional, especially
as they relate to conditions in the United States, but all of
them are possible to adopt in other countries and in other
than socialist societies.

I shall comment, briefly, only on the two that are
less obvious. Cultural patriotism in the context of literature takes the form in the USSR of a deeply rooted awareness of, and pride in, the contribution to world culture of
Russian and Soviet writers, their concern for humanity in
general and dedication to the cause of raising the quality of
cultural life for their own people. Another aspect of cultural patriotism takes the form of an uncommon love for the
Russian language, or for the languages of the separate republics. This love is intelligently and devotedly instilled
and encouraged. It inspires in the young a desire to learn
and speak their language well, and gives an appreciation of
the writing talent of their authors. This kind of cultural
nationalism can be cultivated in children everywhere to great
advantage.

As to being guided in work with children and books
by a clear view of the function of literature, again and
again in educational guidelines for every level of teacher
and reader, the civilizing, enlightening, mind and heart en-
riching role of good books is emphasized. This is the way
Maxim Gorky, for years the leading advocate of high aspirations for children's books, defines the role of literature:

> ... to help man understand himself, to heighten
> his belief in himself and to strengthen in him the
> love of truth, to help him lessen the shallowness
> in people, to help him find the good in humanity,
> to arouse in his heart indignation and courage, and
> to aid him in becoming nobly strong so that his
> life may be blessed with the holy spirit of
> beauty.... [8]

It is no exaggeration to say that there is not a teacher of literature or a children's author or editor who does not know these exalted words and who, to a fair degree, is not dedicated to help reach Gorky's vision for the young reader.

At this point, I must be emphatic that books for the young, along with the high function sought for them, are also entertaining, exciting, dramatic, often sparkling with humor and wit. The humor and gaiety are especially present in books for the younger child. The pathos in some of the works, classical and modern, for the adolescent is leavened with hope and the power of love, with realistic, even romantic, optimism and with confidence that mankind has the capacity to control its destiny.

There are some significant recent trends in Soviet literature that have some relevance to problems faced everywhere with today's young readers. First, what about children's books in a pluralistic society? The Soviet Union has a population consisting of 108 distinct national ethnic, and racial groups. Of the 5, 000, 000 children born each year, about one-half are non-Russian (in language and culture), that is non-Russian in ethnicity. Of these 2, 500, 000 ethnically non-Russian babies, about 1, 250, 000 are not white but of the Mongolian race, such as the Uzbeks, Kazakhs, Tadjiks, Bashkirs, Tatars, etc. In numbers, the various non-Russian ethnic and racial groups range from the 40, 000, 000 Ukrainians to some far-Northern people numbering only a few hundred persons. Most of the 108 different ethnic and racial groups live in historically demarcated geographic areas.

The recognition and encouragement of ethnic identity and culture since the Revolution has released tremendous creative energies--eventually generating a multilingual children's literature. And this is definitely not a matter of tokenism.

I went through the review sections of the twelve monthly issues of Detskaya Literatura, the leading children's literature magazine (the Russian equivalent of Horn Book Magazine), for 1975. I found that of the 220 books reviewed, 52 (or nearly 25%) were originally written in a local Soviet language, then translated into Russian for Russian-speaking children. These books were originally published in the Ukraine, in Belorussia, Estonia, Latvia, Lithuania,

Kazakhstan, Uzbekistan, Armenia, Georgia, Moldavia, Turk-menia, the Tatar Autonomous Region, and in a few other ethnic territories. I know for a fact that such books are often translated not only into Russian but into a number of other non-Russian Soviet languages. Thus there is a re-markable cross-pollinization of children's ethnic literature.

Here I might also cite the scope of foreign works made available to the young Soviet reader. Again, among the 220 books reviewed, 17 were from other than Soviet cultures: German, French, Polish, English, Norwegian, Swedish, Latin American, the United States, and others. The American book was a collection of short stories by seventeen authors, including William Faulkner, Carson Mc-Cullers, John Steinbeck, Flannery O'Connor, James Bald-win, J. D. Salinger. The Latin-American anthology repre-sented twenty authors from twelve countries. The non-Russian Soviet books and the foreign works constituted a full third of the 220 reviewed publications.

Now a few words about what one might term the new realism in Soviet books for young readers. It is perceived especially in books for the adolescent. Contem-porary life in the USSR, as elsewhere, has brought with it disturbing, unique problems and the great need for new in-sights.

Conditions of greater urbanization, the break with traditions, a large increase in the incidence of divorce and the broken family, the incursion of Western mores through tourism and the relaxation of cultural contact with the West, have all disturbed and perplexed adolescents. Books are being written for them to help them find their way, make difficult moral choices, and gain an understanding of the dynamics of interpersonal relationships in today's shifting life-styles, especially as they concern divorce, re-mar-riage, or the casual love-life of parents. Such situations are examined with great frankness. But sensationalism is scorned; clinical details are not considered essential or desirable in order to advance the impact or worth of such books. Careful characterization, and the analysis of mo-tives and of other psychological factors are used instead, to inform and widen the understanding of the behaviour of adults and peer groups. This new realism in juvenile lit-erature is also basically affirmative, seeking understanding rather than condemnation, except in the case of outright scoundrels or viciously self-seeking characters.

The ever greater use of biography to reveal history is a continuing trend. Thomas Carlyle said that "biography is the only history"--the Russians certainly believe this, at least as far as voluntary reading, rather than classroom instruction, is concerned. Since 1935 a juvenile biographical series has been published in the USSR and has recently reached its 500th volume. The name of the series is "The Lives of Remarkable People" and it draws on remarkable people through the ages and from all over the world. Special attention is given to publishing biographies and autobiographies of creative people in the arts. This series, together with numerous individual biographical works, give the young vivid, personalized history and a view of human giftedness, heroism, experience and endeavor in all their variety. It gives them models to follow, knowledge of the past which illuminates the present and encourages positive, inspired, constructive visions of the future.

The human experience and the thrust of human problems and aspirations are also vivified in the unusually ample dramatic literature published for the young reader. The fifty professional theatres for young audiences scattered throughout the land, and the many adult theatres with plays for young people in their repertoires, as well as a large number of puppet theatres, draw a child and youth audience of some twenty million yearly.

Many volumes of plays are published for reading. The published plays make the experience in the theatre fuller if read before or after attendance at the theatre. They make theatre available, at least in book form, to those children who do not live near cultural centers. And whatever special benefits accrue from reading rather than seeing or hearing are there for the young reader of plays. The availability of plays in books also encourages the development of amateur dramatics with all its benefits. In other words, dramatic literature, so long a vital part of adult letters, has become a vital part of children's literature in the Soviet Union.

Literature and the mass media in the USSR co-exist uneasily. Of course television and all its allurements present a threat to the continuation of the pull of books for children, as do the movies. The approach to this problem is expressed by the universal adage: "If you can't beat them, join them." Books are reviewed on television; children's authors appear in interesting interviews with biographical content; favorite stories are dramatized; the books on which televised films are based, as well as their authors, are clearly and dramatically featured before the screening; literary Olympiads and other contests in which young people participate are presented dramatically and with pageantry on television screens (and on radio). Even phonograph records advance the cause of literature, with many of them offering poetry and drama in the voices of famous actors and actresses.

Mass media and literature are thus synthesized, and this results in safeguarding reading and in the enhancement of the written word by its visual and auditory representation. The results of such efforts do not entirely satisfy the champions of reading, but they are substantial.

In Moscow, during the two-week winter holiday season of 1975-76, I counted 200 performances--of theatre, puppetry, opera, ballets, concerts--for children and teenagers. (And this fantastic number did not even include the famous Moscow Circus.) An amazing proportion of the 200 shows stemmed from published works for young readers. The same was true of the 60 such performances on Leningrad stages. Literary art is certainly not taking a back seat. It's in the loge.

In summary, this outstanding literature is radiant with fervor, strong with commitment, talent, artistic and moral perception, and a genuine respect and love of children.

Of course certain elements are lacking. Not enough attention is given in juvenile books to the diversity of life styles of other children of the world, to the variety of political and social movements through history and today, or to the ideas and convictions that have won enduring followings--for example, the world's religions. And there is a complete "blackout" in children's books on Joseph Stalin as a failed leader--and the tragedies that his repressions caused for millions of people. The intention of this "blackout" may be praiseworthy--to keep young psyches free from the corroding effects of bitter disillusionment and cynicism. But the overall result is questionable. For the young people who will soon be adult Soviet citizens must know that they have to be on guard against the corruptibility of leaders. Such lacks notwithstanding, the Soviet young reader is a fortunate person, benefitting from a splendid literature.[10]

In closing, I should like to illuminate these marked benefits by citing a poem written by a fifteen-year-old Moldavian girl. The inspiration she drew from reading made her resolve to become a poet, and in her poem she speaks of what she hopes to bring to her future young readers:

My Gift

Will you take my gift to you
Of the timid murmur of autumn leaves?
And the splendor of sunrise,
And the mystery of evening shadows?

And the saline lips of surging seas,
The tocsin beat of the last storms?
My peers, will you take my gift to you
Of the Milky Way of early reveries?

Come with me, my friends,
To hear the song of mountain waterfalls,
And the playful pelting of the rains,
And the lure of distant, quiet moorings.

Come, let us build cities in the wilderness,
Come, let us be the reckoners of stars.
And like Danko with our hearts
Let us brave battle warnings and darkness.

Come, let us seed the earth with dreams,
Spread happiness amongst all.
Let there resound over our world
Songs of joy, sounds of laughter."[11]

The name of this young poet is Natasha Bukhteyeva. She is but one of many talented readers of her country's fine literature for its young.

Notes

1. Miriam Morton. The Arts and the Soviet Child: The Esthetic Education of Children in USSR. New York: Free Press, 1972.

2. Miriam Morton, comp. A Harvest of Russian Children's Literature. Berkeley: University of California Press, 1967.

3. Kornei Chukovsky. From Two to Five. Berkeley: University of California Press, 1963.

4. Liia Kovaleva. Talant Chitatelia (The Talent of the Reader). Moscow: Detskaia Literatura, 1967, p. 6.

5. Margaret Robinson Preska. Humaneness in Soviet Children's Literature. An unpublished dissertation submitted to the Faculty of Claremont Graduate School, Claremont, California, 1969. Abstract of dissertation, p. 2.

6. Cornelia Meigs, ed. A Critical History of Children's Literature: A Survey of Children's Books in English from Earliest Times to the Present. New York: Macmillan, 1953.

7. "An Appeal to the World's Writers for Children and Youth," issued at the International Meeting of Writers for Children and Youth, held in Moscow, from March 19 to 26, 1973. For full text, see New World Review, Nov.-Dec. 1974.

8. Maxim Gorky. On Literature: Selected Articles. Moscow: Foreign Languages Publishing House, 1960, p. 22.

9. Miriam Morton. "Minorities in the Soviet Union: The Multiethnic and Interracial Children's Literature of the U.S.S.R.," Interracial Books for Children, Vol. 5, No. 1-2, 1974, pp. 1, 12-14.

10. A list of approximately forty works for Soviet children, published in the United States in English translation, follows the text of this essay. The anthology cited above, A Harvest of Russian Children's Literature, offers an additional 100 translated selections. Together, these books offer a fair sampling of Soviet prose and poetry for young readers.

11. Miriam Morton, comp. The Moon Is Like a Silver Sickle: A Celebration of Poetry by Russian Children. New York: Simon and Schuster, 1972.

Bibliography

Books:

Becker, George J., ed. Documents of Modern Literary
Realism. Princeton: University Press, 1963. Chapter
on Vassarion Belinsky.

Benton, William. The Teachers and the Taught in the
U.S.S.R. New York: Atheneum, 1966.

Bronfenbrenner, Urie. The Two Worlds of Childhood:
U.S. and U.S.S.R. New York: Russell Sage Foundation and Basic Books, 1970.

Chukovsky, Kornei. From Two to Five; tr. and ed. by
Miriam Morton. Berkeley: University of California
Press, 1963.

Fromm, Erich, ed. Socialist Humanism. New York:
Doubleday-Anchor, 1966.

Morton, Miriam. The Arts and the Soviet Child: The
Esthetic Education of Children in the U.S.S.R. New
York: Free Press-Macmillan, 1972.

_____, ed. A Harvest of Russian Children's Literature.
Berkeley: University of California Press, 1967.

_____, ed. and tr. Twenty-two Tales for Young Chil-
dren by Leo Tolstoy. New York: Simon & Schuster,
1969.

Pellowski, Anne. The World of Children's Literature.
New York: Bowker, 1968.

Preska, Margaret Robinson. An Analysis of Humaneness
in Contemporary Soviet Books for Preschoolers. Unpublished doctoral dissertation. Accepted by the Department of Contemporary Soviet Culture and International Relations, Claremont School and University Center, Claremont, Calif., 1969.

Trace, Arthur S., Jr. What Ivan Knows that Johnny
Doesn't. New York: Random House, 1961.

Periodicals:

Calkins, Joan Swietzer. "Language Development in Soviet Programs for Young Children," Claremont Reading Conference--36th Yearbook. Claremont, Calif.: The Graduate School, 1972, pp. 59-64.

Morton, Miriam. "'A Great Literature for Little Folk'-- Samuel Marshak as Children's Poet," Horn Book Magazine 42 (June 1966): 335-344.

_____. "Kornei Chukovsky--The Pied Piper of Peredelkino," Horn Book Magazine 38 (October 1962): 458-468.

_____. "Mass Culture and Elite Readers in Soviet Society," Claremont Reading Conference--36th Yearbook. Claremont, Calif.: The Graduate School, 1972, pp. 32-43.

_____. "Minorities in the Soviet Union: The Multiethnic and Interracial Children's Literature of the U.S.S.R.," Interracial Books for Children, Vol. 5, Nos. 1 & 2. New York: Council on Interracial Books for Children, 1974, pp. 1, 12-14.

_____. "Russian Folklore and the Skazka," Folklore and Folktales Around the World--Perspectives in Reading, No. 15. Newark, Del.: International Reading Association, 1972, pp. 75-86.

Spain, Frances Lander. "Books and Library Service for Children in the U.S.S.R.," Top of the News 22:2 (January 1966): 176-185.

For additional bibliographical references, in Russian, see:

Morton, Miriam. The Arts and the Soviet Child: The Esthetic Education of Children in the U.S.S.R. New York: Free Press-Macmillan, 1972.

A List of Soviet Children's Books in Translation

Aitmatov, Chingiz. The White Ship; tr. by Mirra Ginsburg. New York: Crown, 1972.

Aleksin, Anatolii. The Late-born Child; tr. by Maria
Polushkin; il. by Charles Robinson. Cleveland: Col-
lins-World, 1971.

_____. My Brother Plays the Clarinet; tr. by Fainna
Glagoleva; il. by Judith G. Brown. New York: Walck,
1975.

Chekhov, Anton. Kashtanka. New York: Walck, 1961.

_____. Shadows and Light, Nine Stories by Anton Chek-
hov; tr. by Miriam Morton; il. by Ann Grifalconi.
New York: Doubleday, 1969.

Chukovsky, Kornei. The Telephone; tr. by Margarita
Rudolph. Indianapolis: Bobbs-Merrill, 1975.

Frolov, Vadim. What It's All About; tr. by Joseph Barnes.
New York: Doubleday, 1968.

Garshin, Vsevolod. The Travelling Frog; tr. by Margarita
Rudolph; il. by Jerry Pinkey. New York: McGraw-
Hill, 1966.

Grinevskii, Alexander. The Scarlet Sails, tr. by T. P.
Whitney; il. by Esta Nesbitt. Totowa, N.J.: Scribner,
1967.

Kassil, Lev. Brother of the Hero; tr. by Anne Terry
White. New York: Braziller, 1968.

_____. Once in a Lifetime; tr. by Anne Terry White.
New York: Doubleday, 1970.

_____. Shvambrania. New York: Viking, 1945.

Kazakov, Yuri. Arcturus the Hunting Hound and Other
Stories; tr. by Anne Terry White; il. by Bradford Holland. New York: Doubleday, 1968.

Korinetz, Yuri. In the Middle of the World; tr. by Anthea
Bell. Chicago: O'Hara, 1975.

_____. There, Far Beyond the River; tr. from the
German by Anthea Bell. Chicago: O'Hara, 1973.

Kosterina, Nina. The Diary of Nina Kosterina; tr. by
Mirra Ginsburg. New York: Crown, 1968.

Leskov, Nikolai. The Steel Flea; adapted by Babette
Deutsch and Avraham Yarolinsky; il. by Janina Doman-
ska. Rev. ed. Scranton, Pa.: Harper, 1964.

_____. The Wild Beast; tr. by Guy Daniels; il. by H.
Berson. New York: Funk & Wagnalls, 1968.

Linevski, A. An Old Tale Carved Out of Stone; tr. by
Maria Polushkin. New York: Crown, 1973.

Marshak, Samuel. Zoo Babies; tr. by Miriam Morton.
Lexington, Ma.: Ginn, 1974.

Mikhalkov, Sergei. Let's Fight and Other Russian Fables;
tr. by Guy Daniels; il. by Michael Foreman. Westminster, Md.: Pantheon, 1968.

Panova, Vera. On Faraway Street; tr. by Rya Gabel.
New York: Braziller, 1968. (Also published as A
Summer to Remember; tr. by Anne Terry White. Cran-
berry, N.J.: Barnes, 1965.)

Paustovsky, Konstantin. The Magic Ringlet; tr. by T. P.
Whitney; il. by Leonard Weisgard. Reading, Ma.:
Young Scott Books, Addison-Wesley, 1971.

Perovskaya, Olga. The Wolf in Olga's Kitchen; tr. by
Fainna Glagoleva; il. by Angie Culfogienis. Indianapolis: Bobbs-Merrill, 1969.

Prishvin, Mikhail. The Treasure Trove of the Sun; tr. by
T. Balkoff-Drowne; il. by F. Rojankovsky. New York:
Viking, 1967, reissue ed. 1974.

Rosenfeld, Semyon. The First Song; tr. by Miriam Morton. New York: Doubleday, 1968.

Ryss, Yevgeny. Search Behind the Lines; tr. by Bonnie
Carey. Caldwell, N.J.: Morrow, 1974.

Sholokhov, Mikhail. Fierce and Gentle Warriors; tr. by
Miriam Morton; il. by Milton Glaser. New York:
Doubleday, 1967.

Shvarts, Yevgeniy. The Two Maples; tr. by Miriam Morton. 1976.

Tolstoy, Leo. How Valerka Grew Up in a Single Night; tr. by Ivy Litvinov. New York: Watts, 1970.

_____. Nikolenka's Childhood; tr. by Aylmer Maude and Louise Maude; il. by Maurice Sendak. Westminster, Md.: Pantheon, 1963.

_____. Russian Stories and Legends; tr. by Aylmer Maude and Louise Maude. Westminster, Md.: Pantheon, 1967.

_____. Twenty-two Russian Tales for Young Children; tr. by Miriam Morton. New York: Simon & Schuster, 1969.

Ushinsky, Konstantin. How a Shirt Grew in the Field; tr. by Margarita Rudolph; il. by Yaroslava Mills. New York: McGraw-Hill, 1967.

Vangheli, Spiridon. The Adventures of Guguze; tr. by Miriam Morton. Reading, Ma.: Young Scott Books, Addison-Wesley, 1976.

Zakhoder, Boris. The Crocodile's Toothbrush; tr. by Margarita Rudolph; il. by Wallace Tripp. New York: McGraw-Hill, 1973.

_____. How a Piglet Crashed the Christmas Party; il. by Kurt Werth. New York: Lothrop, Lee & Shepard, 1971.

_____. Rosachok: A Russian Story; il. by Yaroslava Mills. New York: Lothrop, Lee & Shepard, 1970.

_____. Star Bright; tr. by Margarita Rudolph. New York: Lothrop, Lee & Shepard, 1969.

In A Harvest of Russian Children's Literature (Berkeley: University of California Press, 1967), an anthology of 100 selections chosen, and most of them translated, by Miriam Morton, a large number of additional Russian and Soviet authors are represented as well as 20 tales from almost all the 15 republics.

Chapter 4

CHILDREN'S BOOKS AND READING
IN A PLURAL SOCIETY--SINGAPORE

by Vilasini Perumbulavil

In 1969, Singapore celebrated the 150th anniversary
of its founding by Sir Stamford Raffles of the British East
India Company; the year 1975 marked its first decade as a
fully autonomous and sovereign republic. Singapore is thus
a young nation, having seen a long era of British colonial
rule and, within recent years, a Commonwealth inheritance
shared with Canada, Australia and New Zealand. Among
other things, it would be useful and interesting to discover
in what similar and different ways a history of a common
British colonial background has affected the problems and
prospects of children's books and reading in our countries.

The island of Singapore, 584 square kilometres in
area, lies at the tip of the Malay Peninsula, at the southern entrance to the Straits of Malacca, Asia's most vital
and busiest sea lane linking the Indian and Pacific Oceans.
Its pivotal position in the heart of the Southeast Asian region and its natural deep-water harbor gave it, from the
start, a destiny in trade and maritime commerce. It was
to establish a trading outpost and a base to protect their
growing commercial interest in the region that the British
staked a claim on the small sparsely inhabited island of
mangrove swamps in the early nineteenth century. Today,
after less than fifteen years of independence, an acceler-
ated program of modernization and industrialization, coupled
with vigorous export promotion and investment-seeking
abroad, has yielded for Singapore a per capita income and
GNP that are the highest in Asia after Japan.

Singapore's multi-ethnic population of 2.25 million
is descended from the migrant Asian stock of people who
began coming from the early days of the settlement, first

as pioneer but transient traders, businessmen and laborers. Later, with the flourishing growth of the incipient rubber and tin industries in Malaya and Singapore at the turn of the nineteenth century, more families settled and took permanent root. Steady but controlled immigration continued from China, in particular, and India till the outbreak of the Second World War. Population growth in the post-war years has mostly been due to natural increase. Family planning was introduced in the sixties to counter the problem of limited land resources to support industrial expansion and the massive urban concentration of the people.

The present ethnic composition of the community is approximately 76% Chinese, 15% Malays, 7% Indians (including Pakistanis and Sri Lankans) and 2% others. The homelands of two major groups are, therefore, Asia's most populous nations and those of all three have rich and ancient cultures and are "likely to have a powerful voice in shaping the Asian future."[1] Close cultural and psychological bonds with their homelands, especially in the case of Indians and Malays, have naturally been an inhibiting factor in the political and social integration of the people but with each successive generation born and bred in Singapore these bonds will tend to become less strong.

In Singapore we are always reminded that human resources are the country's sole and basic asset, that success has come the hard way through the people's unstinting efforts, and that affluence can only continue if there is constant striving by the people to set themselves higher goals of attainment in the national interest. "Political leadership lays heavy stress on the value of hard work [and] the pursuit of meritocracy...."[2] Society is hence highly competitive and the urgent pace and demands of rapid economic advancement are pervasive influences under which patterns of life have to adapt and adjust constantly.

A point also emphasized is that a country so reliant on human skills and initiative for its livelihood can ill afford any disruption in its communal life. Singapore's population of different creeds, cultures and languages projects a light-hearted and picturesque image of the country, but preserving harmonious relations and fostering a sense of national identity and common purpose among its heterogeneous people are matters over which government exercises extreme vigilance. Primarily responsible for cultural integration and the inculcation of civic pride, loyalty and national consciousness is the Ministry of Culture, which operates through its control of publicity and information media and agencies such as Radio Television Singapore. Religion, culture and language are regarded as highly sensitive issues and any public expression about them deemed to stir up communal feeling is discouraged. Equal treatment and equal opportunity for all citizens is a fundamental policy aimed at removing a potential source of interethnic friction and dissidence. In its practical application this policy is manifested in different aspects of national life-- in religious freedom, in equal job opportunities and, above all, in the adoption of three ethnic languages as official languages in addition to English, which is also the language of administration. "Ethnic heterogeneity in Singapore is paralleled by an even more diversified language structure. Each of the three ethnic groups has retained its major 'ethnic' language--Malay for the Malays, Chinese for the Chinese and Tamil for the Indians.... The Republic of Singapore is perhaps unique as a small island state with four official languages. Multilingualism is therefore more than academic in Singapore."[3]

Nowhere is this multilingual approach more evident or its effects more widespread than in the field of education. It follows that multilingualism has a significant bearing on the climate of writing and publishing of children's books in Singapore. With a very high ratio of youthful population, more than half a million of whom attend Singapore's double-session schools in any one year, the government's language policies get immediate and extensive exposure. Instruction in any of the four languages, either as a first or second language, is provided in the various language-medium schools. More and more of these schools are "integrated" to bring together teachers and pupils from two or more language streams under one roof to share a common administration, common facilities and common extra-curricular activities. Parents are free to choose the main medium of instruction they want for their children. Bilingualism is stressed and was, until very recently, compulsory for all primary and secondary school children. Bilingualism in the Singapore usage is not a choice of any two of the official languages; it means English as a compulsory first or second language plus one other language, preferably the pupil's mother tongue. Nor is bilingualism a mere study of a second language and its literature but the functional application or, to use the proper coinage, "exposure" to a language other than the main medium in the teaching of certain subjects in the curriculum.

The official stand on multilingualism and bilingualism is justified on the pragmatic grounds that (a) Chinese, Malay and Tamil, with roots in the culture of the local people, can better instil a sense of belonging and national identity and are more appropriate channels to transmit "Asian moral values and social attitudes such as closeness in family ties, thrift, filial duties and loyalties, "[4] and (b) English is essential to provide administrative continuity. In this capacity it is a means of access to Western scientific, technological, business and commercial development, and so provides a neutral medium in which all races can compete. It is also, in a country of diverse languages and dialects, used in cross-ethnic communication.

Government's concern for the language issue has been a major cause in subjecting educational policies to perpetual experimentation, revaluation and re-structuring in the last fifteen years. Whatever the changes proposed and implemented, there is scrupulous care that these do not in any way give rise to fears that they are directed at limiting the status of the culture and language of any ethnic group. In this respect it is particularly the fears of the predominantly Chinese section of the community that have to be allayed. Chinese culture has always been proudly preserved and promoted, largely under the private patronage and munificence of leaders of the Chinese community, and from colonial days up to the time of independence a large number of Chinese schools flourished independently. There is at present a growing anxiety that current language status and literacy trends in Singapore, as reflected in the various language-medium schools' enrollment, point in favor of English growing at the expense of the ethnic languages, notably Chinese. But here again bilingualism can be defended as a factor which will help not only to mitigate any rate of decline in the popularity of ethnic languages but to stabilize it.

The constant changes in language use in schools so far indicate that results attained in multilingualism have not measured up to what was hoped or desired. The trilingualism of the sixties gave way to bilingualism, the hope being that this would enable the Ministry of Education to establish satisfactory rates of "exposure" time for each language. This has had little success. While bilingualism is likely to remain a cornerstone in Singapore's educational framework, the Ministry of Education has recently made official the decision to adopt monolingualism for children who cannot cope with two languages.

Bilingualism is aimed at producing citizens who can communicate and operate effectively in at least one language and have a functional knowledge of another. In reality, opinions about the prevailing standard of language proficiency, not only among school children but even at tertiary levels, have not been favorable. The performance of English and Mandarin, the official Chinese dialect, causes special concern, as government stresses the importance of English in economic life and wishes, for practical reasons, to promote one standard Chinese dialect in place of a multiplicity of dialects, such as Hokkien, Cantonese and Teochew. The University of Singapore has had to start remedial English courses for students recruited from non-English medium schools.

Children's low reading level in English is noticeable in the National Library's branches in satellite towns where large sections of the population have been resettled in low-cost, high-rise Housing and Development Board flats. In the informal children's reading groups we have started in the last two years with the better readers, we have difficulty in selecting enough books that suit their reading and interest levels. Here it may be pertinent to state, as a general observation, that children in our library find British children's books (both standard and contemporary) difficult in language and style, apart from the fact that they come from a totally different environment and are directed at a totally different audience. The same can be said of Australian and New Zealand writings, which are patterned on the British model and which have long descriptive and narrative passages. On the other hand, American books, with their more informal language and style, more conversation than description, shorter sentences, and less crowded page layouts, have a greater success with our children.

We have been pleased, though, at the appearance of a greater number of easy fiction series put out by British publishers, such as Methuen's "Read Alouds," Hamish Hamilton's "Antelopes" and "Reindeers," and Bodley Head's "Acorns." Many of these, as well as books by Beverly Cleary and Carolyn Haywood, are popular titles in our "S" (for simple fiction) collection which we started when our first branch library opened in 1970.

The problem of poor language attainment is compounded by a high dropout rate, especially after the six-year primary education, a result to be expected of a highly competitive and examination-oriented system of education. It is a situation which Singapore's high literacy figures totally belie and one which we who are engaged in readership development cannot be cheerful about.

Part of the difficulty of coping with languages may be explained by the linguistic complexity which surrounds children in Singapore's multilingual and multi-dialectic environment. In a series of radio talks on "How to improve your child's English," conducted jointly by the Adult Education Board, Radio Television Singapore and the National Library this year, one speaker described this complexity:

> A child in Singapore may be studying in an English-medium school, but he is still a second-language user of English. English is not native to him. If he is in a non-English medium school, it is likely that English is a third language to him (Mandarin, Malay or Tamil being his second language and his home dialect/language being his first). Generally the home linguistic environment determines whether English is his first (but not native), second or third language. A child's home environment may be predominantly English but if he attends a Chinese school, he is then learning English as a second language but speaking it and using it almost as a first language. If his home environment is predominantly dialect-speaking and he attends a Chinese school, English to him is a third language. [5]

In this environment, linguistic and cultural interferences between languages often happen, as when children from Chinese-speaking homes study English or when non-Malay children learning Malay are unable to appreciate the nuances of the language in the idioms, proverbs and other culture-based words because they are not familiar with Malay culture.

The pressing demands upon education to expand and shift massively from an academic to a technical and scientific bias in order to serve the manpower needs of Singapore's industrialized economy have inevitably resulted in a lowering of teacher-training standards and quality of instruction. The limited success of bilingualism can certainly be largely attributed to this. Most serious has been the shortage of teachers with adequate language proficiency, particularly proficiency in the second-language teaching of local languages. The Regional English Language Centre in Singapore, sponsored by the Southeast Asian Ministers of Education Organisation, conducts extensive study in English teaching with regional and international expertise. However, there is no comparable research on the theory and practice of second-language teaching in Chinese, Malay and Tamil, and "methods employed are adaptations from those of teaching in English."[6]

Bilingualism has also not been helped by the acute lack of materials for second-language reinforcement, especially books for general reading, which are so essential to vitalizing language appreciation. "Whereas first-language materials may be imported to fulfil requirements to some extent, albeit with certain disadvantages, materials in the second language have to meet specific needs of individual countries and have therefore to be locally produced in full."[7] The Educational Publications Bureau, set up and subsidized by the Ministry of Education in 1968, tries to meet the need for locally produced materials but the effects of one agency's activities on a large school population are naturally negligible. Few such materials have emanated from commercial publishers, who regard the EPB's association with the Ministry as giving it preemptive privileges and are wary of entering into competition in areas where the EPB has ventured.

We should like to see more evidence in our children's libraries of bilingual reading, especially in local languages where the lack of such materials is greatest and where first-language materials are, more often than not, beyond children's level of second-language proficiency. This is clearly the case with our collection of Tamil children's books which gets a very poor readership that cannot be explained entirely by the low Tamil-medium school enrollment since there are around 20,000 pupils learning Tamil as a second language in any one year. Because of the socio-economic prestige that English enjoys among all ethnic groups it is progressively the language known by most children. Chinese, Malay and Tamil tend to be used largely as school and tuition subjects.

Multilingualism in a small country like Singapore has inhibited the growth of an indigenous literature and its publishing because writers and publishers have a divided readership among four languages in a total of under two and a half million people. With the huge school population, on the other hand, textbook writing and publishing find a surer and more lucrative market. Here again though, it is fragmented and English textbooks yield the most profits, not only through serving local primary and lower secondary school needs but through substantial exports to Malaysia, Hong Kong and as far afield as Africa and the West Indies.

Factors favorable to publishing and writing in Singapore are many. Literacy and educational opportunities are high, purchasing power is high by Asian standards, there are modern publishing and printing works run by joint local and foreign capital and expertise, little or no import duties on printed and printing materials, an excellent communication network for book outlets all over the island and a brisk trade in export and re-export of print. But the output of local writing has remained neglibible. In the case of children's books, the figures are smaller still. Considering the predominance of reading in English, followed by Chinese, the low figures for publishing in these languages, especially Chinese are unfortunate. More Malay writing for children is published in Singapore, but the writers are almost all from Malaysia.

In a perceptive essay reviewing the state of the arts in Singapore during a decade of independence, Robert Yeo, a local poet, sees the country's linguistic and cultural variety as not having, as yet, stimulated the growth of a truly national indigenous literature. Society is a long way from being effectively multilingual and writers and their audiences in the different languages exist in virtual isolation from one another. So there is no sharing, through literature, of the experiences, feelings and aspirations common to all Singaporeans, "though we have been a multicultural, multilingual society for more than a century in the 'market sense'."8

The "linguistic impasse" has had no amelioration so far from adequate translations for the benefit of monolingual readers. In children's books, for instance, only three locally translated titles published since 1972 come to mind-- the Alpha Press Moongate Collection of picture-book folktales in English, Chinese and Malay, two books of Folktales from Asia translated into Chinese from the original English edition published in Tokyo under the Asian Copublication Program, and the Adventures of Monkey God series issued simultaneously in English, Chinese and Malay. Significantly, all are folktales--a definite response to local children's reading tastes. But it is difficult to explain why they have taken so long to arrive on the local scene and why there are so few. China, India and Malaysia, including Indonesia, have a rich myth and folklore tradition and yet these sources, not to mention those of other Asian countries, have not been drawn upon by local writers either for suitable retellings or for original writings for children. As a result, generations of our children have grown up reading Grimm and Andersen and Mother Goose rhymes and other staple Western children's literature and know little about the Ramayana, the Panchatantra or about Hang Tuah, Malaysia's legendary hero. While the Asian Collection of children's books in the National Library shows that Chinese and particularly Indian folktales, myths and legends are available in several imported American and British editions, there is very little as yet on Malaysian folklore in English and Chinese, not even from Malaysia. In this respect, however, the Borneo Literature Bureau has to be commended for its efforts in publishing small, cheaply produced books on the little-known Bornean folktales and other local writing. Eloise Van Niel has written a useful exploratory paper for International Library Review[9] in which she discusses the sources in Malay literature that are waiting to be tapped for children's books. There are surprisingly no notable picture-books or collections of stories on Mousedeer or Pelandok, who is the Malaysian counterpart of Brer Rabbit. Incidentally, I am reminded of a Mousedeer book from England that I saw recently, in which the illustrations shown were of sugar cane and South Indians when references in the text were to banana trees and Malay fishermen.

Singapore's long history as a British colony has delayed the growth of indigenous literary production in all four languages; the impetus came only with education with a Singapore orientation. The book needs of a British-centered educational system and of a British-educated society were entirely fulfilled by United Kingdom publishers. Moreover, Singapore's status as a free port has meant that there has always been a brisk flow of books into the country--Chinese books from Hong Kong and Taiwan, Malay books from Malaysia and to a lesser extent from Indonesia, and Tamil books from South India. Understandably, this free access for imported books has not given local publishers the incentive to compete for a limited market.

The National Library relies almost exclusively on imported books for its four language collections. One of the disadvantages we are experiencing as a result of this heavy reliance is with regard to Chinese children's books. Singapore has followed the People's Republic of China in the use of simplified Chinese characters and the teaching of non-simplified characters is being phased out first in the primary schools. The bulk of Chinese books in the libraries and bookshops, however, comes from Taiwan and Hong Kong, which have retained the non-simplified characters. While those who read the non-simplified characters can recognize simplified ones, the reverse is not generally true. Thus more and more of our children are not going to have enough books to read, and the range now available is already limited in number of titles and subject coverage. Since local Chinese publishers are disinclined to venture into the field of general children's books, the Educational Publications Bureau (EPB) is perhaps the only active source for children's books and magazines. Since 1973 it has held two competitions on writing for children and published the winning entries. One of these is a book of short poems describing Singapore scenes by a well-known local writer for adults; others do not escape from the influence of traditional Chinese concern for moral values in literature for the young. It is an indication of the state of Chinese publishing that out of a total of less than twenty juvenile Chinese titles listed in the 1973 Singapore National Bibliography, fifteen were issued by the EPB. EPB plans to step up its publishing program for children through translating English books and through a co-publication venture with Hong Kong to produce a series of Chinese and Western folktales.

Singapore's readers are often accused by publishers and writers of not supporting the development of a local literature. In the case of the English-educated group these accusations are fairly justified because Singapore's colonial experience has tended to create a built-in resistance to Asian writing in English. During British days school children were reared on English readers, Western classics and standard British authors; today the predilection for Western literature continues. In the upper and post-secondary levels students have texts that are prescribed by a British-based examining body, but even in the lower classes only Son of Singapore, the first of Tan Kok Seng's autobiographical trilogy, and Stella Kon's Three Plays are used. Recommended texts for Malay schools include more local literature: at least one work of children's fiction and one book each of poems and plays by Malay writers in Singapore.

The book-buying habit is not extensive among adults or children. Few homes keep books, and gifts to children on birthdays and special occasions are usually toys and clothes rather than books. The public tends to regard books as highly priced and spends relatively less on them than on other items. How well children's books fare with the local buying public can be judged by the sales performance of Folktales of Asia which, under a condition of the Asian Co-publication Program, can be sold only in the domestic market. With average print runs at three thousand copies for general books, publishers of Singapore's Chinese and English editions of Folktales report that after one year they have half of their stocks left unsold. Chinese booksellers who deal exclusively in paperbacks from Taiwan and Hong Kong have complained that the Chinese edition, at $3.95 per copy, is too expensive for their customers. It is not surprising that no Chinese publisher was interested in bidding for the Chinese translation rights of the books last year, though copyright and the film for four-color illustrations were provided gratis by the Asian Cultural Centre in Tokyo.

Apart from the National Library and its branches, there is little or no other institutional buying of children's books, as school libraries are not well developed. Generally teacher-librarians prefer spending funds on a number of different titles and are reluctant to buy two or three copies of any title, even though the average enrollment per double session school is over 1,000 pupils.

Lack of demand leads to a limited range of good books in the bookshops. Children's booksellers display Enid Blyton, Nancy Drew mysteries, Hardy Boys' series, numerous cheap editions of classics and boys' and girls' annuals. Singapore's best-known children's books, the Alpha Press picture-books, for instance, are not well promoted and the publisher is now concentrating on efforts to sell the books abroad through translation and distribution rights.

A handful of children's books with a Singapore setting has been written by British authors. They belong to either one of two types: (a) proselytizing fiction by

Christian missionaries--for example, The Lim Family of
Singapore, and (b) the popular adventure/mystery type written for the entertainment of British children. In these,
Singapore acts as a picturesque backdrop to a tale of white
resourcefulness against the intrigue and opium smuggling of
inscrutable "Orientals"--as for example in H. F. Pearson's
Singapore Story and Pamela Brown's As Far as Singapore.

Sylvia Sherry's Street of the Small Night Market[10]
is the first story about Singapore for children in which a
stereotyped plot is redeemed by the author's insight into
the life and people of Chinatown and her authentic projection
of the contemporary Singapore locales and atmosphere.
Her book employs an all-Chinese cast, which leads me to
mention a literary artifice used in most current writing for
local children that attempts to depict Singapore's multi-
ethnic community. This is the contrived handling of characters and plot to include children of the three ethnic
groups. The practice appears to be standard in Malay
children's fiction. In fact, the chief Malay publisher in
Singapore has the deliberate policy of requesting his children's authors to include multi-racial characters in their
books with a Singapore background. This is in keeping
with the views of an active Malay literary group, "the
Generation of 50, " of which the publisher and the leading
Malay children's writer in Singapore, Mohd Ariff Ahmad,
are members. The group's motto is "Art for Society" and
Ariff Ahmad's guiding principle in writing is to mirror not
only existing society but also a new and better society to
come. His belief in the social commitment of authors
comes through clearly in his books. His children's stories
are rooted in Singapore's urban milieu and not in the lei-
surely Malay rural settlements or "kampongs" often roman-
ticized in literature. His young characters from different
ethnic groups are shown, in their understanding and appreciation of each other and their social attitudes, to be well
on their way to achieving a cultural and social integration
vital for living in a peaceful and prosperous plural society.

Over the last few years positive steps have been
taken to generate greater interest among Singaporeans in
writing for different forms of literature in all the languages. As Robert Yeo correctly observes, government's
priorities in cultural promotion in the first phase of independence have necessarily been in areas which promote
mass appeal. Literature and writing, on the other hand,
are "minority-based activities in creation and

consumption";[11] consequently, initiative to stimulate development of writing, production and promotion of books has had to come mostly from non-official sources.

Most important of these is the National Book Development Council of Singapore (NBDCS) formed in 1969. To ensure wide support and active participation in book development activities the Council's Board has representatives from numerous agencies and institutions in the private and public sectors. Since its inception the Council has sponsored many projects and programs such as seminars and workshops, talks by visiting poets and writers, courses on publishing and bookselling, competitions and book exhibitions. Its main book promotional activity, co-sponsored by the Singapore Book Publishers Association, is an annual book week, the Festival of Books, highlighted by a book fair. Over the years public response to the book fair has grown appreciably and in 1975 a record of 40,000 people visited it and bought about $130,000 worth of books. During the Festival supporting programs such as bookmark competitions, drama and oratorical contests, film/book tie-ins, book quizzes, storytelling and pre-school programs are held for children and young people. The Council also publishes an annual journal, the Singapore Book World, which includes articles on children's books and reading as well as children's book reviews. The National Library is closely involved in most of these activities.

In 1971 the Council held a three-day Workshop on Children's Books. This was perhaps the first time that children's books had received major attention in Singapore, and papers and discussions covered their writing, illustrating, publishing, distribution and promotional aspects. In 1972 the Council celebrated International Book Year on a wide scale, with several book-related activities arranged for all age groups. During the Festival in August-September, 1976, the Council announced winners of Singapore's first children's book awards for local books published in the four languages between 1972 and 1974.

Just as the Council has been instrumental in strengthening professional and trade associations concerned with the book industry, such as the Singapore Book Publishers' Association and the Singapore Booksellers' Association, so it has worked for the formation of a writers' association. The Society of Singapore Writers came into being early in 1976. Among its objects will be the encouragement of translations of literature in the local languages. The Society will also work for better incentives for writers in the form of effective copyright protection and equitable rates of publishers' royalties.

Stimulus for local writing and its publishing has also come from outside sources, chiefly the Asian Cultural Centre for Unesco/Tokyo Book Development Centre (ACCU/TBDC) and Unesco's Karachi Regional Centre for Book Development in Asia. Singapore has been an active participant in the ACCU's Asian Co-publication Program (ACP) for children's reading materials since it started in 1970.

The NBDCS is the national agency for the ACP in Singapore. The ACP emphasizes the promotion of understanding among Asian children through a common sharing of literature and its initial publications have been in the area of cultural promotion, though there are plans to cover other interests in children's reading. More books in the Folktales series, already mentioned, are scheduled to be issued. There are also now two books on Asian festivals and texts and illustrations on Asian children's games are being studied by the Central Editorial Board, which comprises Japanese consultants and representatives from some participating countries. Singapore publishers invited to produce local editions of ACP titles are reminded to maintain the quality of production of the original and at the same time to keep the price low. The Chinese national editions have so far been undertaken by one of the major publishers in Singapore who operates in three languages.

Japanese experience and expertise in the field of children's books, particularly in their high standards of technical production, are of tremendous value in stimulating writing and publishing for children in the rest of Asia. Commitment to the ACP has given us the incentive to identify and encourage interests and talents in the writing of children's books.

The ACP has not been without its problems. Though the ACP titles show a high quality of technical production, the editorial problem of handling diverse materials from a region where writing for children is in its early stages has not made it possible to apply uniform standards to the texts and illustrations in the books. Singapore's major difficulty has been the shortage of book illustrators and translators of an adequate standard. There are several good artists and painters in Singapore, but book illustration remains a neglected art.

Various regional seminars and training courses organized by the ACCU/TBDC and the Karachi Centre have provided a useful opportunity for participants to be exposed to advanced book production developments and techniques. Singapore's Alpha Press enterprise may well have been inspired by the visits of the writer Chia Hearn Chek to Japan on book illustration courses and his contacts with leading Japanese children's publishers such as Fukuinkan Shoten and Iwanami. It is difficult to explain in any other way how picture-books made a sudden but timely appearance in Singapore in International Book Year. Written, illustrated and published locally, they are Singapore's first notable contribution to children's books and have enabled the country to be represented in the children's book scene abroad. The White Elephant won honorable mention at the Biennale in Bratislava. The books are also available in Malay and Chinese, and translation into some Indian, African and European languages is being negotiated by the publishers.

Creative writing among children and young people is receiving greater attention in schools. Creative writing has been included in the primary school syllabus together with educational drama, poetry and storytelling to enrich the learning of English. The Institute of Education is to introduce soon a course on creative writing in which local literature will be studied and discussed. Another encouraging development is that children's literature is now a recognized subject for undergraduate research in the English Department of the University of Singapore. Three academic exercises--on fantasy, the concept of "self" in children's fiction, and a study of Tove Jansson's Moomintroll books--have been completed to date. Recognition of the importance of children's literature in institutions of higher learning does much to raise its status in Singapore, where people, by and large, have not been exposed to good children's literature in their younger days.

The National Library, which is also the public library, has been a major promotional agency for children's books and reading since the sixties, when the Library was set on a new course of development and expansion. Children form the largest proportion of the total membership and the percentage of children's membership as against primary school enrolment is 50%. The collection provides

books in the four languages, with books in English predomi-
nating in number, followed in order by Chinese, Malay and
Tamil books. Under the National Library's decentralization
policy the first big branch library was opened in 1970, the
second in 1974, and building of a third will start soon.
There are also two small part-time branches and a weekly
mobile library service to ten of the busier community centers in various parts of the island.

Over the years book promotional programs for children and young people have increased and the trend is to
involve readers actively in them. Storytelling in the four
languages is a regular feature in the children's libraries.
Pre-school programs started two years ago have received
a tremendous response from parents, and children who are
enrolled for each series are drawn from the different language groups. Our informal book discussion circles are
conducted in English, Malay and Chinese. There are regular visits to the libraries by classes of school children
accompanied by their teachers. School holidays and the
Festival of Books every year are occasions when more
activities are planned for every day of the week. The
Children's Services have a growing collection of audio-
visual materials such as films and Weston Woods filmstrips.

For parents, teachers and people interested in children's books and reading, the Children's Services keep special collections such as the Asian Collection of children's
books, storytelling collections and an extensive collection of
books and journals on children's literature. The Asian
Collection attempts to be comprehensive in the four languages and one copy of any children's fiction or nonfiction
title on Asia is included in the collection.

The role played by school libraries in the promotion
of books and reading among children is still limited, primarily because most teacher-librarians have insufficient
time to organize library activities. The state of school libraries has received more official attention since 1970 when
a Standing Committee on Libraries was appointed by the
Ministry of Education, with the Director of the National Library as chairman. This has made possible better coor-
dination of the efforts of the National Library and the Ministry in the interests of school library development. The
Standing Committee has drawn up minimum standards for
primary and secondary school libraries, initiated bulk ordering and central processing schemes to help build up

school library collections in different subject areas, and prepared detailed guidelines for enrichment activities in primary school libraries. With active implementation of these recommendations and guidelines, school libraries can begin to fulfil their responsibility of bringing more children in contact with books and reading.

I can think of no better way to end than to leave you with two poems from the magazine Saya[12] which show how two young people have responded in creative writing to their special experience of living in the multicultural society of Singapore.

Marks of Colonialism

I was born Chinese,
Given a Chinese name;
I look Chinese!
I am Chinese!
Yet I write and speak in a foreign tongue
That is native to me.
I think English,
And I communicate in English
With my English-speaking Chinese friends--
Yet when I speak to an Englishman
He thinks me foreign!
Doesn't he realise I know
More about Shakespeare than I do about Confucius,
In other words I am just as English.
Thus, when I speak to a "Chinaman"
I am queer and foreign to him
Although I am a Chinese!
Yet try with all my might,
I can never think Chinese, only in translation--
Did they know it would be like this?
Did they care? Those colonial masters?
That I live in a sadly complicated
Dislodged world today.

Kee Siew Gek

Uncertain

I used to be a devout Buddhist
With respect for all forms of life
Till they made the mistake of sending me

To a Mission School.
Here was a-drilling and a-drumming
Of a God with a capital "G"
And they shrunk my "g" pint size.
Thus, I've grown out of Buddhism
Yet I've not taken to this Christian mode.
Hard thinking on some restless nights
Has helped me to decide,
That life should not be a living in fear--
Fear of "threats of hell" as the Rubaiyat says,
And certainly not mere dictation
From tiny prints in an awfully thick book.
Now sets in a new fear I haven't bargained for--
A fear of a miscalculation;
A fear that on some throne might sit Him,
A fear that provokes still more thoughts
That trigger off a final fear--
A fear that I might go through this precious life
Hand in hand with someone called Cynic.

Chan Leng Geok

Acknowledgment

I wish to acknowledge with gratitude the valuable assistance I received from Mrs. Siti H. Mustapha and Mrs. Lim-Tham Yew Chin of the National Library, who provided me with the information in this paper concerning Malay and Chinese children's books, respectively.

Notes

1. Gopinathan, S. "Publishing in a Plural Society: The Case of Singapore," in Perspectives in Publishing; Philip Altbach, and Sheila McVey, editors. Lexington, Mass.: D. C. Heath, 1976, p. 157.

2. Ibid., p. 162.

3. Kuo, Eddie C. Y. "Language Status and Literary Trends in a Multilingual Society," Relc Journal 5, no. 1: June, 1974.

4. Lau, Wai Har. "Education for Living--an Appreciation." Singapore, 1974 (unpublished). Quoted by S. Gopinathan, p. 162.

5. Lee, Kok Cheong. "Learning English in the Singapore
    Context." Radio talk in series, "Improving Your
    Child's English." Singapore, 1976 (unpublished).

6. Mohd, Salleh Daud. "Problems and Prospects in Malay
    Language (ML2) Teaching." Paper presented at
    seminar on "The Role of Educational Materials in
    Singapore Schools." Singapore, 1973 (unpublished).

7. Perumbulavil, Vilasini. "The Selection of Materials
    for Student Use in Developing Countries," Singapore
    Libraries 4: 1974, pp. 34-35.

8. Yeo, Robert. "The Arts in Singapore--The Last Ten
    Years and Beyond," in NG, Charles and Menon,
    T. P. B., Singapore--A Decade of Independence.
    Singapore, Alumni International. Singapore, 1975,
    p. 54.

9. Van Niel, Eloise. "Malay Folk Literature with Special
    Reference to Children," International Library Review
    5, no. 4, 1973, pp. 483-495.

10. Sherry, Sylvia. Street of the Small Night Market.
    London: Cape, 1966.

11. Yeo, Robert, op. cit., p. 55.

12. Saya (meaning "I" in Malay), a magazine devoted to
    creative writing by young people in the secondary
    schools in Singapore.

Chapter 5

MODERN JAPANESE CHILDREN'S BOOKS

by Momoko Ishii

I would like to begin with a brief, personal history, for through it I can perhaps best describe the development of Japanese children's literature from the point of view of a translator, an author, an editor, a teacher and a librarian. I have been all of these at some time in my life.

Soon after my graduation as an English major, I encountered those two wonderful English children's books, Winnie the Pooh and The House at Pooh Corner by A. A. Milne. They were Christmas presents from a friend to two children whom I knew. Until the moment I set eyes on the books, I did not know who Pooh was, or A. A. Milne, but as I began to tell, in Japanese, the stories to those two children, at their request, I felt a most unusual sensation. The sensation was quite physical and it was as though I entered into a strange world, just as Lucy in C. S. Lewis' The Lion, the Witch and the Wardrobe went into the country of Narnia through a wardrobe in her uncle's house.

The two children and I had a hilarious time that evening. And the "Pooh fever" became quite contagious among my friends and they kept nagging me to translate the stories into Japanese.

That is how I came to be the translator of the Pooh stories at the very beginning of the Second World War, and Iwanami Shoten, one of our most conscientious publishers, kindly published them in spite of the scarcity of paper. They were, however, soon out of print, because the stories had nothing to do with the war and, moreover, they were the literature of an enemy country.

A short time later, I wrote a story of my own, this time to console a soldier who did not want to go to the war. The story was about a little girl called Nonchan. "One morning, Nonchan, who was very sad, fell into a pond and met an old man who was rowing a big cloud floating on the surface of the pond. They had a good time together." This story was not published because, again, the story had nothing to do with the war. The times were becoming harder and paper scarcer. So the manuscript was just circulated among my friends.

When the war became very severe and food scanty, a few friends and I went into a mountain village to become farmers. But eventually the long war came to an end. Mr. Tamao Fujita, an editor of a publishing firm called Chūō Koronsha, who had read the story of Nonchan, wrote to me at my mountain home, asking if I had the manuscript with me. "In Japan, people are starving for printed pages as well as for food," he said. And this is how Nonchan Kumo Ni Noru (Nonchan Rides a Cloud) was published in Tokyo while I was in the mountain village of Miyagi-Ken. I remember that we bought a cow with the first royalty payment on Nonchan.

All this time, I had had no idea that I was a children's book translator or a writer. I did what I liked. Now, if you will permit me to go back a little farther into my own life story ... I was one of the fortunate children who had been told stories by grandparents who knew many folktales. Life was quite plain in Japan fifty or sixty years ago. Stories and books were handed down in families in the same manner as the kimonos we wore. Being a fifth sister, I scarcely had anything new until I was about fifteen. As the kimonos were used and used by my sisters and then myself, so the stories and books were told, read and handed down to us. Nowadays, the situation is quite different. Grandparents no longer tell stories to their grandchildren and, even worse, the children who want to listen to them are very few; both just watch TV. So, it was because of my grandparents and large family that I had come to develop a receptive mind and could recognize something enjoyable when I met it, as with the Pooh books.

But other people thought that I was trying to be a children's writer, although I thought of myself as a farmer. Many friends wrote to me suggesting that I come back to Tokyo and take a job which had something to do with

children's books. The most eager encourager was the
publisher Iwanami, who had so courageously published the
Pooh books during the war. And at last, I went back to
Tokyo after five years of farming. It was suggested that
I edit "The Iwanami Boys and Girls Library," a series of
childrens' classics, old and new, Japanese and foreign. I
was supposed to choose about two hundred volumes, find
the right translators for the right books, select good Japanese stories, and so forth.

When I began to work, my agony began. I found
choosing good foreign books such as Treasure Island and
The Secret Garden amazingly easy. The Story of Doctor
Dolittle or Emile and the Detectives were so alive and
visual that I could almost feel a tug from the books themselves. Whereas, when the so-called Japanese modern
classics were placed side by side with these foreign
stories, they seemed so fragmented, mystical, remote,
without body or structure or plot. Sometimes you could
catch brilliant flashes of intense emotion, but they were
not tangible. I began to realize that I had never read
Japanese stories critically enough before. As a child, with
the exception of the Japanese folk tales, I had always preferred foreign stories. And then one day, to my great
dismay, I read an article written by a famous teacher which
said that modern Japanese children should discard folktales.
They were not suitable food for their minds in the new
democratic age.

I had then been at Iwanami for five years. We had
brought out about one hundred foreign old and new classics
in good translations and fifteen picture books, but only
about five Japanese classics. I did not have much belief
in my work by then, when, as luck would have it, I was
granted a one-year fellowship abroad to study children's
literature, editing and public libraries in the United States
and other countries. This trip was really a profound experience to me. What I enjoyed most was going about the
children's rooms in New York City and the Toronto Boys
and Girls House. Those of you who are from countries
that have had children's rooms in your public libraries for
many years, I wonder if you recognize the value of what
you have been doing? Maybe you overlook it; it is too
much of an everyday thing for you. What you have on your
bookshelves is an accumulation of seventy to eighty years
of responses of children to their books.

When I looked at your children's rooms and at the children as they swarmed over them and the open shelves full of books, I thought that this was the way the children expressed what they wanted to say, but could not. Children cannot tell you analytically why they like these books; they just say, "We like this," or they read until the book becomes threadbare. And as I stood in front of the bookshelves of your children's rooms, I thought, "Isn't it the duty of adults to take at least ten or twenty books that have been loved by the children for over twenty years and see critically what they have in common?" I noticed also that the folktales of the world formed the core of the collection, and around them were new stories, new books, like flowers and fruit that had sprung from their roots.

When I went back to Japan after one year's stay abroad, I did not go back to my editorial work. Instead I went to the mountain village where I had lived before and began reading stories once a week to the fifth-grade children of the village school. What I really wanted to do was to lend books to the children for them to read. But the village children could not read well. All they could devour and gulp down by themselves were the comic-magazines which were circulating in Japan by the millions. At first, I took foreign picture books which would take about five minutes to tell, but they could not even sit still that five minutes. After some weeks, they were able to listen to a thirty-minute story. What they liked especially were folktales! When a folktale came to an end, I could hear a whole class give a big sigh, and yet when I asked if they ever had heard such a story from their grandparents, there was no hand raised. By the end of the two years, when they were graduated from the primary school, what do you think they could listen to?--Leo Tolstoi's Where There Is Love, There Is God, which lasted two hours.

After these two years in the mountain village I went back to Tokyo again, because as long as I was in the country, I would have to read to the children. They were not able to read on the level of their interests. As you know, we use Chinese characters, which we learned from China through Korea more than a thousand years ago, and two types of phonetic symbols, which we call "Kana," all mixed together. It is a very clever but intricate system for expressing ideas. You have to begin at an early age if you want to master this skill with ease.

In 1958, with the help of an assistant, I started a little reading room for the neighborhood children in Tokyo which we called "Katsurabunko." All my children's books were available to them and they could take two books home for two weeks. There were about forty English and American picture books and I cannot tell you what a great help they were. Very young children did not mind what language the books were written in, as long as they could read the stories from the pictures. This was twenty years ago and I can not help but think what a long way Japanese picture books have come since then. Now, many Japanese picture books are thought to be outstanding throughout the world.

All in all, my children preferred translations better than the original Japanese stories. It was about then that my several friends and I, who had often gathered together and talked about children's books, began to re-read the Japanese stories which had been considered "modern Japanese classics that every child should read." The friends were: Teiji Seta, who had edited the Children's Encyclopaedia at Heibonsha; Tadashi Matsui, at that time chief editor of Fukuinkan-Shoten; Tomiko Inui, my successor at the Iwanami Shoten; a writer, Shigeru Watanabe, once a children's librarian at New York Public Library and at that time teaching in the Library School of Keio University; and Shinichi Suzuki, a journalist. We began reading and discussing famous Japanese writers and their stories, one by one.

Ours was only a small discussion group, meeting in a tiny corner of Japan's publishing and children's book world. After five years we felt that it might be worthwhile to publish the records of our discussions. Fortunately, an editor took up the idea and put them into an attractive paperback in 1960. Our approach in this book was to reappraise the value of the literature of Mimei Ogawa, Hirosuke Hamada and Joji Tsubata, who had been considered the founders of modern Japanese children's literature, and also Kenji Miyazawa, Shozo Chiba, and Nankichi Niimi. We expressed adverse opinions on the first three authors; we felt that they had "led us astray." Our book caused considerable controversy.

While we were having our small study group sessions, we thought we were alone in our concern, but when the book came out we found there were many cries like ours among our young, lively critics. The tide was

changing, but not as quickly as we thought. If there had
been a public library system with experienced librarians
functioning for the past fifty or sixty years in Japan, the
circumstances might have been different. New dimensions
might have been opened and different perspectives expressed. But these young critics and our voices were
rather too many-sided and unorganized. The discussions
were chaotic and not really constructive.

But my own feelings about those famous three authors, whom we had appraised as negative, were rather
complicated. I had to think of the drastic changes Japan
had undergone during their lifetime and of the Japanese
temperament which we too had inside ourselves. I mean
by our temperaments our ever-changing moods, which are
our response to our climate. Our seasons are short and
so is the life of our flowers. The cycle of this kind of
climate reminds us of sadness, loneliness and death.
From this temperament was born the culture of "wabi" and
"sabi." I think that, in general, we are emotional and
subjective, instead of logical and objective. This is why
I could quite sympathize with those writers.

Let me go a little further back into our Japanese
cultural history. Over a hundred years ago, in 1853, after
two hundred and fifty years of complete isolation under the
Tokugawa Shogunate's control, our country was opened up.
At that time, about fifty per cent of the Japanese men and
more than fifteen per cent of the Japanese women could
read and write. This is not the result of my research,
but that of Dr. Dore of England. He says, in his book
Education in Tokugawa Japan, [1] that this literacy percentage
must have been the highest in the world at that time. But
that did not mean that all of our people were free and
happy. At any rate, the country was opened and the Meiji
Era began. In 1872, the compulsory educational law was
enacted and the reading public rapidly increased. Western
civilization rushed in.

However, when we look back at the Japanese language of that time from the literary point of view, it was
not in a very happy state. The written and the colloquial
had been sadly split in two. The writers for adults and
children suffered under this burden. For language was
their tool and for some of them it became a problem of
life or death. How could one create anything real when
the language was so remote from the people?

As early as 1872, <u>Robinson Crusoe</u> had been translated into Japanese, in 1875 <u>The Arabian Nights</u> and in
1878, Verne's <u>Around the World in Eighty Days</u>, and these
are but a few. These and others were translated into
grandiose Japanese and went into the highly educated families. In order to keep people up to date with these foreign
masterpieces, various magazines sprang up, retelling them
in a less difficult form of the Japanese language. This
kind of situation continued for some thirty years. Then,
in 1891, Sazananami Iwaya, our first important name in the
history of children's literature, wrote a story called
<u>Koganemaru</u>. It is an adventure story of a dog's revenge
on his father's destroyer, a ferocious tiger. <u>Koganemaru</u>
was also written in a grandiose style.

Iwaya was brought up in a well-to-do family and
learned German while quite young. After he became an
author and wrote many children's stories or retold Japanese
folktales, he went to Germany to teach Japanese in a German university. When he came back to Japan, he became
an ardent supporter of colloquial language. This was a
very serious movement, at that time, in Japan. He decided
to rewrite his successful <u>Koganemaru</u> in colloquial and con-
versational language. But it fell flat! I was surprised
when I was told that it had been rewritten by Sazananami
himself; I could not recognize it. As time went on, his
voluminous body of retold fairy tales became moralistic
and his style talkative.

By the time the Meiji era came to an end in 1912
and the Taisho era took its place, people's ideas and their
ways of life had changed considerably. The champion, who
claimed that children's literature should also be "artistic,"
was the writer Miekichi Suzuki. Although he himself did
not write original stories for children, he issued the magazine <u>Akai Tori</u> (Red Bird) and asked many contemporary
writers and poets to write for children. Many stories and
songs appeared in this magazine which are still read and
sung, such as <u>Toshishun</u> (a tale retold from China about a
man called Toshishun), <u>Kumo No Ito</u> (A Thread of Cobweb)
by Ryunosuke Akutagawa, and children's songs by Hakushu
Kitahara.

Mimei Ogawa was one of the contributors to <u>Akai
Tori</u> who became a writer of children's stories by his own
choice in the middle of his literary career. The publication of his first book in 1910, <u>Akai Fune</u> (Red Ship), was

regarded as a landmark of Japanese modern artistic children's literature. With a few other children's writers, this era was thought of as the "blossoming of modern Japanese children's literature," until just after the Second World War.

But as I told you before, when our little group re-read these short, sad, nostalgic stories, some forty years later, we felt we recognized the shadows of the Japanese temperament, which is very difficult for us to escape. And yet we also felt it was about time our children were raised upon something more healthy, and yet, still basically Japanese.

Here I will touch upon the business side--the publishing and selling of books in Japan, which sometimes tends to prevent the publishing of quality books.

In Japan, the publishers seldom sell their own books to the public through their own salespeople. There are several very powerful wholesalers in Tokyo, as well as in a few other big cities, and when the publishers print new books they go to the wholesalers with their samples. Perhaps, one wholesaler will take five hundred copies. Then the wholesaler pays the publisher about seventy-five per cent of the retail price and distributes the books all through Japan along with the books of other publishers. Then the bookstores put the new books upon the bookshelves and after one month or so (the time depends, more or less, upon the space on the bookshelves of the individual bookstores), they return the unsold books to the wholesaler. Often the publisher has to refund the money paid by the wholesaler for the unsold books. In order to avoid this, the publishers keep on bringing out new books all the time, so that they will not come face to face with the ultimate loss. I heard that it takes a half a year for a publisher to know the rough balance of one book, and that the average rate of unsold books is seventy per cent. I do not know how many publishers can work in this kind of system, but there are still even more complicated riddles to our publishing business in Japan that I do not know. I shall only add here that there are about three publishers who use what we call "kaikiri seido." That means that they will not take back the unsold books. These publishers have their own customers and are very careful and have confidence in what they bring out.

I think that this risky distribution situation, especially in the area of children's books, could be avoided if
we had a public library system as customers for children's
books.   When our publishers bring out children's books,
they do not think of the public library market; they are
only interested in individual sales.   Japan has a population
of one hundred and eleven million people, and we have about
one thousand public libraries and approximately six hundred
children's rooms.   When the publishers want to sell their
books, it is only natural that they play out their game at
the bookstores.

Twenty years ago, when I went back to Japan, I
was talking to a head of the children's department of a
very big publishing firm.   He told me frankly that at that
time their most important job was to publish fifteen or
twenty volumes of the "world children's classic series."
They had been doing this over and over again, sometimes
changing titles of the series, abridging, rewriting, etc.
This type of work absorbed up to eighty per cent of their
publishing business.   A twenty-volume series was also very
expensive.   Bookstores were eager to respond to the publisher's encouragement, for if you sold fifty sets of the
series the profit was really good.   So until twenty years
ago, everywhere you went, you could see these thick
volumes of "World Classics for Boys and Girls" set upon
the bookshelves of so many homes as pieces of furniture.
How many of those were really read by children, I do not
know.   But almost every Japanese older than forty knows
Little Lord Fauntleroy, The Little Princess, Little Women,
Pinocchio and so on.   All of which had been going on for
forty or fifty years.

But at my own private library the children did not
like those big fat books which all looked the same.   They
preferred books which had individual faces, even just to
look upon.   When I told this to the young editors who
sometimes came to visit my library, they said that individually produced books just did not sell.   I discovered
that the books that children liked to borrow on their own
account were often the kind that publishers did not like to
publish.   I sometimes think that if there had been stronger
influential public libraries as the main buyers of the books,
the publishing situation of children's books in Japan would
have been quite different.

However, some publishers were courageous enough

to publish young writer's original stories or quite new foreign classics, such as C. S. Lewis's fantasies of Narnia or the adventure stories of Arthur Ransome or Astrid Lindgren's "Pippi" stories. In the eighteen-year history of my little library, the best read record goes to C. S. Lewis's books. The fever has now subsided, but when the books began to come out, one by one, more than ten years ago, we put three sets of the series on the shelf and yet there was always a long waiting list.

So the tide which had been flowing in one narrow direction had begun to turn, slowly but steadily. There are now quite a few original writers in Japan, although I think we are still weak in creating really robust and truly Japanese children's books which might become classic. There are hundreds of children's authors and would-be authors, for children's books do sell, because, as I stated before, parents buy them, but not public libraries.

However, private libraries, which we call "Home Libraries," are increasing every year. Since the public libraries' activities are regulated by the national or municipal governments and since trained librarians are scarce, people are finding it necessary to create their own libraries. A home library can get started with only a few housewives who have agreed to take on the responsibility. Please remember that there are only a little more than six hundred public children's libraries in Japan now. You cannot tell, of course, exactly how many home libraries there are; some of them are here today and gone tomorrow. But, there are certainly over three thousand.

With these situations in our background, our children's librarians themselves started, some years ago, their own volunteer workshop called the Association for Study of Children's Library and have been fighting for the betterment of services for children in the public library. There also are other groups which try to help and advise those who are running home libraries with scanty facilities. Among them is a party called Japan Centre for Parent-Child Reading, which is working under Mr. Shogo Saito, an ex-teacher. Another interesting group is Mrs. Mitsue Ishitake's Ohanashi Caravan (Storytelling Caravan), which visits public and home libraries with puppet shows and storytellers.

Our little group is doing its part too. To spur our country and to unite the activities of the public libraries and the home libraries, with Kyoko Matsuoka as our champion, we created a foundation two years ago. The foundation is called Tokyo Kodomo Toshokan (Tokyo Children's Library). Our aim is to have a model children's library in the future, to show people what we can do with children and with books outside of school. Kyoko Matsuoka and her assistants have been working with definite educational programs, such as running storytelling courses for children's librarians of the public libraries, as well as for mothers or any other persons who are managing home libraries. In April of 1976 we completed a two-year course on storytelling. We also issue pamphlets with suggestions on how to select stories and books for children, and so on. This is important, since the millions of people who buy books for children--mothers, aunts and uncles, etc.--frequently buy only what attracts the eye.

Certainly, in every country the way from didacticism to a genuine children's literature has been long and difficult. Now, we are living on a small and yet open planet. In spite of a new type of nationalism which is arising everywhere today, we are stepping out into another stage where the range of give-and-take between countries is greater than ever. Your concern is our concern. We have to work together, I think. And I think that we can not go back to isolation.

Well, I am afraid that I have spoken subjectively, rather than objectively about children's literature. How like a Japanese!

Note

1. Dore, Ronald Philip. Education in Tokugawa Japan. Berkeley: University of California Press, 1965.

A List of Japanese Children's Books

Aman, Kimiko. Fushigi na yūenchi (Mysterious Playground). Tokyo: Jitsugyō no Nihon Sha, 1969.

_____. Kuruma no iro wa sora no iro (The Color of the Wheel Is the Color of the Sky). Tokyo: Popurasha, 1968.

Imae, Yoshitomo. Furūto to konekochan (The Kitten and the Flute). Tokyo: Akane Shobō, 1973.

_____. Hen desu nee hen desu nee (Isn't It Strange? Isn't It Strange?). Tokyo: Betonamu no Kodomo o Shiensuru Kai, 1972.

_____. Kieta tonosama (The Lord Who Disappeared). Tokyo: Komine Shoten, 1968.

*Imanishi, Sukeyuki. The Moon and the Fishes; tr. by Ann Herring; il. by Sakura Fujita. Tokyo: Gakken; San Francisco: Japan Pubns, 1973.

Inui, Tomiko. Kaze no omatsuri (The Wind Festival). Tokyo: Fukuinkan Shoten, 1972.

_____. Kokage no ie no kobitotachi (The Little People in the House under the Big Tree). Tokyo: Kadokawa Shoten, 1972.

_____. Kurayami no tani no kobitotachi (The Little People in the Pitch Dark Valley). Tokyo: Fukuinkan Shoten, 1972.

_____. Nagai nagai pengin no hanashi (A Long, Long Story of Penguins). Tokyo: Rironsha, 1963.

*Ishii, Momoko. Issunbōshi (The Inchling); tr. by Yone Mizuta; il. by Fuku Akino. New York: Walker, 1967.

_____. Kotorachan no bōken (The Adventures of Little Tiger). Tokyo: Fujin no Tomo Sha, 1971.

Iwasaki, Kyōko. Akamammatōge (Akamamma Pass). Tokyo: Dōshinsha, 1972.

_____. Chiisana hachikai (The Little Bee Keeper). Tokyo: Fukuinkan Shoten, 1971.

*Kanzawa, Toshiko. The Foxes and the Horse Dealer; adapted by Kenichi Mizusawa; tr. by Ann Brannen; il.

_____

*Listings prefaced with an asterisk have been translated into English.

by Daihachi Ohta. Tokyo: Gakken; San Francisco:
Japan Pubns, 1973. (Gakken Picture Book Series.)

* _____. Raintaro. San Francisco: Japan Pubns, 1972.

* _____. The Selfish Old Woman; il. by Yosuke Inoue.
Indianapolis: Bobbs-Merrill, 1971.

Matsuoka, Kyōko. Nazonazo no suki na onna no ko (The
Little Girl Who Liked Riddles). Tokyo: Gakushū
Kenkyūsha, 1973.

*Matsutani, Miyoko. The Crane Maiden; tr. by Alvin Tres-
selt; il. by Chihiro Iwasaki. New York: Parents' Magazine Press, 1968.

* _____. The Fisherman under the Sea; tr. by Alvin
Tresselt; il. by Chihiro Iwasaki. New York: Parents'
Magazine Press, 1969.

* _____. How the Withered Tree Blossomed; il. by Yasuo
Segawa. Philadelphia: Lippincott, 1971, c1969. English and Japanese text.

* _____. Taro, the Dragon Boy; tr. by Donald C. Boone;
il. by Masakazu Kuwata. 1st ed. Tokyo; Palo Alto,
Calif.: Kodansha International, 1967.

* _____. The Witch's Magic Cloth; tr. by Alvin Tresselt; il. by Yasuo Segawa. New York: Parents' Magazine Press, 1969.

*Nakagawa, Rieko. A Blue Seed; il. by Yuriko Omura.
New York: Hastings House, 1967, c1965.

_____. Kogitsune Konchi to okāsan (Konchi, the Little
Fox and His Mother). Tokyo: Kodansha, 1971.

Satō, Satoru. Jun to Himitsu no tomodachi (Jun and His
Secret Friend). Tokyo: Iwanami Shoten, 1972.

_____. Kappa to mikazuki (A Kappa and the New Moon).
Tokyo: Akane Shobo, 1974.

Watanabe, Shigeo. Tera-machi sanchōme jūichibanchi
(#11, 3-chome, Tera Street). Tokyo: Fukuinkan
Shoten, 1969.

Yamanaka, Hisashi. *Gando no ganko* (Stubborn Gando).
  Tokyo: Bunken Shuppan, 1973.

_____. *Mama wa oshaberi* (Mother's a Blabbermouth).
  Tokyo: Komine Shoten, 1970.

Chapter 6

BOOK TRAILS IN A SMALL COUNTRY
(NEW ZEALAND)

by Elsie Locke

So there we are away down in the South Pacific, as
the poet said,

Two small islands pointing towards the Pole,
A child's kite in the indifferent blue.

The first people to discover and colonize this land
were Maoris, that is Polynesians akin to the Hawaiians and
Samoans, and we were the last island of any size to be inhabited by men. One hundred and thirty-six years ago, in
1840, New Zealand became a colony of the British Empire,
which makes us about the same vintage as British Columbia. For twenty years after accession we had something
like dual control between Maoris and British; then the
colonists became dominant by a mixed process of negotia-
tion, force and guile. The Maoris resisted through a
series of little wars and they never lost completely. Although there was a time when many of the conquerors believed, with a lugubrious sort of hope, that the Maoris
were dying out as a separate entity, they turned the tables
and are now increasing much faster than average. Today,
of our population of a little over three million, about one
in ten is a Maori. If we take children under fifteen, the
proportion is about one in eight.

Our immigration has been overwhelmingly British
and Irish, with a few beneficial injections from other European countries and from China. So here is the social context for our literature--a short colonial history followed by
independence, a high standard of living, a language shared
by all, and three million people with a good level of education. And we are keen readers. True, there are many

whose reading never rises higher than the road signs or
"Best Bets," but we keep a lot of bookshops in business.
We claim one bookshop for every seventy-five hundred people, whereas Australia has one for every fifteen thousand,
Britain one for every nineteen thousand and the United
States one for every fifty thousand. I cannot find comparable figures for libraries but unless the Australians have
caught up in the last ten years, we are about thirty per
cent higher than they are in the number of borrowers.

What books do we have in our children's libraries?
Obviously most of the titles must come from the big world
outside, mainly from Britain, and some from Australia,
but very few from America because of market agreements
and currency problems. And these books include lots of
translations. Our children are nourished on the literature
of the whole world so far as it's available in English and
they take all this in their stride.

But what do we provide that is really our own? For
our first hundred years we can say bluntly, very little and
very poor fare. Anyone from countries with a colonial
background could have guessed as much. No one can write
from a sense of national identity until that identity is truly
established. To quote a poet again,

> No people can possess a land
> Where every single sod and stone is strange.

Our first settlers were transplanted Englishmen, Scotsmen
and Irishmen and how they loved their Home, their Mother
Country--so much so that they kept trying and trying to
turn New Zealand into a Little Britain of the South. But
of course they couldn't. The land and landscape were different, the work was different, the ways they earned their
livings were different, even the great traditional festivals
came at the wrong season, Easter in autumn and Christmas
at midsummer. And it took more than a century to get us
out of the habit of eating the Christmas plum duff in swelt-
ering heat. And we still stick imitation holly all over the
place and pictures of lighted candles in the snow. Walt
Whitman said,

> There was a child went forth every day
> And the first object he looked upon, that object
>   he became
> And that object became part of him for the day

or a certain part of the day
Or for many years or stretching cycles of years.

But how is it when the real world in which he walks,
and the world of books in which he feeds his imagination and
enlarges his understanding are two radically different
spheres? I give you the words of a fellow writer, Rollo
Arnold:

> I grew up in a back country valley a few
> chains from where my grandfather had pitched his
> tent beside a bush stream, and began the im-
> mense task of hewing the hundreds of acres of
> rimu and totara from the valley floor; a work to
> which my father was taken from his primary
> schooling at the age of twelve. But only in the
> most limited sense did I inherit this past as a
> child. I can remember reciting:
>
> > The silver birch is a dainty lady
> > She keeps our English churchyards
> > shady.
>
> But nothing about rimus and totaras. And even
> before I saw the schoolroom, the process had
> begun as my mother passed on the nursery rhymes
> endeared to her by her own childhood:
>
> > The north wind doth blow
> > And we shall have snow
> > And what will cock robin do then,
> > poor thing!
> > He'll sit in the barn
> > And keep himself warm
> > And poke his head under his wing,
> > poor thing.
>
> But the English robin is one of those birds that
> failed to acclimatise in New Zealand, and al-
> though I knew a little of the shy New Zealand
> bush robins, we all knew that they never came
> near our sheds--for of course, we didn't talk of
> barns.
>   The countryside about me and the toils, hopes
> and fears of the two generations who had lived
> there before me were excluded as if they had
> never been, a great unexplained irrelevance. I

do not think we can really say that we have possessed this land of ours until we have as it were,
much more fully colonized it in our imaginations.

Inevitably, and marvelously, the time had to come
when enough of us felt as New Zealanders, and saw ourselves as New Zealanders, to begin this imaginative revolution. It was no use any more trying to pretend that New
Zealand was a little Britain of the South. The pioneers
had their intentions and expectations but the land and landscape were not the same, the work was not the same, the
seasons were not the same and the Maori people had their
effect. As other colonies have discovered, and as the
poet said,

> But as the children grew
> It was something different, something
> Nobody counted on.

After a few preliminary efforts, this revolution got
under way in the 1930s and as you would expect, it began
with young adults writing for their own age group. It was
a vigorous time anyway, for other reasons. We were
Pakehas with New Zealand in our bones. (The term Pakeha
is a nice word for a New Zealander of European descent;
it means a fair-skinned being from another world.) One
of our best poets was the great-great-great-grandson of
pre-colonial missionaries. I saw "we" because I was a
part of that movement although my contribution wasn't literary. I was collating pages for the "little magazines"
which carried the work of the writers, and feeding the
dedicated printer with pork pies at three in the morning
and that sort of thing.

I mention this because the role of small presses,
sometimes run for no pay at all in the promoters' spare
time and sometimes run as an idealistic business giving
the promoter no more than a modest living or even bank-
ruptcy at the end, has been very important in developing
a New Zealand literature. I suspect this must be the
case for all small communities, whether they constitute a
nation or a section within a nation separated by space or
language.

It is no accident that our writers have developed a
real finesse in short stories and sketches and poetry.
These are the forms which the "little magazines" and little

books could accommodate. These writings did not reach a
big audience. Most New Zealanders still had the feeling
that what came out of England was quality (from machines
to shoes to books) and that home products were second
rate. But then came our first Centenary in 1940. True,
it was bedeviled by the war, but the books to celebrate it
had already been commissioned, the literary competitions
had been launched. And some of these were very good
books. They made a great contribution towards turning
our thoughts and imaginations and sense of history and
geography increasingly to our own country. The impetus
continued after the war and the sales of New Zealand books
began to rise. Today, we are great buyers of our own
books.

But even with good reading habits three million people provide a very small market for a publisher and the
economic problem for children's books is compounded by
the cost of illustration. Yet even in the two decades before
the Centenary we had four women writing extensively for
children, and in a library survey of 1927 three of these
were included among the eighteen favorite authors among
girls. The boys, alas, had no favorite New Zealand au-
thors--or Australian either.

The "little magazine" that lifted our juvenile literature off the ground was the New Zealand School Journal.
I find a deal of scepticism here that a Government publication could be devoted to literature and art, but it's true.
The Journal was already well established as a teaching tool
when after the war (and the centenary) it went through its
own revolution to become a lively venture into literature
and art. And being a Government publication it did not
have to worry, as publishers did, about making those financial ends meet. Its editors have been consistently expert
and enthusiastic--many of them writers and artists of distinction. The hand of officialdom appears sometimes, but
not too often. Many of our authors began by trying their
hand in the New Zealand School Journal--Ruth Dallas and
Margaret Mahy and Katarina Mataira and myself included.
And the illustrators, too, often began there--like Jill Mc-
Donald who draws those marvelous funny Puffins. You
may think of her as English, but she's really one of us.

Then what about the commercially published books?
About one hundred and ninety fiction and poetry titles for
children (that is excluding all those classed as educational)

have appeared since the Centenary. In quality they cover the whole range from good to terrible. Seventy-five were published overseas and many of the others had dual publication: New Zealand and Great Britain, and New Zealand and Australia. Taking figures for sixteen substantial publishers in the three years ending March 1975, we had three hundred and sixty-three new books in the categories of fiction, poetry, general non-fiction and juveniles. Of these three hundred and sixty-three, thirteen were for children (three and one-half per cent), with an average print-run of three thousand and three hundred. Those published overseas exceeded this number--at least twenty-one--although twelve were by one author, Margaret Mahy, whose stories, many of them written earlier, were being suddenly put on the market at this time.

What sort of books do we write? Let's take fantasy first. Alas for the writers who have tried to give us fairies; the results have all been deplorable. Let us face it, New Zealand cannot have fairies in the old world sense at all. Like the Robin Redbreast they just will not acclimatize. Oh yes, as a child, bemused by those English books, I had my own special pixies in a cave beside the harbor; but I knew all the time they were English pixies. We have no tradition of folk and fairy tales, as have France and Japan and the USSR, reaching back for centuries. The industrial revolution had torn up the peasant roots before New Zealand was colonized. We do have our own kind of folklore but it's a very human folklore, the tough elemental kind where man contends with a tough environment, hunting whales, suffering shipwreck, felling the forest, prospecting for gold, digging kauri gum, exploring the most forbidding mountains.

We have only three fantasy writers of quality and the most successful of them, Margaret Mahy, has simply stepped out of the local scene into a universal one. She peoples her fantasies with pirates and witches and kings and clowns who could be anywhere, and that suits our children because their fantasy world is everywhere and anywhere. And she has the most delicious language. Like this:

> There was once a very cross woman called Mrs. Discombobulus. Oh, she was a scold, a shrew, a vixen and a virago, and a proper tyrant and tartar to her poor husband (whose name was

Mr. Discombobulus). She niggled and naggled
him day and night, from first yawn to last. He
was ragged, poor-spirited, uncivil, unkempt and
unkind, if you listened to what his wife said about
him. Mrs. Discombobulus's tongue, people said,
was as sharp as a barber's razor and twice as
long.

Mrs. Discombobulus was sucked into the washing machine
and came out into a different world where her wicked tongue
did some good, and returned in a better frame of mind.
So you see, this is a modern fantasy, because it has a
washing machine!

Personally I do see a light-hearted commentary on
New Zealand in Margaret Mahy's fondness for juxtaposition
of the ordinary and the respectable with the delightfully incredible. Take The Man Whose Mother Was a Pirate. He
worked in an office writing down rows of figures and ruling
neat lines beneath them until one day his mother was
seized with a longing to go back to the sea, and the only
way he had to take her was in a wheelbarrow.

His mother's short grey hair ruffled merrily out
under the green scarf she wore tied around her
head. Her gold earrings challenged the sun,
throwing his light back to him. Between her
lips was her old black pipe, and she wore behind
her ear a rose that matched her scarlet shawl.
The little man wore his brown suit and boots,
all buttoned and tied. He trotted along pushing
the wheelbarrow. As they went his mother talked
about the sea. She told him of its voices.
"It sings at night with a sad booming voice.
Under the sun it laughs and slaps the side of the
ship in time to its laughter. Yes, and then when
a storm comes it screams and hates poor sailors.
And the sea is a great gossip. What is the
weather at Tierra del Fuego? Is the ice moving
in Hudson Bay? Where are the great whales sailing? The sea knows it all, and one wave whispers and mutters it to another, and to those who
know how to listen."
"Hmm, yes indeed mother," the little man
said, pattering the wheelbarrow along. His shoes
hurt rather.

These are books inspired by books, words inspired by words, sometimes words that children, in practice, may find difficult and daunting but helped along by lavish illustrations since Margaret Mahy was "discovered" by an American publisher, Franklin-Watts.

Then what about the Maori tradition? Certainly that was oral, and many were the stories told of old in the long dark evenings or in shelter from the rain and storm. The hybrid writers who have tried their best to write England into New Zealand have had a go at Maori fairies, too. But although Maori legends do tell of other-worldly beings, they are not fairies in any sense approaching the European species; and it's misleading to use the term "fairies" at all.

Originally the Maori myths and legends were oral stories, taught and memorized and lovingly recounted generation by generation. When the Pakehas came the collectors seized these stories avidly and glued them down in print, whether faithfully recorded or otherwise. The popularizers followed. But we can not just switch a tale that has grown in one culture into the language and forms of another--any more than an alpine daisy can be made to flourish in the salt spray of the sea coast. The English mind did not easily reach the subtleties and the deep meanings and the allusions. The English words did not express the same concepts, they lacked the rhythm and beauty of sound. And when the legends were stark, the temptation was to adapt them to respectability. And they were not children's stories, anyway, in the first place. Yet these were our only truly New Zealand legends and naturally Pakeha writers have done their best to pass them on to all our children, although their best was not, and could not be, good enough. It is only very recently that Maori writers have attempted the task, and that the general reading public has a better understanding of the way the Maori looks at life.

Maori culture today is vigorous and assertive. The Maori writer or artist does not try to pretend that he is an ancient Maori, he accepts the modern influences and blends them with the traditional. You can see this in the art work in the Maori language journals. The Taniwha of Whangaparaoa, one of the few bilingual books for children, is also an interesting example. Whangaparaoa has a Pakeha name, Cape Runaway, named by Captain Cook because, when the ship's cannon was fired, the people ran away. The Maori children in the little school there hated this story, so the Maori teacher, Roka Paora, suggested that they write their own. The Taniwha of Whangaparaoa is the result--a legend made up to suit the present day but still very Maori in its style.

One of the problems of self-expression in a colonial environment, and it carries over long after its usefulness has passed, is a certain Puritanism, a devotion to work as a praiseworthy ethic in itself. For example, reading is a waste of valuable time when you might be chopping wood, and a rigidness in enforcing conduct is considered right and proper. This is a positive atmosphere in which to clear the forest and bridge the rivers and build the house, but once that's done and we are living in the house we have a different situation. It is all right to put the lawnmower over the lawn but if we put it over the flowerbed how can we expect to have flowers?

New Zealand children, like all other children, have developed their own little worlds and their own kinds of slangy speech. One of our first children's books to depict boys in an authentic city setting, talking to each other in their own vernacular, was Our Street by Brian Sutton-Smith. When serialized in the School Journal in 1948, one of the first outbreaks of that literary revolution I spoke of, it raised such a furor that the final episodes were suppressed. It appeared in book form prefaced by several apologies. The boys of the story lived the very limited lives of working class families with unimaginative parents (which was not meant to imply that all working class parents were unimaginative). Seen from the lofty heights of adult respectability, the things the boys got up to were thought to set a very bad example--such as getting into the movies or the zoo without paying, or pinching golf balls and claiming money for finding them. In the sequel, Smitty Does a Bunk, the boys decide to teach Horsey's father not to drink so much by holding him up with two real guns which they are forbidden to have. The plan comes unstuck when the parents come home earlier than expected. One of the children hides, the other two run away.

> After they'd gone about seven lamp-posts and they felt like hot traction engines inside, Gormie says, "Gee, let's stop. I'm puffed. Is he coming?"

"Listen," hissed Smitty. They listened.
They could hear footsteps. Footsteps. Footsteps? Could they hear footsteps? Could they?
They weren't sure. The giant night made such
a beating, heaving noise in their ears. Blowing
through his giant hands. They couldn't be sure
they could hear anything. "Ssss! I can't hear
anything." And the night rushed about them like
mad men riding blind horses, here and there,
never quite stopping, but never seeming to go
anywhere all the time. "What can you hear?"
"I can't hear anything." There was nothing to
be heard but the galloping of the blind night's
hooves. Hooves that hammered upon their ears
until they were as deaf and blind as the winds
that rushed about them.

"She's right," shouted Smitty against the wind.
"He wouldn't chase us anyway."

"Well why the heck did we run this far, then?"
said Gormie.

"He just might of."

"Yeah, that's true," said Gormie. "You never
can be sure. My father would have chased us if
it had been his guns. That's if he had anything
private. Though he hasn't got anything private
as far as I know. At least I haven't found anything yet."

"No, he'll just give us a hiding when we get
back. Come on, my back's as sore as the
billio."

Smitty does get that hiding and it does not improve
him one bit. These books were written from a keen memory of the inside of that sub-culture which children create
between themselves, independently of adults, and about
which many respectable adults do not want to know. The
author, who was then a young teacher, defended himself in
these words:

Most of the anti-social behaviour of children is
perfectly reasonable in the over-organised and
restricted environment in which they find themselves. By moralizing about such behaviour we
merely emphasise our adulthood. We can do
something about it only if we "take sides" with
the child. I believe that in Our Street we have
one of the many approaches which will bring us
nearer to the children we teach.

Today's rebel becomes tomorrow's honored figure. Our Street and its two successors have been re-issued in paperback by an educational publisher, although without the original illustrations and with kitsch covers. Brian Sutton-Smith is now a New York professor and a world authority on the games of children. Two years ago he was welcomed home as a visiting lecturer of distinction.

Ten years after Our Street we had another book which again presented adults as seen by children. This time there were three boys, two Maori and one Pakeha, living in an outback farming district, but near a beach popular with summer campers. Their activities ranged through the whole spectrum from good to bad, from cheeky to heroic. Nobody objected to the way they talked and behaved. Indeed The Boys of Puhawai has remained one of our best loved books. But books of this kind are still rare among us, and perhaps everywhere.

We have seen a few other storms but we are recovering from stuffy primness and strict ideas as to what is good for children. We even have a little gentle satire and humor about ourselves, and one funny spoof, but not as funny as Farley Mowat's Owls in the Family. We have not got around to that really uproarious laughter about ourselves that is the sign of maturity. Well, not the Pakehas. The Maoris have always been inclined that way and nothing has spoiled it, thank goodness.

What do we have for the older children, the ones who can read fluently for themselves? I have looked at all the books published since the Centenary and I can not honestly say that we have broken into any totally new areas. We have made our own contributions to the usual categories of family stories, adventure stories, animal stories, historical stories. We have few mysteries (although mystery gets into the adventures). We rather run to holiday adventures because we have the sort of country where children do spend exciting holidays. The countryside has the lion's share of the settings even though most of us now live in towns and cities--but then the countryside gives better opportunities for children to do exciting things. We do not go in heavily for "problem" themes, although recent fiction gives more scope to personality development and relationships.

We have no space fiction at all, unless we count the

recent book by Katarina Mataira, Te Atea, written in Maori
and illustrated by the Maori artist Para Matchitt. In this
story, written poetically, the people go through the last
war, emerge from underground and then have to go underground again through a nuclear war. This time there are
few people left but they are of all races, black and brown
and yellow and white. They realize that all may eventually
perish from radiation and so they send out a space ship
with a selected body of young people who travel for twenty
years, with adventures and experiences on the way, to
another world. And what is that world? It is Rehua--a
traditional Maori heaven--perhaps a little like all of us
traveling back to the Garden of Eden. It is a beautiful,
humane and warm story.

Twenty-five of our books are set in the past but less
than half could honestly be called historical fiction. This
is largely my own field. I have two historical novels published and a third just completed, as well as many short
stories. I have also written, with a co-author, a contemporary novel about boys tramping in our mountain country
(which is on its way). Also to be published soon is a
group of four animal stories for younger children. And I
have written a good deal of short fiction, non-fiction, and
some educational books on conservation and social studies
themes as well as history.

There are three main factors to be considered--the
writer, the environment and atmosphere in which he works,
and the publishing set-up through which his book has to
pass to reach the audience. In a small country we can not
help but realize how much that publishing apparatus counts.
It is not just a matter of business, of machinery--it is a
matter of encouragement. If the possibility exists of having
his work appear in print, the writer can tackle his other
problems and obstacles with energy. But not many people
will sacrifice their lives to communicate their thoughts if
they can not see any avenue for communication.

It is especially difficult with picture-books, where
the text and the illustrations must match--and New Zealand
publishers can not afford the strong glossy covers, fine
paper and unlimited color that we see in the lovely picture
books that come to us from Japan, and the United States
and Great Britain. The author can seek an overseas publisher but that has its pitfalls. Peter Walsh wrote a story
called Freddy the Fell Engine--published in England by the

Oxford University Press. This delightful little tale is factual. It is about a special kind of engine that climbed a mountain pass so slowly that passengers could literally step off the train and run along-side and join it further up. Freddy was made redundant by a new tunnel and sat lonely on the hillside until the children wanted him for the new playground at Cross Creek--a real place--after which Freddy was happy. A little fragment of our lives caught up in words to be preserved for ever. And what happened? Without reference to the author, the book came out with exuberant pictures by a top class English illustrator, William Papas. The cover said "by Papas," the title page acknowledged "text by Peter Walsh" but nowhere was New Zealand mentioned. The engine is not a fell engine, the railcar is not a railcar--it's a happy and handsome book-- but New Zealand has been robbed.

One of our answers to the publishing problem, or perhaps it is just one of the things we do, is what I call the home-made book--the book that originates from enthusiasm to fill some particular empty space. Teachers, parents, people working with pre-school children may produce such books by hand or by using some kind of copying device. Occasionally one attracts the right sort of notice and becomes a published book. An example is Nikademus. That is one that came out well, but others may be too amateurish to deserve further promotion. However, I have a theory that really fine writing develops when lively writing of lesser note is going on all round. Books do not grow just any old place. Like flowers they grow in a garden where the champion bloom stands out among the not-quite-champions.

Last year, after a small child asked his mother, "Mummy, do monsters clean their teeth?", that mother got together with another play-center Mum to produce a book with that intriguing title. It is in the class of modest books that other Mums can afford to buy. Its drawings may not be great art but they are in the mood, and as for the verses, here is a sample.

> Mummy do monsters clean their teeth?
> Yes my darling, they do, they do,
> With tubes of slime and sludgy goo
> With an old string mop from a rubbish pile
> Which gives them a beautiful slimy green smile.

Mummy do monsters wash their hair?
Yes my darling they wash their hair
With baked beans and porridge rubbed in with
    care;
And to make it look prettily matted and coarse
They rinse it in mayonnaise and horseradish
    sauce.

So the limitations of local publishing have their compensations even if we can not be lavish and luxurious, while the attractions of overseas publishing have their risks and pitfalls. The writer who publishes in New Zealand need not worry about whether his homegrown flavors are going to be acceptable to overseas palates.

Of course, a writer does not have to be bound to a region, but most of us are. This is because a writer must write as a whole person--not as a brain or a pair of eyes or a set of ten typewriting fingers. And this is even more so when writing for children because honesty is basic; you can not fool a child and you must not try. You are sharing an experience and it must be real experience; and that is true even when you are writing about times past, as I often do myself. And of course none of us exist as wolf children, all alone in a jungle. Any true wolf children who have been discovered, living with animals, have never become truly human. Each of us is part of our community and part of the land which we tread, of that piece of the world into which, as Walt Whitman said, as a child he went forth every day.

To me as a New Zealander, the land and the sea which surrounds us are part of myself. Our small country is magnificently endowed by nature and even when we live in cities we are not shut away from beach and mountain, river and sea, farm and forest. Their presence penetrates us, it makes us cry out with joy for the beauty of our land when it is left unspoiled or happily adapted for human living, and it makes us cry out with pain when it is torn apart and degraded for profit. It used to be said that New Zealand could not produce quality because we were too young. Certainly we do not have medieval castles dotted about, or temples or the Great Wall of China. In fact we are the youngest country of all, the last to be discovered by both Maori and Pakeha.

So, we are young. Why not glory in our youth?

And the land is not young, it is old and hard--we can climb
above four thousand feet and see the rocks scraped out by
the glaciers in those long away days when the ancestors of
man could not even dream of such places--and it fills us
with the strangest thoughts to stand there and think about
the oldness and the loneliness and at last, the coming of
people.

Our small country has magic enough, human and
non-human, to charm a host of artists and writers if only
we will allow it to speak to us. But I am well aware that
all the world is not like us and that all people are not well
fed and comfortable. Food comes before books, and children cannot enjoy what we give until they have a fair life
to begin with. We must be conscious that we are concerned
in this discussion with the literate children who have access
to books. Many of these books portray as normal a world
in which all children ride round in motorcars and live in
houses stuffed with expensive gadgets and receive cameras
for birthday presents. Outside this charmed circle are
millions without a hope of going to school. If we continue
to waste the resources of the world in the midst of increasing populations, if we allow the rich to get richer while
the poor get poorer, our children will not have a chance or
our grandchildren either.

And that is if we are still here to tell the tale.
Our children are growing up in a world under a threat of
total extinction inconceivable in the days of Alice or Winnie-
the-Pooh or Little Lord Fauntleroy. If we have our audience of children in our sights we must remember that we
now have a global community and that there is nowhere else
to go, the earth is all filled up. Mankind must cope with
these global problems or perish, but--I am an optimist.
I think that every writer for children has to be--if we
thought we were doomed we would not bother to write. We
must pass on that faith and hope, but I do not mean we
should portray only sweetness and light. Some writers can
and must deal with difficult, unhappy, unpleasant and tragic
themes with sometimes the saddest endings. We need
thinking books, with the heroism of fighting the new kinds
of dragons, the magnificent power of human beings to endure the almost impossible.

The writers who do this, and we need them, are
the writers who feel impelled and able to do so. Literature, whether for children or adults, grows out of life and

its needs. It grows and it cannot be forced. People who write consciously to promote a cause are liable to turn out very dull books.

And does not the way to the positive lie through the positive? Despite everything we are living in a marvelous world; life itself is a marvel, the birth of a child is a miracle no matter how many times it happens, and the children who read our books are themselves of value beyond price. So is nature in its infinite variety and the web of life into which we fit. So are the beautiful creations of mankind in centuries of devotion to art and poetry and song and story. So are the triumphs of human achievement by individuals and groups and societies. So are heroism and endurance and vision. Let the children seize upon these delights and glories with their imaginations and their emotions and their minds--they will not have to be told that our world is worth saving.

I can say this from my small faraway country because I am convinced that our world can be best understood in its immensity, in its infinite variety, in its bewildering and frightening complexities and conflicts, in its widening and exciting possibilities, from a secure and sound position on one's piece of home ground. There is nothing insular in that, so long as we recognize that folks in other countries and cultures have the same love and reverence for their piece of home ground and with just as good reason. Out of that mutual respect comes one of the foundations for cooperation and peace.

I would go further. I am thinking of a Maori girl who rose up in a seminar about race relations where people were saying, "We must do this for the Maori" and "We must do that for the Maori," and cried out--"Why won't you grant us the right to be different?" This assertion of difference pooled together creates a defence against our being overwhelmed by what I call the plastic culture which is being spread with a dreadful sameness all over the South Pacific. I know that Americans will understand what I mean when I say this, because we are all on the same side, the side of the child. The elevation of money and things as the great goals of life, cheapjack advertising, the presentation of violence and hatred and cruelty and sheer silliness as normal and acceptable ways of life--these things are part of that false culture that presents The Little House on the Prairie in a saccharine version on television. This plastic culture overlays the true American culture also.

Is it too much to ask for simplicity in children's literature, that simplicity through which a child can emerge in the best traditions of humanity? If a writer in faraway New Zealand, writing for New Zealand, can also illuminate some corner of our common world for a child in Peru or Singapore or China or North America, then we too have given something.

A Maori orator would conclude by chanting an ancient poem of his people. I have not said anything about poetry, because what is the use of talking about it? You have to hear its message direct. One of our most distinguished and prolific poets, James K. Baxter, had a short spell at teaching and wrote a group of poems as the only way he could think of to keep his class in order. Or so he said. I think myself that he could not face any audience without giving them his poems--so here is one of them.

> Swing, swing, swing
> swinging wide and high--
> If you swing high enough
> Your feet will touch the sky.
>
> If your foot should touch it
> Then the sky will break.
> It'll make no difference when you say
> You did it by mistake.
>
> The sun will growl and grumble,
> The stars will tumble down,
> And the weather man come running
> In a long, black gown.
>
> The river will run backwards,
> The sums will add up wrong,
> You'll come to school on Saturday
> And play the whole night long.
>
> It will take a ton of thistledown
> A ladder bought from Spain
> And a new magician's hammer
> To patch it up again.

Chapter 7

AN EVENING WITH LEON GARFIELD

by Leon Garfield

The only title I can give is, quite honestly, "Leon Garfield." This isn't vanity, it's just ignorance of any other subject. So I thought I would tell you how I became a writer. It will have to be external, I'm afraid, because the internal part is in the writing itself, and if, as I hope, you read my books, you will perhaps be able to make the connection between the two. I hope that out of it all will come something of my own attitude to writing, the way I think of stories, or the way they are thought of for me. And the fact that at no time do I particularly think of writing for children or of writing for adults, but just writing stories, because I happen to like doing it.

I started writing very early in my life. I had always wanted to write, to make my living as a writer, which seemed a very remote thing, for a long time. Those of us who are professional writers know what an extraordinary dream it is.

I had tried a great many different ways of writing, imitating every possible favorite. This is the only way to learn, by imitation. And for some reason, I imitated various so-called "adult" writers, with no success at all. And I imitated children's writers. In the whole idea of writing for oneself, there didn't seem very much distinction to me; there still doesn't. I found that I gravitated naturally to the sort of thing that could be described as writing for children. It gave one a wider feeling, a wider play for one's imagination. I wrote a number of short stories in the style of Hans Christian Andersen and Lewis Carroll. I can't remember any other children's writers I imitated because I hadn't read any, but had I read them I would have imitated them.

110

Then I had a story published by the Daily Mail Annual. Oh, it was a terrible thing, and I'm deeply ashamed of it, and fortunately it's no longer in print. And then I wrote an immensely long fairytale, of about a hundred thousand words, which was equally bad, and very over-written, and mercifully that wasn't printed either. In fact I had a whole pile of my early work, and I kept it in a garden shed, in London, securely locked in a chest. And we had a jobbing gardener who used to come round and, I don't know what he did, but he always used to knock on the door after he'd done it, and ask to be paid. But one day he said, "I went into the shed and burned all that old rubbish." And it was the nicest thing anybody could ever have done. But I don't suppose I ever really gave up.

And then one day, or one week, or one fortnight, I read The Master of Ballantrae; it was the only thing of Stevenson's I have ever read, and I was enormously impressed by it. I remember lying awake, and thinking of the idea of the two brothers, and that I would like to write a story about two brothers, one good and one bad, and what interested me was: how would you tell the difference between them, if you didn't know, without their reputations, if they looked identical; how do you tell which is good and which is evil, at any given moment in time? And I remember when I thought of that, I suddenly realized that at last I'd thought of an actual subject for a novel, something that would expand, something that would grow. It takes a very, very long time to gain experience, to realize what is the subject for a novel, and what is just an anecdote. I sensed that there was something different in the idea, and I began to write my story after I explained it excitedly to my wife, and she said, "Yes, but you've got to have some viewpoint, and somebody to tell the story." So with some irritation I decided to have a small boy, thinking the whole thing unnecessary anyway, but I could see some vague point in having someone to tell the story, and also somebody who could be bewildered by the appearance of the two brothers, and not know which was which. I wrote the first paragraph of it very very quickly, the only time I ever have written quickly, and I showed it to my wife, and for once she said, "That's excellent." And there was a perceptible difference. I had learned, after many years of trying--and it's a very difficult thing to explain, and I hope you will all understand, when I say that it was the first time that I felt the pen actually making contact with the paper--that I could speak directly to the paper, that at last I had managed to get rid

of an awful lot of clutter from my writing. I had many
many more mannerisms then than I have now. And then I
suddenly realized that, good heavens, I had set it, unconsciously, in the eighteenth century, for the very simple reason that The Master of Ballantrae was set in the eighteenth
century. And I realized also that I didn't know anything
about the eighteenth century except that it was seveteen-
hundred and something. But the whole flavor of the story
seemed to me inevitable for that period about which I knew
nothing except by a certain sensing of it, and an affection
for the music of the period, and writers like Fielding.

So I started to do some research, and I didn't know
how to do research. I just read and read and read indis-
criminately. I think I wrote about two pages in as many
months, until I suddenly realized that my story, like The
Master of Ballantrae, was set on board ship, and I also
realized, with some embarrassment, that I did not know one
end of a ship from another. Then I just stopped; the whole
thing seemed impossible. I felt that one had to go sailing
round the Horn or something, and that in order to write anything about ships one really ought to know the feel of them,
and all those extraordinary terms. And I read Swift's
Gulliver's Travels, and Robinson Crusoe, and admired the
details and wondered how much I could pinch from them.
And, again, I nearly gave up, until I read in some history
of sailing that neither Swift nor Defoe had ever been to sea
in their lives. They'd both got their information from the
same sailing manual. So I thought, well, if Swift and Defoe
can do it, it's possible. I really became aware then of the
use of books; it never occurred to me that you could get information from them. So I started, much heartened by that,
on a long, very tedious process of research. I paid a visit
to the Maritime Museum in Greenwich, in search of two
things that seemed to me absolutely vital about ships. One
was, what the hell the mizzen-mast was, and the other was,
where exactly was the poop. Well, I remember walking in
the front of the Maritime Museum and there's a great big
pole outside it, very treacherously placed, and I sort of
stumbled against it, and my wife said, "That's a mizzen-
mast." And I said, "Don't be ridiculous, it's a main-mast,
it's enormous." And sure enough it was a mizzen-mast.
Then I went in to the Maritime Museum, into the splendid
gallery of wonderful ships' models, and I looked at them,
but of course, they don't give the parts of the ship on them.
I summoned an attendant and asked him where the poop was,
and he didn't know. Eventually I found that they sold a won-

derful paperback at the entrance with all the parts of the
ship clearly labeled. And then I went to the museum again
and got a marvelous map, of about sixteen-hundred and
something, with all sorts of nautical directions that were
very authentic, and I used the lot. I hadn't the faintest
idea what it was about but it sounded very convincing, and
I'm perfectly certain Swift and Defoe didn't know any more
about it either. And I wrote the story, and the story grew
as I wrote it. It was the sort of story that you discover
as you go along, and I knew how it was going to end, but I
didn't know how I was going to get there.

It's a funny thing about writing a novel, one always
regards the middle as that awkward part that keeps the beginning away from the end. Then I came to one point in the
story, about a third of the way through, in which, with immense gusto and enjoyment, I described a shipwreck. I
was looking forward to describing that, and it really worked,
it was a splendid shipwreck. The only thing is, that for
something like a year after that, I was stuck. I just could
not think of how I was going to get out of the shipwreck, or
even who was going to be saved from it. During that time
I wrote about two or three different chapters, and different
ways out, which subsequently I found, and thought--well they
weren't bad, I wonder why I scrapped them? But I realized
what had happened at the time; I had made the most elementary mistake. I had concentrated so hard on the one
episode, the climax of the shipwreck, that I had not thought
of what happens next while I was writing it. At that point
I realized that one has to think of even the main climaxes
of a book as merely bridge passages to the next. You must
really think of them as, not something you're going to write,
but as something you've almost written, and looking forward
to what comes after them. And it was only when I realized
that, that I was able to go on with it.

I had set myself a ridiculous aim. I was going to
write, I think, about a hundred and twenty thousand words.
I don't know why, it was just a figure that I'd set my sights
on, and finally achieved. Incidentally, there's rather a nice
story that my publisher told me about an equal situation.
Someone once actually phoned up his office and said, "How
long is the average novel these days?" There was some
consternation in the office, and finally they came up with a
figure of sixty thousand words, which he was told. And
there was a long silence, and then he said, "Good, I've
finished." Don't you get the impression sometimes, that

that's the way it's done? I finished my sort of monumental book, and I met someone who knew a literary agent and said, "You should send it to her." So I did, and to my intense surprise and amazement she wrote back saying would I come to see her, as she thought it was splendid. She sent it to Heinemann, who kept it for something like four or five months and then finally sent it back, saying they didn't know whether it was an adult or a juvenile book, but they'd love to see the next thing I wrote.

Well, it was only at that point that I realized that there was a difference between the two. I mean, I'm not utterly stupid, but it had just never occurred to me. I had written the book because at that time I was imitating various children's writers, although The Master of Ballantrae is not really a children's book. And I'd written it with the vague idea of a boy's adventure story; but once you set pen to paper the audience disappears and you concentrate on the story. And it was only then that I realized that the book had been aimed by an agent, and that it had obviously not struck any sort of target.

But the next publisher it was sent to was Constable, and the most marvelous editor called Grace Hogarth was there. It was sent again to their adult department, who took it downstairs (I don't know why the juvenile department was downstairs) to Grace Hogarth, who, I was told, looked at its huge bulk in dismay, and took it home and apparently did read it. And liked it very much, and wrote to me, or wrote to my agent saying that if I was willing to shorten it, she would like to publish it as a juvenile book. Well, I remember very clearly that when I sent the book off to my agent, it had been typed out about four times. It was absolutely perfect, not a single "X" anywhere, it was a model of typing and clarity, and I had vowed that I was not going to alter a single word. It was as good as I could possibly make it. But when I was told that it would actually be published if I would agree to cut it, you know, I would have re-written the whole book on the spot. And I cut it by nearly a half, in about ten days, to their absolute astonishment. In the process of cutting, I'm afraid I left one or two ragged edges, in my haste to get the publisher to honor his agreement. In fact, not long ago I was talking to some librarians in Holland, and one of them pointed out to me that there was a mistake in Jack Holborn, and wasn't I willing to admit that there was? And I said, "Yes, but it must be in the translation." But he said, "Oh no, I read it in

English." It was a very, very embarrassing few minutes.
But I cut the book, and the publishers were satisfied and
the book was duly printed.

But then I wondered if the book would ever be reviewed, and I thought of all sorts of things that might happen, that the whole lot would be remaindered, and all sorts
of disasters that would rightly happen to it. When one sees
one's own work in print one's acutely ashamed of it, as
though every fault is exposed and every virtue has mysteri-
ously disappeared. And I remember thinking that if it gets
reviewed everybody's going to say, "It's a straight copy of
The Master of Ballantrae," because it seemed to me absolutely glaring. But the first review was a very very nice
one, in the Birmingham Post. I went through it very
anxiously, to find my book right at the end, but thankfully,
because the reviewer started off by saying, "But best of all
these..." and that was absolutely wonderful. And he went
on to say "... that this writer reminds us of..."--and there
I held my breath, and he said... "Captain Marryat." I hadn't
read any Captain Marryat, but I went to the local library.
I didn't look up any Captain Marryat--but I looked up people's opinions on Captain Marryat; it seemed much more important, and I was reassured that he was extremely highly
thought of. I counted myself very lucky to have got away
with that. And then, not long after, I heard a talk on the
radio in which they were reading some of Stevenson's letters, letters that he wrote at the time he was writing The
Master of Ballantrae. And he said in his letters that he
owed it all to Captain Marryat. I thought it was a fascinating example of influence, sort of by proxy.

My book didn't sell very well, but it was very well
reviewed; a first book quite often is, later ones not. And
then my agent, who was enormously pleased with herself and
enormously pleased with me, said, "Now you must write an
adult novel." And I was so full of confidence, and I thought
well, I must do that. It's got to be different from the last
book I wrote, it's got to be consciously for adults, that means
sex and violence, and a very complicated style, and an ela-
borate irony, and, in point of fact, of talking down in a
very strange way. I read the Newgate Calendar, which was
very enjoyable, and I found one story that really seemed to
be quite possible, about a gentleman pickpocket. I did a
great deal of research on pickpockets, and strolling players,
and a great variety of things, and wrote the book; not a
hundred and twenty thousand words, about ninety thousand I

think, because I realized that I'd been excessive on the first one. It took me about nine or ten months. I gave it to my agent, and it was rejected by every publisher in London, quite rightly.

Then my wife presented me with two typed pages, saying, "What about this for a story?" I looked at it and said, "You know I really can't write that sort of thing." It was about a strolling player, and the mistaken identity thing, and I wasn't terribly interested. I wanted to write something about the French Revolution at that time, which I thought was much more exciting. But as my adult novel came back and back, and back and back again, I looked again at this idea that I'd been given and began to see some possibilities in it. And then, Grace Hogarth from Constable's actually telephoned me and took me out to lunch; it was the first time a publisher had ever taken me out to lunch, and she said, "What about another book?" And you know that was such an unheard of thing, it seemed so absolutely wonderful. So I trotted out this idea that wasn't my idea, I regret to say, but nevertheless I saw something familiar in it that I could use. And she said, "Yes, that's fine, would you like a contract right away?" And that was a very cunning and very courageous thing to do on her part, because I got the money in advance, and once you've got the money, and once you've spent it--and the two things occur simultaneously--I realized I had to write the book.

That book took me about eight or nine months and in point of fact it came straight out of the unwieldy adult novel I'd written--a very small part of it.

Since then, I've had about five or six books out of that one book that was rejected. It was a bad book, but I've always thought of it as being a sort of lead mine of information. Very, very weighty, but one can always make something of it. It was quite malleable. I remember I called the second book The Dead Little Gentleman, and all the publisher's travelers said they couldn't possibly have that as a title, it sounded too much like a murder story. So I tried very hard to think of a title, and then an Irishwoman I knew, for some reason or other, said, "Well, what about Devil-in-the-Fog?" And I said, "What on earth is that?" And she said, "Oh, it's a sort of a--heather or something," in--she thought--the north of England. I've since found out that she was totally wrong. But there it stayed, and it had quite a ring to it. The story wasn't mine, or the title, but I do lay claim to the writing.

Devil-in-the-Fog, curiously enough, suffered from the reverse fault of Jack Holborn. It was too short; I'd gone to the other extreme. Grace Hogarth, who was in the States at the time, sent me a cable saying could I lengthen it. So I had to put in two chapters, which was much more difficult than cutting chapters out. I can't remember which they were now, but there are two that really oughtn't to be there. She then, when I saw her after that, said, "You can't possibly go on writing in the first person." And that filled me with the greatest dismay, because when you're writing historical novels it's much easier to do it in the first person--you don't have to describe that much. You only have to describe what one person would see, there's no author's omniscient eye to look at the scene. Grace Hogarth, apart from being a very great editor, is a very alarming lady, and I thought I had better take notice of her. So, once more, my wife and I both went back to that unhappy lead mine, and produced something about pickpockets, and that's how I wrote Smith, which did even better than the other two. But sometimes I feel that I would like to go back to the first person again, I've got so used now to writing in a sort of very subjective third person.

I thought it might be interesting to explain how I personally work out a story. This is a story that I have not written. Often one is asked, "How does a story occur?" It's a very reasonable question, and it's also a very difficult question to answer. It's just as difficult to explain really how one writes, because when one is alone and writing, quite a different personality takes over, or comes to the surface. It's utterly different, and one can't honestly communicate that except through the work that's written. I can talk about the details, but not the real substance; that is in the book.

But as far as the technicality is concerned, or how ideas occur, the particular one I have in mind was of an occasion when I went to a wedding rehearsal, in a country village, not far out of London. It was a late afternoon, and it was a very pleasant occasion. I remember particularly the atmosphere in the church, of the vicar making very silly jokes, and everybody in rather a good mood. And all the usual mishaps occurred, that one hoped would be corrected on the final day. And then going back to the house, where the bride and bridegroom to-be were unwrapping presents, and the masses of tissue paper everywhere, and the extraordinary presents that emerged from them, that one

didn't really know what they were. And the sort of thing of
five fruit bowls, and what had happened to the sixth? And
a frenzied search through the tissue paper for the other
bowl. And then the terrified looking for labels as to who
they were from, to realize they were all in a pile and you
didn't really know who had sent what. In short, it was a
very pleasant, amusing, warm occasion. And I remember
going back to London, and thinking, there was something
about that atmosphere I would like to use, very much indeed. And I couldn't think of any way of using it.

And then, there was something else; in point of fact
I've told this round the wrong way, but it doesn't matter.
The only time I ever told my daughter a bedtime story, or
used to, was because I was bullied into it. I was told it
was my place to do it, but I wasn't very good at it, in fact
I was very bad; but there was one story that I liked telling
her, a particular version of a fairy tale. And it did succeed in getting her to sleep, probably from sheer boredom.
I enjoyed doing it, merely because I'd taken a reverse way
of telling it, and I could build a certain amount of suspense
into it, and that's one thing I rather like doing in writing.
I wondered how I could use the fairy tale, and again I
couldn't think of anything. And then this wedding rehearsal,
again may I describe the feeling of coming back, and the
memory of the warmth of the present opening, and somehow
or other the two ideas came together. Ideas are rather
like that, they sort of magnetize to each other; that is, if
they're appropriate they come together, and it may take
many ideas before you have one with a whole that is actually
workable. It's never just one idea. A novel, or even a
short story, is composed of many ideas. And it suddenly
occurred to me that these two fitted.

I began to think of a story opening with a wedding
rehearsal and all the amusement of undoing the presents.
And then I thought of the bridegroom opening one present,
and it is the equivocal present. You don't quite know, you
never know who it's from, and you don't quite know what it
is. In this particular instance it's a map, but it's a map
of a place that the bridegroom can't recognize, it's no place
he's seen, ever. He's rather troubled by it, and he goes
away, he leaves the house, and he becomes more and more
absorbed in the map, and the feeling arises within him that
this is a place that he has got to go to, and he has got to
go there before the wedding. It becomes immensely important to him, and he doesn't know why. He is also in

London, and then I had to think of the setting, of what period this would be, and I felt that the very latest in time I could make it was about the turn of the century. Because I visualized this young man going down towards the river and the docks, and there are sailing ships tied up, and he stands under a lamp and looks at the map again, and there are sailors coming off one particular ship, and one of them stops and looks over his shoulder, and recognizes the map, and asks him if he wants to go there, because it's quite near, it really wouldn't take very long. And he agrees, and he goes on board the ship. It's rather curious, it's a sort of Flying Dutchman-like ship, drifting in and out of mists, half real, half dream. But every now and then throughout this voyage he reassures himself that this is not a dream, by some actual touching of a metal object, pinching himself, treading on his own feet, blowing in the air, feeling the canvas, all these real things, so that the reader also realizes that this is a sort of reality, even though the voyage is very strange, almost unnatural.

Eventually they come to the shore that he recognizes on the map, and he's put ashore, and he walks inland, and almost immediately there's an immense dark forest, and he knows he must go through this forest, because this too is on the map. And he begins to walk through the forest, and then he has to go rather more slowly as it becomes very dense and thorny. And as he goes in further he finds very disagreeable objects hanging in the forest, bones, whole skeletons, caught in bramble. And the curious thing about them is that they are all facing the same way, they are all facing towards him. He pushes past them, and goes on and on, until eventually, in the thickest and most impenetrable part of the forest, he comes to an enormous pair of wrought iron gates, very rusted, and he pushes and pushes, and manages to push them open. And as he does so, he kicks something at his feet and looks down, and sees that it's a three-legged stool, and another small piece of furniture that he half recognizes and half doesn't.

And he goes on, and he finds animals and birds lying in the grass, or in the thickly overgrown grass, that seem to be dead but are not. And at last he comes to the doorway of an enormous mansion, again with everything overgrown, and it's only at that point that he realizes where he is and who he is; that he has reached the palace of the Sleeping Beauty, and he is the prince who is destined to awaken her. He forces open the door--and I'm quite looking

forward to writing the description of what it might be like
inside. And he goes through the rooms, and at last he
finds the room where the Sleeping Beauty is, and he looks
down, and she's every bit as beautiful as she's supposed to
be. And he knows he must bend down and awaken her with
a kiss. At this point he pauses, and realizes that if he
wakens her everything in the palace, everything, will be
subject to decay. At the moment it is held in a dream and
he cannot bring himself to break the dream. Then he wants
to run away, to go back through the forest, and it's then
that he remembers all the skeletons he saw facing outwards,
and he realizes he wasn't the first one to come there, and
he wasn't the first one to have that idea. But no one has
escaped. And then he does bend down and awaken her.

I regret to say there's a gap in the story at this
point. But I do know how the story must end. Possibly
when I think of the middle bit I will write it. But the story
ends with the wedding of this young man and the Sleeping
Beauty, in an enormous glimmering cathedral, and for some
reason he is walking up the aisle and she is there, waiting,
and as he walks, the cathedral dwindles and dwindles and
dwindles, and becomes brighter, until it eventually becomes
the country church in which he is supposed to be married.
And his bride is waiting at the altar; he's late. But his
bride is not the Sleeping Beauty by any means, his bride
is the girl he's supposed to marry. But as he walks, he
becomes aware that along the aisle beside him, and in and
out of the columns, is running the Sleeping Beauty, flickering in and out of them, watching him, smiling at him. And
he knows at that moment that because he had awakened her,
he would always have a double life, that he has had the
courage to awaken his dreams and his imagination, and that
he will always have this double life, whereas those who rejected it did die. And that would be the story. That is
how a story does come together.

Chapter 8

REFLECTIONS AND RECOLLECTIONS

by Edward Blishen

I have a preoccupation--even a consuming preoccupation--with respect to children's literature. It is a preoccupation with the separation of what children read, from what is read by those who are no longer children. I look to a time when that separation will be less severe and less solemn than it now is.

At a program committee meeting of the English Center of an international organization of writers, a committee of which I am chairman, someone recently suggested that we have an evening devoted to the question: "Why write for children?" The suggestion was made very seriously; it meant that we should examine why it is that certain writers turn for their primary audience, or for one of their audiences, to children. But despite the seriousness of the suggestion, most of my colleagues, some of them quite distinguished enough to know better, began to fall about with amusement. "Ah yes," they said, "let us indeed discuss what maladjustment, what condition of arrested development leads a man or woman to write for children rather than for adults." And I was furious. I would, if I had had one, have banged my gavel. "How," I asked, "could anyone who was a writer, how could anyone regard writing for children as some lesser, aberrant, almost diseased thing?" At the most practical level, should adult writers not respect those who prepare their own audience for them? Adult writer-- the whole vocabulary in which one has to discuss this subject is absurd. You know, perhaps, the story of Hugh Lofting, how angry he became with his American publishers when he discovered that they were cataloging his work under the heading--JUVENILE. And he said he would permit this to continue only if they cataloged the adult works in their catalog under the heading--SENILE.

121

But beyond this matter of creating an audience for themselves, of being happy that an audience is being created for them, how can anyone who cares for literature, let alone anyone concerned in the creating of literature, regard any part of literature as of less importance than any other part?

Either literature is a continuous enterprise, all of its parts of equal importance, or there is something very seriously wrong. A few years ago an American novelist, for whom in all other respects I have considerable admiration, told me that the New York Center of the organization of writers we both belonged to, was dominated by children's writers: "Women," he said, "wearing strange hats and chunky beads." Well, I spend most of my time, or a lot of my time, in the company of children's writers and the only one I know who habitually wears a hat, wears one just as wittily fantastic as her writing; none of them wears beads. Oh yes, I was telling the story the other day to a very good writer for children, Jane Gardam, and she turned pale and confessed to a passion for beads, and chunky ones at that. (I do not know what chunky beads are.) "I never," she said pleadingly, "I never wear them when writing." And a great many of us, of course, who write for children, are not even women. It would clearly be difficult to describe Leon Garfield or Ivan Southall as a woman given to wearing strange hats and chunky beads--not impossible, but difficult. I would not like to try it.

Clearly, this notion of what a children's writer is, is based, first of all, on a really quite shameful ignorance of the quality of much children's literature produced in recent times; and secondly, on a simple failure of observation. Before the Second World War, in the English-speaking world certainly, there might have been something in it. George Orwell, you may remember, writing about his experience of working in the early '30s in a London bookshop, said that the children's books that passed through his hands, during those months he spent in the bookshop, seemed to him mostly worthless, intolerably cosy, sweet and unreal. "I would rather," he memorably said, "I would rather give a child a copy of Petronius Arbiter than one of those." But since the war the scene has been transformed. I think if one was asked to name a score of the best writers now working in Britain, there would have to be a number of children's writers among them. Consider: is there a better novel written since the war by a writer of any kind, a better novel about the mystery and grief of time, than

Philippa Pearce's Tom's Midnight Garden? It embodies,
does it not, memorably within a narrative most beautifully
and exactly apt, the whole subject of that pain we feel because time in the mind and the heart is forever at odds
with the ruthless progress of clock and calendar time.
Well, Tom's Midnight Garden is for children. Oh, very
well. Is there not something wrong when the fact that such
a book is written primarily for children keeps it out of the
hands of most adults? This is the problem that I worry
away at all the time. Joan Aiken has described how when
she is introduced at parties as a children's writer people
tend to move away nervously at the first opportunity; as if,
she says, they expected her to break, in a high voice, into
a poem about fairies. She now insists that she be introduced at parties as a writer of thrillers, which she in fact
is, as well. It has quite changed her status. How absurd
that most adults should never have heard of, let alone read,
Joan Aiken's The Wolves of Willoughby Chase, one of that
sequence in which she tinkers, quite radically, and quite
delightfully, with the facts, not only of English history but
also of English wildlife. How absurd not to read Joan
Aiken.

I think something is going on that will in fact trans-
form this scene. It is a complicated thing that is going on,
and one element in it is, I believe, the change in our thinking about children and childhood. Read one of those books
that Orwell deplored, and then read a good post-war children's book, and you will see how we have changed in our
ideas about what children know and need to know, and understand and need to understand. Though as an adult who
can count as still being alive, we ought to be still in the
thick of things, still changing and developing and discovering
and being amazed, because childhood in that sense never
ends, yet it is profoundly true that in strict childhood we
have an apprehension of the world. An apprehension which
is, in its own way, as intense, sensitive and, in the best
sense of the word, serious, as the apprehension of the
most lively adult. Indeed, there are moments in childhood,
I believe, when the apprehension is swifter and more powerful, more intense, more charged, than the apprehension of
almost any adult; if only because the child is listening so
keenly to whispers of what lies over the border, in adulthood. It is the difference that Blake was concerned with
when he wrote his Songs of Innocence and his Songs of Experience. It is one of the absurdities of the situation that
arises from the excessive separation of children's literature

and adult literature that this separation cuts adults off from many of the best children's books, even from Songs of Innocence. The innocence is now seen to be a profoundly important clue to the whole man, the whole woman; we need to be in touch with childhood, our own and others, and out of this changed view of the child--who, in any case, in our day has his ear to the same ground as his elders to an extent that was never true before--out of that changed view arises, among other things, a changed and still changing children's literature.

I have been a close bystander during these last dozen years when I have seen Leon Garfield extend the frontiers of children's fiction, not simply by the total seriousness of the imagination and insight that he brings to his writing, but also by extending the very vocabulary in which children's fiction may be written. A reviewer of his latest novel, The Pleasure Garden, writing in the Times Educational Supplement--a man who has the insolence, after supposing that The Pleasure Garden was "set in the time of Thackeray," to upbraid Leon Garfield for failure of what I do believe he called "historicity"--this reviewer--if the word can be used --said, of his use in the book of words such as "tits" and "pee" and "arse," that they were "sly intrusions." This reviewer was being mealy-minded, and I mean mealy-minded, under a pretence of being broad-minded. It may not seem to matter much that the vocabulary of children's fiction is enlarged by such additions. I think myself it is essential that it should be so enlarged, because these childish words, which the continuing child in us never abandons, are a vital element in the creation of a narrative in which children can feel that their own imaginations are properly involved.

There is a writer in Britain, Leila Berg, who wrote for schools the series of books called Nippers. And the great originality of these books was that they were actually about the kind of children who really exist. Children whose parents may actually be out of work, whose fathers might occasionally get drunk, and who might eat fish and chips, which is a meal which does not usually figure in children's fiction in Britain, although it figures very largely in children's lives in Britain. Anyway, she wrote books of this kind, and they were quite sharply attacked for seaminess, and for introducing an undesirable element of reality into school work. And she tells a marvelous story of an infant school headmaster, who wrote protesting about one of the books, indeed sending the book back. On the first page, every sentence began with the word "and." He underlined, this headmaster, every "and," and pointed out to Leila Berg in his letter that one of the things they strove to do, one of the things for which the school existed, was to stamp out this civilization-destroying habit of beginning sentences with the word "and." And Leila Berg wrote back to him and said she was terribly sorry not to be of assistance to him in his campaign, but she had to confess that she herself had been profoundly influenced in this matter by her childhood reading, and she quoted the first book of Genesis. All sorts of primnesses and pruriences are involved here. I can even remember a teacher who wrote to Leon Garfield protesting because he used an eighteenth-century past tense. I cannot remember exactly what it was, but he used an eighteenth-century past tense in exactly the sense in which the eighteenth century used it, and in a sense which could not have been misunderstood by anybody. But she said that this made it necessary to outlaw his books entirely. Whatever virtues they might have, those virtues weighed as nothing against this pernicious misuse of the past tense.

I think that on one side there is a great deal of prurience and primness; but if one thinks of what is happening, what might change the situation, what is going to change the situation is simply that writers are obstinate, and that writers also follow a kind of instinct. And one of the exciting things about being involved with literature in any way, is that writers do reflect the hidden movement in our society, and in all societies. They reflect the hidden movements and make us aware of them before, in fact, they ever emerge clearly. One can say of the changed state of children's fiction since the war that it is evidence of things happening under our social skin: things happening of which society will not, in general, perhaps, reap the fruits for some time. Children's fiction is perhaps reaping prematurely some of the better fruits of this change in our view of two things. First, in our view of the importance of childhood, the meaning of childhood; and second, in our view that it is necessary to make some kind of separation between the two. This view, which still makes me angry when I think of it, of my highly intelligent adult colleagues ("adult" again), my colleagues who write adult fiction and adult works--the fury that that caused me when I think of the way in which they were able to let themselves think that there was between children's books and adult books, between children's writers and adult writers, some kind of difference

which could be expressed in terms of that laughter of theirs
at that meeting--there is no sense in that at all, and I look
forward to what in ten or twenty years' time might really
be seen to be a new unity in literature. Not a unity which
will make children's literature pretend to be other than what
it is, or adult literature pretend to be other than what it is,
but a unity of which one of the evidences would be that the
audiences would be interchangeable, and that certainly there
would not be among adults, to the degree that there is today, this foolish belief that children's literature is only for
children.

When I was a teacher, I was also a story-teller. I
developed the habit of story-telling in my early days, very
much as, well it is not a very good analogy, but very much
as a snake charmer might learn to play a pipe. As a
very, very young and helpless teacher in a difficult school
in London, on my first day after moments of incredulous
inspection on the part of the children, I picked up a copy of
The Invisible Man and began to read it. Fast, at first I
read it fast, very fast, but then it became possible for me
to read it slower and slower, and at last it became possible
to read it at a pace which was tolerable to the human
tongue. So, some days ago I wrote a poem about children's
reading, and I would like to read it to you. I designed it
as a lecturer's confession; it is the confession of someone
who stands up and speaks for a very great deal of time
about nothing very much. The happiest writing I ever did
in my life was working out a four-line epigram or a hun-
dred-word parody, and taking all the weekend over it and
sending it off to the New Statesman competitions. And I
have often thought since that a good New Statesman competition would be to reduce some lecture on some theme
to the right size, which would be something covering the
back of a postcard. However, I am aware that I spend a
lot of my time talking at enormous length about nothing
very much. So I have written "The Lecturer's Confession," and I hope that you will find it relevant in various
ways.

THE LECTURER'S CONFESSION

I remember, it was some barely credible year
    like 1929,
Old Mrs. Brown, only I suppose she wasn't as
    old as I thought--
At that time I believed anyone discernibly over

twenty was preparing for the dark--
I remember how she read to us, always at the
    day's end:
The marvellous day's end, with arithmetic behind
    us,
Transcription behind us--truly, in those days, we
    did something called Transcription,
And I have an old exercise book in which I've
    solemnly printed the word
At the top of pages that were clearly copyings
    from the board--
Fancy letting us into the secret that Transcription
    was the word for that!
At the age of seven, believe me, I could spell
    Transcription--
Well, with those behind us, and Spelling too, and
    what we called History
Of which I mostly remember: Battle of Barnet,
    1471:
The school was in Barnet, you see
And we had the good luck to have this bit of his-
    tory on the doorstep,
Which made the whole business slightly easier to
    believe in--
Though I confess it was years before I really be-
    lieved it had taken place--
For a long time, for me, History was a story
    they'd hurriedly thought up to fill the gap be-
    fore I arrived, in 1920--
Anyway, at the marvellous day's end, when the
    gas was lit, and
Between me and mum and tea there was only the
    squabbling peril of the journey home,
Then it was that Mrs. Brown read to us: Black
    Beauty, I remember:
Without the slightest intention of disrespect, I
    must say I thought Mrs. Brown was Black
    Beauty:
Nothing terribly wrong about equating a teacher
    much-loved with a horse of such sensitivity...
Even now, as I think of it, the story gathers
    around me, I am inside it, I cannot tell myself
    apart from the story,
And that's how it is when we read with warmth,
    to children:
As dear Mrs. Brown did, in her round, clear,
    comforting voice...

I remember seeing the words, as she read them,
    going together,
Coming together, making sentences, paragraphs,
    chapters.
I think Mrs. Brown believed she taught us about
    sentences and paragraphs
At that other, less marvellous end of the day,
    when she waxed so solemn
About commas, full stops, and "i" before "e,"
    except after "c,"
And all those circular statements about the adjec-
    tive,
Which described... because it described... because
    it described...
Which was all due to its being... a describing
    word.
She also read us Jackanapes, by Mrs. Ewing.
After I'd got over the surprise of a writer being
    called Mrs.,
Which, after all, made her just like my mum--
And Mrs. Brown--who'd never written a book in
    their lives:
I think I believed a teacher who wrote a book
    might have got into trouble for it--
It wasn't what she was there for--
Well, as I say,
After I'd got over that, I enjoyed so very much
    the strange Victorian
Air of the story, the little boy on his horse--
My goodness, we were reared on the horse, if
    you see what I mean;
But then, we actually had horses all round us in
    those days:
One of my earliest memories--the milkman telling
    my mum
"Your little boy's scared of my horse": he was
    right.
I was worried by the way it would explode through
    its nostrils,
Make its entire and quite remarkably long body
    quiver,
And sometimes urinate with shameless vehemence.
But oh, all that reading: all that being read to.
I sometimes say the task of the teacher seems
Enormously simple. All that he has to do
(And by "he" I mean "she"--I suppose we shall
    solve that problem)

Is to share his feeling for books.
And reading aloud
Is one of the best of methods, and only requires
That one learn to read aloud well.
Oh, I remember
Discovering that when I went to teach in London,
In a battered corner of London, where few of my
    boys
Knew what a sentence was, or a paragraph.
I tried to make them easier about spelling by tell-
    ing them that Keats
Couldn't spell: but it didn't help: they just didn't
    know
Who Keats was: most of them would have said
They didn't know what Keats were...

We had a Head then, nice man, who regrettably
    held
That reading aloud was the softest of options for
    class and teacher.
You could read aloud on the very last day of term,
    but only
Then if the class had been almost unimaginably
    saintly.
A wandering Head: he used to come and look
Through the glass panels in the classroom doors:
    would go away quite happy
If he saw what he wanted: boys glumly agog, or
    scribbling,
Teachers eloquent, or writing on the board,
Or peering over shoulders as they wrote...

It was there that I learned to read aloud without
    seeming to do so.

Thank you, old difficult sir.

It's really all that I know about reading and chil-
    dren.
It all depends on someone warmly reading,
Which in itself gives rise quite naturally, to warm
    listening.
I had an Irish teacher once who threw a book in
    my lap
On his way to the platform for morning assembly.
"Ssh!" he said. "Keep it quiet!" It was Tess of
    the D'Urbervilles

And forty years too late to hush that up!
But what an agreeable sense of conspiracy!
He, and the few he lent books to, against the
    world!
(And against the Head, who believed the English
    literary innings had ended with Kipling:
Nobody since had gone to the crease in whites:
D. H. Lawrence in his cloth cap, and Aldous
    Huxley
Who didn't even know how to hold the bat...)

It's really all I know about reading and children.
That warm sharing
And sense, perhaps, of conspiracy...

Sometimes I'm asked to talk about the young and
    their reading.
And golly, I amaze myself,
Stretching these few simple thoughts over as many
    as a couple of most solemn hours!

Chapter 9

CHILDREN'S LITERATURE IN SOUTH AMERICA

by Carlota Carvallo de Núñez

Before I discuss children's literature in Peru and in other Latin American countries, I would first like to comment on the universal state of children's literature in our contemporary world as I, a South American, see it.

In these last few years writers, editors, educators and psychologists have realized that children's books play a very important part in the cultural and moral formation of a child. In some countries movements have begun whose object is the creation and circulation of a literature specially dedicated to children and adolescents in order to counteract the negative influence of the comics, the cinema and television, whose heroes are nearly always driven by hate and ambition, negative emotions that can endanger the normal development of the mind and sentiments of the child.

It is now realized that to read good children's literature is not only an important pastime but a true necessity. Since children's books can attain an artistic status as creative and elevating as any other great literature, they serve as an essential model to children of the reading they are yet to enjoy and profit from. At the same time it is believed that books for children can serve as an instrument for peace among all peoples.

There are some questions that should be answered by authors of children's literature. One is: Up to what point is it advisable to stimulate the imagination of children with fantastic stories? Wouldn't it be better to give them a true picture of the world that surrounds them? And another question: Hasn't the time come to renew the themes and characters of children's literature, incorporating the contributions recently made by science and technology, and so

131

create a new type of fantasy and reality that is more in
keeping with the life of today? And lastly: Should children's literature teach children something or should we just
be content with giving them a few minutes of recreation and
amusement?

In my opinion there are many ways of leading children along the road of fantasy. Their imaginations are un-
ending and cannot be annulled or destroyed. While there
is a child in the world, there must be fantasy. The imagination is a psychological force the principal characteristic
of which is the reconstruction of what is in existence.
Thanks to imagination the child transforms reality. He also
likes to make up stories which often mix the real world with
the imaginary.

Though some psychologists and teachers are of the
opinion that too much fantasy can affect the psychic development of the child, others assure us that they run no danger
because the child knows full well up to what point he can
be fooled. He will have plenty of time later on for more
realistic reading, once he reaches the age when his own
mental development demands it.

So far as the second question is concerned--that is
if we should continue repeating traditional themes and characters or whether we should try to renew children's literature with a fantasy and a reality more in keeping with the
world we live in--I believe that we cannot fail to recognize
the advances made by science and technology during this
century. These advances have by far surpassed the most
daring creations of man's imagination--indeed, to such a
point that we have found ourselves obliged to revise our own
concepts.

We have sometimes asked ourselves if our means of
expression and our most characteristic forms of creativity
such as Art or Literature really reflect the true and exact
progress made by man in these latter years. What was
previously fiction for us today is reality. Many of the
most fantastic creations of literature have been surpassed.

The child of today shows great interest in machines.
Television has been substituted for toys and also for books.
He shows a preference for what demands the least effort.
The quick synthetic images that slide across the television
screen fascinate him. The child of today is ashamed of

experiencing gentle and tender feelings. He prefers violent
emotions. We frequently see him using a toy pistol or substituting this with a simple action of the first finger and
thumb in imitation of the barrel of a gun, shooting with
rage at the body of an imaginary enemy. His foes throw
themselves on the ground; they are dead. And in this manner the child becomes familiar with death and violence and
these hold no horror for him. James Bond is the archetype
of modern youth; wonderful adventures have converted him
into the most popular hero of our times. The child finds
himself dazzled by this display of useless fantasy. Children
of this era are not interested in fairy tales, princesses or
gnomes. It would be like putting them into an anachronistic
and incomprehensible world.

It is necessary to create other characters. Only
very young children are entertained by <u>Snow White</u> or <u>Little
Red Riding Hood</u>. Present-day means of communication
such as "jets," radio and television have formed, up to a
certain point, the mentality of children. In Peru as in
Australia children show the same admiration for gangsters
as they do for the Flintstones.

Now, my reply to the third question: Should children's literature have a teaching aim? I believe so. At
this moment in the story of mankind this is necessary from
every point of view.

It is true that the wonderful voyages dreamed about
by our ancestors have now been turned into reality and even
surpassed. Men from the farthest corners of the globe are
no longer unknown to us, but on the other hand dangerous
rivalries have arisen. Desires to dominate have been
awakened and the new discoveries, far from being instru-
ments of peace and universal fraternity, threaten to lead humanity towards inevitable disaster. Rich and powerful countries subdue the weaker ones. A blindfold covers the eyes
of the rulers who have in their hands the destiny of their
people. Nature's forces have been unleashed and put to the
service of death and destruction.

We believe that our hopes lie in the children of today,
if we can teach them from their earliest days to repudiate
violence and injustice and to eradicate the differences among
men. Good reading and good and well-directed cinema and
television could help us to build a new world for the future.

Children's literature could be an excellent means of offering them characters who act at their own mental level. But we cannot hope that the salvation of humanity be in their hands while we see young people reading stories of crime, violence and destruction which poison their minds. Today, when world peace is in danger and when there hangs over humanity the threat of an atomic war, it is more than ever necessary to warn the young people, to teach them from a very early age tolerance and the love of justice. This must be our task--the task of teachers, writers and parents: to place in their young spirits the desire for universal fraternity. For this reason children's literature should not be just a simple passing amusement. It should have a message, although it should not be presented didactically.

Children's literature--whether it be through elements of reality or fantasy--should lead to this goal. It must try to improve man, taking away his selfishness and his uncontrolled desires for power and riches at the cost of the oppression and misery of his fellow men. At this moment this should be one of the most important objectives of children's literature at a universal level.

But do children from what we call the developing countries have additional needs? And should children's literature play a special role? I feel so. In these countries a large part of the population suffers from many economic, political and social problems. It is true that a large section of Latin Americans in our large cities live at a similar level to those in developed countries, but there is also another group who find themselves huddled in unhealthy homes, in slums, where their children have never had the chance of catching hold of a book. The unstable work of their parents, food deficiency and the sordidness of the homes they live in condemn these children to abandonment and ignorance.

Children who live in the villages in the Andes are in equal if not in worse conditions. The countries that have reached a high level of development cannot even begin to imagine this situation and problem. If it is true that at present in the cities many of the children enjoy economic and cultural conditions similar to children of other countries, there are also forgotten children living in our most remote villages--children that many people only know about because they have seen a picturesque poster in some tourist agency, which is far from a true picture. That picturesque hat and that bright-colored "poncho" which do not keep out the cold are really poor rags. Very often these children do not even go to school, because to get there they have to cover great distances and they are not sufficiently well fed to stand the effort. No one has ever put a book in their hands, and if such a thing did happen they wouldn't be able to read it, because at night when they no longer have sheep to look after or fields to sow, there is nothing with which to light the hut, or if there is, it is only the flickering light of a candle or a small lamp.

It is true that there are exceptions. We see children and youths who attend classes at night in both schools and universities because during the day they must work. Frequently there are farm workers and laborers whose ambition in life is for their children to go to school and to university in the hopes that they will later reach a higher level of life than they themselves have had, and in order to obtain their objective they feel that no sacrifice on their part is too great.

The ruthless grandeur of nature in many parts of the American continent divides man--the great rivers and tangled vegetation of the jungle, the sandy deserts of the coast, the icy regions of the Andes with its gigantic mountains. It is there that these children live. They have the same desire to know as other children; they need books in order to quench their thirst for knowledge. We cannot speak to these children about fairies and princes and princesses, for they would not understand. They must be taught even what to aspire to before they can live among their own kind, much less reach the same level as children from other countries.

In recent years our Latin-American countries have become conscious of our common historical destiny. Fortunately, we have one language which is common to almost all the people of our continent. The origin of our literature has the same roots--stemming from Garcilaso de la Vega (Inca Garcilasa), the son of a Spanish conquistador and an Incan princess, who wrote of the conquest of Peru and who retold the legends of the Incas. The cross-breeding produced throughout the generations has strengthened this cultural heritage and today we are witnessing a renaissance of Spanish-American literature. Writers such as García Márquez, Vargas Llosa, Carpentier, Fuentes or Cortázar do not belong to any one country; they belong to the whole continent.

Foreign critics are full of admiration as they examine this phenomenon produced after a long and silent wait. Spanish-American literature is considered as one of the first symptoms of our integration, an integration which is eagerly sought in other fields, as in the economic or social fields by means of congresses or meetings, of which one of the chief objectives is the forming of a Common Market or the Andean Pact. If this integration is important in the material aspect, it is even more so in the cultural aspect. The image of a world convulsed and threatened by poverty has made us turn our eyes towards ourselves, in order that together we might face this common adversary of under-development which afflicts our continent. That is why the children of today must be nourished with a literature that will help to form them both intellectually and spiritually, which will act as a support so that they will not be lost in the confusion and chaos which surrounds them, that will teach them the true and just dimension of men and of things. Thus they may become aware of the part that they have to play later in society and the goals for which they must strive.

For this reason children's literature in the Latin American world cannot be a simple means of amusement, with the object only of quenching the thirst for new adventures. Neither must it give children a distorted image of a world dominated by violence. When the time comes for them to review the ideas and ideals which their parents have encouraged, they must know how to surpass them.

Many valuable sources, both literary and natural, have not been tapped for children in South America. Folklore is one example. Countries, like people, are born, grow and develop. From the primitive age of man arise many myths and legends full of symbols and magic elements which are peculiar to each country, yet common to all. The folklore of European countries has long been widespread in South America, and some Asiatic folklore has also reached us. But the rich Latin American store remains unknown. If these were told and retold and used as themes in children's literature, there would be a unity among the various countries and yet a link with the world commonality of folklore.

There is also the matter of setting. We need stories that describe and paint our own landscape: its flowers, its trees, its birds and its climates. Should we not write of

the "toucan" or the "buzzard" rather than the nightingale or
the rook; of the native "cantuta" or "amancay" and not the
forget-me-not or the cyclamen; of the "molle" or the "carob"
rather than the sandalwood or the fir? Why not make use
of our rivers, or our tangled jungles or our enormous deserts? Let us look around us and we shall find beauty in
what surrounds us, and out of the landscape can come the
characters to people our children's books. As with all
man's creations, literature should have roots in life itself.

With the achievement of this goal, our own children
would know their own country, and children from other
countries would begin to know us as we already know them.
The reformation and enrichment of children's literature can
unite all the countries in the world.

Chapter 10

A BASKET OF FIREFLIES: QUETZALCOATL
AND THE NAHUATL POETRY OF MEXICO

by Toni de Gerez

It would be very sad if I tried to tell you about children's books in Mexico. There are perhaps three publishing houses but their books are not representative of what I feel Mexico should really have. There is now a new movement under the Instituto Nacional de la Protección a la Infancia that is beginning to publish pamphlet-like books at a very low cost. One of them is based on a codex which is in the Library of Congress and it is a beautiful book, the best that they have published. But I can not fill this essay by trying to tell you of the few odd things that have come out at odd times, and that are not important enough for you to remember the authors or the titles.

Now, I can not possibly start discussing books without reminding you of something that, every time I think of books, I try not to forget. I know you know it, but it bears mentioning: it is the derivation of the word "book," which, of course, is from the Anglo-Saxon. It comes from the word tree, the beech tree I believe. This is very significant in relation to books in Mexico, the codices, which I shall be talking about because they were made from the amoxtl, which is the bark of the wild fig. I love to tell children about this relationship because I can not bear to think of trees being cut down for mediocre books, for books that are not important. In all of the legends in Mexico we always refer to the "ceiba," because that is known as the first tree, and it is always in the "ombligo," the very center of the universe. It is a fascinating idea, and immediately when you start thinking about the word tree then you become part of the whole galaxy, using Joseph Campbell's term--the whole galaxy of mythologies that are so beautifully related. One of the definitions of knowledge in

138

Nahuatl is "the singing wood" and actually the Nahuatl literature that I will try to explain was poetry, and so it was
something to be sung; it was an oral tradition that came
down to us through the centuries.

The first printed books in Mexico, in the sense of
the codices, were really our first picture books, and now
the Museo de Antropología is beginning to publish some of
these so that children can understand them and enjoy them.
What were these picture books? They are called codices,
and are presented in pictographs or ideograms, depicting a
story of a god or the story of the history of the tribes of
Mexico, and very eloquently. What better way could you
explain tribes moving from one part of the country to
another than by just making pictures of feet going somewhere? They are fascinating, these picture books, and they
are going to be the basis finally, I think, of some beautiful
books for children.

If these books had no written language--which they
obviously did not--how can I be talking about Nahuatl books?
Well, the pre-Columbian ones were the codices but, unfortunately, during the Spanish Conquest many of them were
burnt and were lost to history. But we did have a few wise
Spaniards who realized that some should be saved so that
the people could know what their culture was like before the
Spaniards and the Christians arrived. And so they did make
an effort to save some. Outside of Mexico City, at
Tlaltelolco, is an old convent (actually, it had been an Indian
college before the Spaniards came), and the friars there
decided to try to write down what could be remembered of
the old myths and legends. They had the wise men of the
area of Tlaltelolco tell these stories and histories, and
since there was no written Nahuatl language they were written down first in Latin, and then they were eventually translated from Latin into Spanish, and now some are available
in English.

When I began to work on some of this literature I
thought that there would perhaps be fifty books, but we actually have hundreds of titles, and who knows how many more
are lost? But we keep finding more and more. The
codices are in many places in Europe. Mexico, unfortunately, has, I think, perhaps two--one is in the National Library and one is in the Museo de Antropología. They are
like a screen, and they unfold, and are made out of amoxtl
and the colors are usually in red, a darkish red and black.

The Nahuatl word for knowledge is "the world of red and black," because these are the colors of the codices.

I would like to remind you of some of the marvelous things about Mexico, besides the pre-Columbian literature. When I first went to Mexico, straight from Boston, I felt that Boston had all the culture in the world and I really went there with a great deal of misinformation. I soon discovered that the first printing press on this continent was set up in Mexico; known as the Juan Pablos Press, it began in 1539. That is pretty early. Then we have these early schools. We have the Colegio de San José de Belém, founded in 1529, and this was designed for higher education for the Indians alone. Then we have a school called San Juan de Letrán, which was for mestizo boys. Then there was, of course, the school of Tlaltelolco, which I have mentioned; it had already been a school for the Indians, and then was taken over by the Spaniards in 1536. This was one of our first bilingual schools. The friars felt the only way they could get to the heart of the children who were going to this school was to learn Nahuatl. It is a difficult language, and if the friars went to another part of the country they had to learn another dialect. So bilingual education is really not new. Then, there was Fray Pedro de Gante, who is known as the Pestalozzi of this continent, his school was in Texcoco, right outside of Mexico city, and it was established at the same early date. Then, in 1540, in Michoacán, not far from where I live, there was another beautiful school, the one of Vasco de Quiroga. This was for the Tarascan Indian children; in fact, he translated some works of Pliny into the Tarascan language, because he felt they were important. It is also very interesting to note that he felt that Aesop's fables should be available to the children, so he translated them into the Tarascan language. So we have the first printing press, the first grammar schools, the first bilingual higher education schools in the Americas.

Just recently, in the Excelsior, a paper in Mexico, they have been talking a great deal about a little village called Tiripiteo--a Tarascan word--which is near the lake of Pátzcuaro. There they have found an early library, and they feel it is one of the first libraries on this continent. We cannot, of course, forget the University of Mexico, but here we have to bow to Peru, because the one in Peru, the University of San Marcos, was perhaps the first. But the University of Mexico began, I believe, in 1539 and it

was founded on the University of Salamanca, which dates
back to 1230.

Above all, Mexico has Quetzalcoatl and Nahuatl poetry. I do not know how in the world I can begin to try to
explain Quetzalcoatl to you. I think I shall probably spend
the rest of my life following in the footsteps of Quetzalcoatl,
and I hope I shall have many more years to live, because
there are so many more things to discover. Quetzalcoatl
was a god, of course, and was also known as a priest king.
We begin to hear about him when he lands in Tampico,
which is off the Atlantic coast of Mexico. No one knows
where he came from. He was blond and tall and there is a
theory perhaps that he might have been a Viking. Certainly
he bears many resemblances to Odin. Perhaps, though,
this marvelous Quetzalcoatl might have been Vainamoinen,
the hero of the Finnish epic, the Kalevala. At the end of
the Kalevala, Vainamoinen is leaving in a boat. The boat
is sung, and by singing the boat is made, and Vainamoinen
disappears. Well, where did he go? He could very well
have sailed down from the Baltic, and have landed in Tampico. Now I am not telling you that this is the truth, because I do not know the truth at all, and besides, in myths
and legends nobody worries about the truth; that is what is
so marvelous. There is yet another intriguing possibility,
that Quetzalcoatl was Oisin from Irish mythology. Anyway,
there he was in Tampico and he left the coast and went to
Tula. It is now an archaeological site, and is where the
Toltecs lived. Quetzalcoatl was the priest of the Toltecs.
There was an actual Quetzalcoatl, and there was also a
mythological one. He was known as the god of knowledge,
as the god of arts and crafts; he was a little like Prometheus
who stole fire for man. Quetzalcoatl stole something, not
more important than fire, but certainly terribly important
for Mexico and for Latin America--corn!

At first there was no corn and he had to find it. Man
had just been created and had nothing to eat--and what could
he eat but corn? Well, Quetzalcoatl discovered that it belonged to the red ants and they had hidden it in an enormous
hill. First he went to the ants as Quetzalcoatl and begged
and begged. But the ants would not give him corn. So then
he changed himself into an ant and went over to the hill.
The hill is called the Hill of Our Holy Sustenance, Tamoan-
chan, and this is the hill of corn. The ants said, "No, we
won't give you corn." So he stole the corn for man, and
then he had the problem of what to do with it. Then he

begged the rain god, Tlaloc, to help out, and so, you begin
to have corn in Mexico.

I am sure you have this legend here too, in North
America: when man was made, what was he made of?
Well, according to the Epica Nahuatl and other early epics,
when the gods were first deciding to make man they discussed it and first they thought, well, perhaps we will
make him out of wood. And so they made a very nice looking man out of wood. But there was a terrible fire and so
man was lost. A long time went by, and again they said,
"Well, let's try again, let's make man." And this time
they made man out of clay. And this was a magnificent man;
he was simply marvelous, this dark red clay man. And all
went well for quite a while, but then there was a flood, and
man disappeared. And again the gods had to put on their
thinking caps: "What shall we make man out of?" They
made man out of corn. And we are made out of corn today.

The mythological story of Quetzalcoatl is that one
day he suddenly looked into a mirror and saw how old and
wrinkled he was, and he said, "It is time for me to go."
And so he left. Along with him went most of the Toltecs;
they abandoned the city. They took their jewels and precious possessions, and legend has it that they threw them
in the lake near Tula. Even though a lot of this is, of
course, mythology mixed up with some history, there have
actually been people who go there excavating, trying to find
out whether these jewels are really there. Along the way
there is a little village with a gully with many, many
stones, and myth has it that on their way the Toltecs spent
several nights playing the drum and the flute and singing
songs, and resting and then singing again. And they were
so sad because they were leaving Tollan, the old name for
Tula, that they finally threw themselves into the gully, and
became stones. There is a rock which they call Quetzalcoatl's Rock, where he sat down to rest, and where he
rested there is the imprint of his hands.

Historically, we know that the Toltec civilization was
one of the finest, but eventually something happened and the
Toltecs left Tula about the year 1000 and started their mi-
gration south. We know they stayed in Cholula, near Teo-
tihuacán, and then they left that area for Yucatan. Quetzalcoatl changes into Kukulcan of the Mayans, and in Peru,
Viracocha is essentially Quetzalcoatl--and I would not be
surprised if you landed down at Tierra del Fuego that you
would still find pieces of the Quetzalcoatl myth.

And now I would like to read to you from 2-Rabbit,
7-Wind, my reworking of some Nahuatl poems. They are
not really translations; I took the liberty of cutting and making them into new poems. Actually if I were to do this
correctly, I should have a drum with me, and I should be
able to dance, because these poems, these early Nahuatl
poems, were part of a ritual. It was not something isolated
and alone; there was always a fiesta going on, probably for
nights and nights. So, try to imagine a drum in the background, an actual event, and that you are participating in
the event. And Shamanism is part of it too, a kind of
ecstasy, where you get drunk on all these words, and you
finally fall down, because you have been nights and nights
chanting them.

This early literature should be seen as a kind of
proto-poetry, the very first poetry that we have, and in
that sense it is extremely sacred. It is a kind of poetry
that is completely related to the whole earth. It is not
apart. I think poetry is too often thought of as a completely separate thing. It is a part of the first things, of the
naming of things; the first time you saw the sky, the first
time you saw a color, the first time you heard a bird.
All these are namings, and origins, and this is what Nahuatl
poetry, the pre-Columbian poetry, is about. For instance,
there is a song, at the end of which it says, "It really has
no meaning, just take it, I give it to you." So in a sense,
it is a little bit like our modern happenings. In a sense
also, it is all sacramental, and it is a part of the eucharist,
the sharing of words and dance, the flute, and the drum.
It is primary, the very firstness, and in a sense it is really
almost a kind of surrealism, as we know it today. And,
incredibly, it is filled with metaphors. That must have
been a terrifically important moment in time, when someone made these first metaphors. All the poetry that I have
been in contact with is filled with metaphors.

> O-mother-of-the-gods
> o-father-of-the-gods
>   I speak to you!
>
> oldest-god-of-the-jade-navel-of-the-earth
> mother-and-father-and-oldest god
>   I speak to you!
>
> lord-of-the-fire and lord-of-the-years
> your house is in waters bluebird color

your house is in the clouds
your house is in the
    dark
    difficult
country of the dead
    I speak to you!

lady-of-the-starry-skirt
lady-of-the-jade-petticoat
    lady-of-our-flesh
lord-of-our-flesh
she-who-makes-the-earth-solid
he-who-covers-the-earth-with-cotton
    I speak to you!

I direct my words
toward the place-of-duality
above the 9-levels-of-heaven
    I speak to you!

That is a famous poem and is usually quoted when people talk about Nahuatl poetry. This is my version of it and I think it sums up, really what Nahuatl poetry was like in its lyricism.

Part of the next poem is quoted on the walls of the Museo de Antropología.

I coyote-hungry-for-wisdom I say:
we are only a little while here
not forever on earth not forever on earth
only a little while
    though it is jade it will be broken
    though it is gold it will be crushed
    though it is quetzal feather
    it will be torn apart
not forever on earth not forever on earth
only a little while

The last poem in the book is a very tragic one. The scene described happened just a few years after the Conquest, in Tlaltelolco, at this convent. It was an encounter, a colloquium between the old Indian wise men and some Spanish friars. They sat at a table, facing each other, and the Spaniards were giving the Indians a chance to explain their way of life, even though, of course, it was not really fair, because it had already been taken away from them.

But it is a very sad poem, and it indicates the advent of
the Spanish language, culture and religion into Mexico. So
you can picture these friars facing the "old ones," the
"wise ones." Here they are, answering the Spaniards:

Our lords most esteemed most high
your journey has been hard and long
to reach this land

we who are humble
we who are ignorant
look at you

what is it that we should say?
what is it that your ears want to hear?
can there be meaning
in what we say to you?

we are common people
because of our god-of-the-near-and-far
because of him
we dare to speak
we exhale his breath and his words
    his air
for him and in his name
we dare to speak to you
despite the danger

perhaps we will be taken to our ruin
we are ordinary people
we can be killed
we can be destroyed
what are we to do?

. . .

allow us to die
let us perish now
since our gods are already dead

wait be calm our lords
we will break open
    a little

we will open
    a little
the secret of our god-who-is

. . . .

and now must we destroy
the ancient order
    of the Chichimec?
    of the Toltec?
    of the Acolhua?
    of the Teopanec?

we know our god
he gives us life
he continues our race
we know how it is that we must pray

hear us o lords
do not harm our people
do not destroy them
be calm and friendly
consider these matters o lords

we cannot accept your words
we cannot accept your teachings as truth
even though this may offend you
we cannot agree
that our gods are wrong

is it not enough that we have already lost
that our way of life has been taken away?
is that not enough?

this is all we can say
this is our answer
to your words o lords
do with us
as you please

      I just want to mention a book by Jerome Rothenberg.
It is Shaking the Pumpkin: Traditional Poetry of the Indian
North Americas. In this book he says that we have spent
much time on Greek and Roman myths, and the Scandinavian
myths, and we have neglected the great ones on this continent. He suggests that we get acquainted with the beautiful
myths that we have on this continent, and that we tell them
again with the rattle and the drum. I would like to leave
you with that thought.

Chapter 11

SURPRISED BY JOY:
THE WORLD OF PICTURE-BOOKS

by Margaret Johnston

"To everything there is a season, and a time to
every purpose under the heaven." To every child there is
a season for picture-books. For many children a picture-
book is the beginning of understanding, an understanding of
the world around them, an understanding of the way children
of other countries live and think, an understanding of the
world of animals both tame and wild. Of all classes of literature picture-books are the most versatile and all-embracing. Not only do they stimulate the understanding of children, they also appeal to their senses because in picture-
books they may discover drama, poetry, fiction, fact, history, art and music, the rhythm and beat of words. They
can travel to distant countries and experience folk and
legendary literature, science and religion. It is true that
these subjects are presented in an extremely simple form,
but what other class of literature unfolds such a palatable
point of view on the whole universe? What a glorious introduction to the whole field of art and literature that awaits
the child in his more mature years.

Just as picture-books form the basis of all literature,
so also they form the basis of art criticism. Because of
the vast output of picture-books, parents, teachers and librarians need sound, informed criticism if we are to put
into the hands of children books which will stimulate their
imagination, exercise their minds and arouse their curiosity;
books which will mean so much to them in later years. We
do not know what is in store for our children, but we can
through picture-books help to prepare for their maturity.
To my mind that is what education is, a preparation for the
understanding, the handling and the enjoyment of all the
wonderful things yet to come. The reading of factual books

147

alone and the memorization of dates and facts is not going to educate a child unless the imagination has been stimulated to put these facts to use in a way that will help the world to progress.

It is within the last 100 years that picture-books as we know them had their beginning. Up until the middle of the Victorian era children had only a very few and these were generally staid, dull and moralizing. It took Walter Crane, Kate Greenaway and Randolph Caldecott to revolutionize the picture book. This immortal trio has clearly expressed through their work their ideas of what picture-books should be, and set goals for many picture-book artists since their time. Since their time and throughout the world writers and artists have bent their talents towards pleasing young children and many have succeeded in producing books which generation after generation will enjoy.

When looking over the whole field, general favorites spring into focus. They are favorites because they are the best, and they are the best because their creators have felt a responsibility to childhood and have produced their books with some dignity of purpose. In considering writing for children Anatole France once wrote, "Do not assume a style for the occasion. Think your best and write your best." The great creators of the picture-book have grasped his wisdom.

Sincere writers and artists, in all probability, cherish the hope that their work will live, that it will strike a chord in the mind and heart of the reader or beholder and therein exist. Children are not born with likes and dislikes, prejudices and enthusiasms, good taste or poor taste; these are critical developments which they acquire through experience. This experience is directly dependent upon their relations to adults and what is provided for them. These experiences can be deep or shallow, broad or narrow, according to the direction and the influence of the particular adult world. If in the early years a child has well chosen picture-books, how boundless experience can be.

Those of us who are children's librarians know for certain that children do gain experience from their picture-books, even though we cannot measure how much, nor always judge the kind of experience. They are quick to find what gives them pleasure. They identify themselves with their picture-book friends and delight in entering into the

surprising world they encounter. The characters they meet
between the covers of favorite books are not just words and
pictures; these characters live, move and have their being
with all the reality of their imaginations. Their friends
may be a duck like Ping, a monkey like George, an elephant like Babar or even cats by the million. They may
take to their hearts a soldier like Clever Bill or a snow-
plough like Katy. Among their dearest friends they may
count Little Tim, the stowaway, Ola the little Viking or
Madeline of appendix fame. Such are likely to be a young
child's nominations for a "Hall of Fame."

What is the magic of artists in words and pictures
that so enchants children that they return to these books
again and again for the pleasure and joy they bring? If we
turn the pages of these books we may grasp the quality of
their makers, the quality of mind and heart and imagination
that finds satisfaction in giving only the best that is in them
so that the children may be "surprised by joy."

What is a good picture-book? In simple terms it is
one in which stories and pictures equally will give lasting
pleasure. The pictures should possess all the mental qualities of the text. What the ear hears the eye must behold.
This perfect harmony between seeing matter and hearing
matter, however, is not enough. They must both have a
quality. The "spark of life" is the nearest I can come to
a definition. It is that quality of bringing about a positive
response from a child which makes the book a living thing.
Without this spark, however perfect a book may be in all
its detail, it can be a dead thing, a very dead thing. It is
this same vital factor which determines whether a book
shall endure, whether it can be read countless times without
losing its charm, and whether in later years adults will be
glad it was one of their first books.

The story in a picture-book is of equal importance
with the pictures and its literary value may be judged in the
same way as an adult book is judged; indeed, it must meet
the same requirements. The age level of a book ought not
to raise or lower its standards. Surely the child of four
deserves as good a book as a person of forty.

The story must attract and sustain interest. It must
have action and plot, which are not too involved and which
develop in a natural way--not manufactured to bring in points
which the author obviously wishes to put across. The story

should have a beginning, a middle and an end and it should be allowed to tell itself with vitality, action and a fine use of words. The way the story is written is of great importance because the most exciting plot can be deadened by the use of dull, unimaginative language.

The characterization, too, is important. There must be a control character who propels and governs the action from an inner nature, whether it be a person, an animal or an object. All the characters must be clearly defined, not by wordy descriptions but by what they do and say in their relationships to one another and by how they meet certain situations.

The text of a picture-book should, to a large extent, determine the type of illustration, and success often depends upon the process and medium used. As we choose and carefully consider the text of picture-books so we should choose and consider the pictures. If we want children to develop a natural sense of art we may as well start from the beginning. Why give them pictures of saccharine sweetness without strength of line, vitality or character just because the subject matter is child-like? The subject, of course, is important in children's pictures because the story they look for revolves around the subject. But most of all, the pictures alone should tell the story that the children may not yet be able to read for themselves.

Picture-books can help to develop a sense of humor. Humor is not essential but a picture-book is all the richer for its presence. Most children love to laugh and nothing is more rewarding than to cause their laughter. It hardly matters whether the humor is slapstick or subtle as long as it is really funny. Picture-books can also exercise the imagination. Imagination on the part of the author or the gift of sharing the imagination of a child is a most desirable quality. It can lift the child from humdrum everydayness to the realm where the impossible and the most fanciful are the most likely and the most real.

And now I would like to praise famous men.

> Let us now praise famous men
> Men of little showing
> For their work continueth,
> And their work continueth,
> Broad and deep continueth,
> Greater than their knowing.

(Perhaps I should have said "persons," but I doubt if Kipling would have approved.)

Here are a few illustrators (some author/illustrators) whose works contain the qualities I have emphasized in this brief paper. These by no means represent all the "classics" of the picture-book genre, but my long experience with children and picture-books has convinced me that we can never do without them.

Leslie Brooke has never been surpassed in his use of fine line, color and particularly humor. Who else could draw a bear like Leslie Brooke, and who else would have thought of the family motto, "Bear and Forbear," or the newspaper called "The Bear Truth" or the portrait of the ancestor labeled "Major Ursa D.S.O." all found in one picture in his The Story of the Three Bears. Beatrix Potter's incomparable books have made a definite contribution to literature and her illustrations have a special place as art in the development of book illustration. Kurt Wiese's illustrations in The Story of Ping (written by Marjorie Flack) have helped make a memorable friend for many children. Ingri and Edgar d'Aulaire's fine use of lithography reveals the authentic life of children in Norway. Edward Ardizzone's use of water color in such books as Little Tim and the Brave Sea Captain is an example of an eminently suitable medium for his sea stories. H. H. Rey, in Curious George, may well have created the best loved character in literature. Ezra Jack Keats, who works mostly in collage, shows a perfect interrelation of story, pictures, medium and colour. Virginia Lee Burton brings inanimate objects to life in a most natural way. Harold Jones, in Lavender's Blue (edited by Kathleen Lines), shows a sense of design and sparks of spontaneous humor and brings them together with a sure, fresh touch of brush and color which will enchant children for years to come. Marcia Brown is so versatile that she can always use the best medium for the story she is illustrating. Roger Duvoisin brings that precious smile to the face of children as they read and see the incongruities he presents. Perhaps Petunia is the greatest favorite. Ludwig Bemelmans, in creating Madeline and Hansi, has not only produced well-loved characters but has also developed an interest in children of other countries.

Among the later illustrators in England, we have: Raymond Briggs, who has brought a vigorous, robust approach to the nursery rhymes--one feels that this is how the

characters should have been drawn when they were first
chanted; Brian Wildsmith, whose illustrations for the old
fables present pictures whose design and color triumph glow-
ingly and vibrantly; John Burningham who, with his "Mr.
Grumpy" books, has created a new hero; Charles Keeping,
who appeals not only to the eye with his shifting patterns
of color, but to all the senses and, most importantly, to
the intellect; William Stobbs and Barry Wilkinson, who have
opened up new ways of looking at the old folk and fairy
tales.

Recently, in the United States, Leo Lionni, Maurice
Sendak and Barbara Cooney have also created, in their individual styles, books which children return to again and
again.

I have been speaking, chiefly, about picture books
from Great Britain and the United States. I would like to
mention briefly some Canadian picture-books. You all know
the Republic of Childhood; A Critical Guide to Canadian
Children's Literature in English by Sheila Egoff. I do not
wish merely to echo what has been said in that book about
illustration and writing for young children, but to reinforce
the implication of the need for more and more good Canadian picture books. It is only when we produce a great
volume of work that we can have a body of Canadian literature for young children which can take its place in the
mainstream of Canadian literature.

For reasons of publication difficulties we cannot
hope, nor perhaps should we wish, to compete with the
vast output of Great Britain and the United States, but I am
confident that we can compete in quality of production and
content. We need many, many picture-books which will not
only give children pleasure in books but also pleasure in
the world around them, books of national yet universal interest, books that will create satisfaction in the recognition
of themselves in family surroundings, conditions and attitudes, and stimulating enough to help them grow in their
own period of time. Canadian children, like all others,
must live in their own age and be able to envision their
world of the future.

We are grateful to Canadian publishers such as the
Oxford University Press, Tundra Books, Macmillan of Canada, McClelland & Stewart and the Oberon Press, who have
made tremendous strides in producing books of fine quality

which have pleased not only the children of Canada but have also achieved international acclaim. Most notable among these are The Wind Has Wings, edited by Mary Alice Downie and Barbara Robertson and illustrated by Elizabeth Cleaver; Cartier Discovers the St. Lawrence, by William Toye and illustrated by Lazlo Gal; How Summer Came to Canada and The Mountain Goats of Temlaham, by William Toye and illustrated by Elizabeth Cleaver; The Princess of Tomboso, from The Golden Phoenix, by Marcus Barbeau and illustrated by Frank Newfeld; Mary of Mile 18 and A Boy of Taché, written and illustrated by Ann Blades; A Prairie Boy's Summer, written by William Kurelak and illustrated with his paintings; Au-Delà du Soleil/Beyond the Sun, written and illustrated by Jacques de Rousseau; Alligator Pie and Nicholas Knock and Other People, written by Dennis Lee and illustrated by Frank Newfeld; Sally Go Round the Sun, by Edith Fowke and illustrated by Carlos Marchiori; Cinderella, retold and illustrated by Alan Sudden; and The Sleeping Beauty, by Charles Perrault, adapted by Michael Macklem and illustrated by Carel Moiseiwitsch.

We are grateful, also, to the many smaller presses throughout Canada that are producing picture books. It is impossible to mention all these presses so I hope I may just call upon my personal experience with the children of Toronto and name some of those which I know have delighted them. From the "Tree Frog Press"--Bonnie McSmithers You're Driving Me Dithers, by Sue Ann Alderson, illustrated by Fiona Garrick; "Canadian Women's Educational Press"-- Mandy and the Flying Map, by Beverly Allinson, illustrated by Ann Powell, and The Travels of Ms. Beaver, by Rosemary Allison, illustrated by Ann Powell; "Zenovia Press"-- Wayne's Wagon, by George Michailiuk, and The Wind, by Richard Michailiuk; "Before We Are Six Press"--Minoo's Family, by Sue Crawford, illustrated by Frances McGlynn, and Irene's Idea, by Bernice Geoffroy, illustrated by Frances McGlynn; "Kids Kan Press"--Strange Street, written and illustrated by Ann Powell; I'm A Child of the City, by Esther Fine, illustrated by Ann Powell; Harriet and The Great Bike Robbery, written and illustrated by Claire Garcia, and The Sandwich, written and illustrated by Ian Wallace and Angel Wood.

These are some of the publishers, writers and artists who are producing books for children which show them in their world today, in city life, with family problems, in non-sexist situations. They are books of true realism and not so overburdened with a "message" that they cannot be enjoyed as genuine stories; books which lead on to reading of other realistic stories, folk tales and fantasy, and so to a significant reading future.

Chapter 12

THE PRICE OF BEING AN ARTIST

by Graham Booth

An illustrator obviously deals with the visual aspects
of a picture-book, he reacts visually, he thinks visually.
At least I know I do, and therefore it is more difficult for
me to talk about pictures than to draw them. It is somewhat like trying to explain the taste of a banana to somebody
who has never eaten one. However, there are some problems that seem to be universal with illustrators, apart from
the economic ones which I shall also mention.

First of all, I do not know many illustrators as such,
who really started out to be illustrators with illustrating as
their prime goal. I teach at a college in California, and I
am often asked, "How do I become a children's book illustrator? I think it would be great." This is from somebody
who is just starting to get a formal art education. It seems
to me that you really do not set that as your goal. What
you do is to try to become as competent as you can as an
artist, and there is a difference of course, between the fine
artist or painter and that which is now called graphic design. "Graphic design" is the word that has replaced "advertising design," which replaced "commercial art," because
"commercial art" sounds commercial, and means that you
have sold out. So the word now is "graphic design" and it
is, from my experience, the largest single avenue for art
students to travel because it seems to be the way that offers
some money. I think it is necessary for the art student to
move as long as he can along the formal education path, but
then to strike off on his own. Education, especially art education, can be either beneficial or disastrous; it depends--I
have seen a lot of people spoiled through poor teaching or
poor exposure. It is very hard to teach art, and I often
wonder if you really can. Where I teach we simply try to
provide students with an atmosphere in which they can grow.

It is not an indoctrination program. Encouragement is very
important in art education. The ego can be easily snapped,
easily hurt, and there is a point where students have to
make the decision to leave that formal set-up, the kind of
the mother of the art department, and go out and develop.
Otherwise they remain and become perennially graduate students, and maybe eventually teachers. And anyway, there
is that responsibility.

In my own case, which brings me back to illustration, I was working in Vancouver as a graphic designer, or
advertising designer, or commercial artist. Anyway, it
was essentially advertising, and I was trying to get paid for
it. It was very difficult for me. This was ten years ago,
and in that little office on Pender Street there were six
other artists, who were very capable and who were having
the same economic problems as myself, except that I happened to be single at the time, so all I needed was something to carry me over in the evening at the Abbotsford,
and I was happy. But for the others, because of family
situations, there was a sense of depression that always pre-
vailed. You get to the point where that sort of frustration,
which obviously is not just common to the art scene, wears
you down, and you start to lose a sense of where you are
in this scheme, wondering if you ever should have been involved in art, whereas everybody who went into law seems
to be doing jolly well. You find yourself walking up to the
advertising agencies, which you depend on for your work,
hat in hand, and it gets really to be too much.

At that time I was asked to teach graphic design at
the Vancouver Art School at night, which I did, because I
thought it was a nice idea and also I got paid a little bit,
which helped. That is really the key thing that made me
shift my horizons; I found I enjoyed teaching. I also felt
that it would allow me to balance my other art endeavors;
I could be more selective, I would not have to do Bow-Mac
ads any more, which are just terrible. But the worst thing
is you start to think they are good. That is why art direc-
tors give everybody awards. In advertising art, you will
notice, everybody is getting awards and giving awards, because they are all trying to convince themselves that whatever they are doing has immense social and artistic merit.
Some of it has, of course, it is communication, but somehow it always struck me as being peculiar.

Having found that I enjoyed teaching, I decided that

it was necessary for me to get an advanced degree, and so
I went down to the University of Southern California, which
had a Master of Fine Art program. I do not know if you
know much about the University of Southern California. It
is a private university in the Los Angeles area, most noted
for football, which is a whole different thing, but being a
private university it has the fastest master's program on
earth and there is a student body of something like twenty-
three thousand, with only four thousand undergraduates.
But during that time, because I had some leisure (you can
only see Last Year at Marienbad so many times), I decided
to be involved, as part of my graduate work, in children's
books. I am not an expert on children's literature; in fact
I am still rather naive about a great deal that is happening.
But I met a fellow in the library school called Mark Taylor
and we collaborated after about a year on the first book.

   I put together some roughs, and they were a reflection of living up here in British Columbia. It had something
to do with snow, and I called it Henry and His World. I
presented it to Mark and I said, "Well what do you think of
this?" And he said, "Well, apart from a few things, it's
already been done." And he showed me Ezra Jack Keats'
The Snowy Day, which was a remarkable and beautiful book,
and I got very depressed.

   I understand that about twenty-three hundred titles a
year are published in the United States in the children's
book field, so it is possible to have a duplication of theme,
especially by someone who has had little exposure to children's books. Fortunately, Mark Taylor, being a professor
of librarianship, knew these things and that really helped a
great deal.

   But from that particular beginning we worked up a
dummy, a dummy being a kind of a hand-made original copy
of a book. We felt that the best publisher in New York was
Atheneum, and we would submit it there and then we could
go to so-and-so, and then we would go to so-and-so and
then finally we could send it to Texas or somewhere. Here
my advertising background came to the fore. You do not
just send it in; it has to be in a slick box, well packaged
and so on. So I made a box out of black material, similar
to the box that Life books come in, with a red legal seal
and wrapped in plastic. And we decided that we would put
as much postage on that package as we could, without being
redundant. Then Mark said, "Well, always when you do

this you include a cheque for the return postage." The
postage was five dollars and eighty-one cents so I included
a cheque for five dollars and eighty-one cents made out to
Atheneum, and we sent it off. Four weeks to the day, it
came back to Mark Taylor's house, in a brown manilla
envelope with two dollars and twenty-five cents worth of postage. Mark telephoned me and said, "Well, you'd better
come over, I haven't opened it yet." So I went over and it
was one of the highs of my life. Inside was a beautiful
letter from Jean Karl saying they liked the book and wanted
to publish it. I flew around the room nine times. But
then the reality hit me, after the cheque for five dollars
and eighty-one cents cleared. I had the acceptance, but I
was out about two dollars and forty cents.

I would like to talk a little bit about the reality of
working as an illustrator. I have talked to other illustrators, and although we all work differently, we all have some
of the same problems, the same fears. Because I teach
full-time, I can only really work on a book on weekends,
or preferably during vacation periods, because you can not
really get rolling in two days and then drop it and pick it
up with the same feeling week after week, even though
sometimes that happens. I would prefer, which is a natural
preference, to write my own material, which I am doing to
some extent, except that my stories are locked in a closet.
I look at them, and I go over them and I work a little bit,
and I put them back, because nothing is pushing me to finish
them. I am sure that without the pain of deadline imposed
by the publisher my work would never get finished. It would
just keep going through a metamorphosis of endless changes
and, given an infinite amount of time, I would probably dup-
licate every book ever done, just on the one theme. So
since my own material does not have that imposing deadline,
it is inclined to sit and grow and change and be just a thing
that expands files. Because in the meantime a book will
come along for me to illustrate, and I will look into that.
However, I have a commitment this year with myself to try
and look at some of that material and see if it has any
merit.

I prefer to work with the writer on the conceptual
point of the book; that is to say, getting together with the
author on an afternoon or perhaps a weekend, and working
on story themes. During that time he will be writing and I
will be doing rough sketches, which we call story boards.
We tape them up to his glass doors or windows so they are

spread around. This allows him to relate to the visual even
if they are only scribble-type drawings. It allows him to
get some sense of the design or the pacing of the book. At
the same time I can get some feeling of the writing. And
so we feed each other. I can suggest something or argue
that this or that should happen, and we seem to be polite
enough to settle our differences without fighting. But the
essential is that there is a joint composition. This is not
too different from putting together a film, in which you have
dialogue and visual material and they have to work in unison
in order to be a successful experience. Whether the writer
and the artist are one and the same or two people are involved in the concept of a book, this dovetailing of the two
elements is one of the essential pieces.

The other way, of course, is for a publisher to send
a manuscript to an illustrator who then does the lay-out. I
have worked for a publishing firm which has the text typeset.
Then they send me xeroxes of the type set in running gal-
leys, so I not only have the manuscript but I know the space
and the size. But these books are not story-books, they
are a science series. And it seems to me in that case that
the text stands on its own completely. It is my job to make
that text more palatable; it is really dry stuff. Imagine a
grade-five book on the metric system! So I try to introduce
a little lightness to it, although I do not know if this is the
best approach or not. Scientists tend to frown now and
again on that lightness of illustration--you are mocking science, you know. I say that if sugar-coating the pill is a
way of reinforcing the information, then it works. So that
is a different approach to illustration.

In my own attitude toward the kind of illustrations I
do, there is always one essential limitation imposed, and
that is economic. There are two ways of doing children's
book illustrations in color. One is to paint the pictures in
color, just as you can see them, and that is called the
full-color process art. But it is the most expensive kind
of art to reproduce. It involves the photo-engraving process, taking that original illustration, which is like a painting, just painted in the colors of the artist's palette, and
presenting it to the publisher, who then turns it over to the
printer. The printer goes through a process of photo-engraving separations; he separates, using filters, the three
primary colors out of the illustration much as a television
does. And then there are actually four plates. Those four
plates are then assembled under pressure one at a time.

The paper is printed in four separate impressions. It is
not only an expensive process to make the separations; the
registration on four-color process, because you are regis-
tering dots equivalent to a hundred and twenty-five thousand
per square inch, causes a higher degree of waste. More
paper has to go through the set-up. It is also more critical, and you cannot run the presses so quickly and therefore the costs are reflected in the price of the book. The
costs of printing are accelerating; but paper prices over the
last few years have tripled, on an international world-wide
basis. Art paper increased in price by another fifteen per
cent in one month recently, and this goes on every year,
year after year, so paper is no longer a throw-away com-
modity.

The other method of illustrating a book is for the
artist to hand-separate the illustrations. That is to say,
he does his primary illustration on the board, and then the
colors are done, usually on acetate, as overlays. When the
picture comes to the printing process it is already separated
into three or two separate drawings that are necessary to
make the individual plates to print the book. This is infin-
itely cheaper because the artist does not charge for it. And
so you will find, it seems to me, that more and more books
are being done in a limited color situation, and being hand-
separated for economic reasons. This is not to say that
they are lesser in an artistic sense; I think some of the
most beautiful books have been done with these limitations.

It is important for the illustrator to understand design limitation, and to see that it can be an advantage, if
you work within it. With full color there is no limitation
and you just do what you want. But within hand separation,
your drawing takes on a different character. I like color--
everybody does--but it is not necessary for a noble, fine
book. That is essentially the difference between working as
an illustrator and as a painter.

I have mentioned something about economics and
would now like to link it to the Canadian scene. I do not
think the situation is too different here from what it is in
the United States. The difference essentially is between a
country of twenty-two million people and a country of two
hundred million, and the economic base, whether it is in
children's books or refrigerators, or any consumer manufactured product, is reflective of that size differential. I
see the frustration when people say they go to Seattle and

things are cheaper. Part of the price of being a Canadian
is to live in a country where population as such does not
allow for the high production levels of countries such as
the United States or Japan. That is a fact of life and may
be a source of frustration. It was for me; it should not
have been, but it was. However, I think the problems are
essentially the same; that is to say, I do not know too many
illustrators on my own circuit in California who do not do
something else besides illustrate books.

Nicholas Sitchikoff, for example, is a very well-
known graphic designer working in San Francisco, and a
children's book is something extra that he does upon occasion. Gene Holton, who is incidentally from Canada, has
told me that the books he has done really represent an
economic loss because it takes him off the board to do the
books; it takes time for which he could get paid by I. A.
Magnin. He does not mean to knock children's books because
he likes to do them, but that is one factor. In my own
case, of course, I teach. I think you need that other basis.
There are a number of people who would be more involved
in children's books if the economic returns justified it.

Of course, I am paid on a royalty basis and so I get
a percentage of the gross sales over a long period of time.
A typical situation is this: I finish the illustrations, I submit them, the book is published about a year later, and a
year after that I start getting my first residuals. There is
an advance but that is applied to the first royalties. It is
very hard to do something now and anticipate that you are
going to be paid so much a year, three or four years from
now, and consider that as a career opportunity. Obviously,
if you have sufficient books out, and provided they do not all
drop out of print, they overlap to the point that it can become a nice thing. I always look forward to April because
I am so far removed from when I did the books that it is
almost like somebody giving me something for nothing--like
winning something in a contest. I am very happy with the
structure of my life, the teaching, and the books. If I can
do sufficient books and if they are successful, I shall back
off from my teaching load.

There are Canadian illustrators who feel that there
are problems of publishing in Canada, but they are ones of
degree, I think. I do not know if things will change. To
be a Canadian and to be published by a Canadian publisher
is deemed to be especially worthy. I am not sure, though,

that it matters so much if the book is published in the
United States and sold in Canada, providing it is by Canadian authors and artists who are acknowledged. If it is an
economic necessity, that to me seems the important con-
sideration. Publishing may be esoteric, but it is still a
dollars and cents situation. This is reflective of the economy here. The printing costs are even more expensive
here, but distribution is the key factor. I can see that
this is a sort of "sweaty-palm" situation with Canadian publishers, but I do not know what the answer is.

I understand that there are increased Canada Council
grants for artists. In some countries in Europe the artist
is automatically pensioned for being an artist, because, as
somebody said, "Well, how long did it take you to do that
little drawing?" And the answer is not fifteen minutes or
twenty; it has taken years to get to that point, and to reach
that kind of ability. Utopia, to me, is to have artists re-
lieved of the frustration of having to worry about the economic factors and receive some sort of residuals from the
state. But the system would break as soon as the artists
started worrying about <u>how much</u> they were going to get.
It becomes a different ball-game if the artist wants to
change from an Austin A-40 life-style to a Porsche 917
and things like that. So I suppose there is a price to be
paid for an involvement in an activity that is creative. It
is obviously a filtering process; the best rises, in most
cases, and the rest struggle to reach that point--and this
is your commitment. In my own case, I try not to worry
but just to do my best. It is very very difficult for an
artist to view his own work; this is not just false modesty,
it is a fact. I know of no artist who actually regards his
own work as important. I happen to be a good friend of a
well-known Mexican artist, José Luis Cuevas, a man who
is probably the most important expressionist in Mexico.
When he goes to his showings he takes his glasses off so
that he can not see his own work. He has none of it in his
house--he has sixty Picassos but no Cuevases.

I have another artist friend who after his work has
been even ten years on the wall of a gallery, takes in a
friend to engage the guard in conversation while he whips
out his paints and quickly starts making changes on the
canvas on the wall. Unfortunately I cannot intercept my
books as they are delivered to bookstores and change the
illustrations, although I would like to. When the books
come out and I get an advance copy, my adrenalin starts to

flow; I almost can not look at it because it has been a year since I did it. That year has allowed reflection and growth. So this, too, is part of the price an artist pays for being an artist.

Chapter 13

BETWEEN CHAOS AND CREATIVITY:
THE ROLE OF THE CHILDREN'S EDITOR

by Jean Karl

Not long ago, not long at all as time goes in these
troubled days, there lived a boy. Jack was his name.
Jack Boggs. He lived in a town not too large and not too
small, and he did as all children do, he learned and played
and worked when he had to, and sometimes he dreamed
dreams and pondered on the world. If there was any difference between him and other children, it was that he was
more restless, more quick to feel discontent than his companions. He spent more time than others wondering about
himself and trying to think of new things to do. But one
thing he did not spend much time thinking about was dragons.
In fact, he hardly ever thought of them. And if he had
been asked, he might have laughed and said there was no
such thing. For he was a bright boy and wise in the knowing of his day.

He lived his days, Jack did, each in much the same
way until his school time was over. Then he had to find a
life work. It was a sensible village he lived in, and no
child was ever made to follow a work that did not suit.
When the right time came, each child was sent forth, lovingly and with some funds, to find a future. Some wandered
about only a day or two and came home, content with what
there was there and took a parent's occupation perhaps, and
no one criticized. That child had chosen. Others wandered
longer and came home, some with skills they had learned
and some with nothing, eager to take whatever the village
offered. And to each the village gave what was needed,
recognition or a place to learn. Some never returned. But
each, whatever the end, had had his chance to choose and
his days of freedom. There was only one firm rule: if a
child came home to stay after two or more years had gone

164

by, the village would have the final say as to that child's placement. But even then the decision was made only after the story of the journey was told and considered. And so the village was content and prospered.

When Jack's time came to be off, he went in joy. Not for him, he knew, the quick return. Though what he hoped the world would bring him, he did not know. Somewhere, he was sure, there lay the kind of life that would be forever merry, forever enough to stay the restlessness of his mind.

First he went to an Inn, thinking that the life of an innkeeper must be ever changing and ever new, with each new guest; and the innkeeper did need help. So Jack waited on tables, and scrubbed floors, and carried bags and polished boots. He also met travelers, and as he worked he listened to their chatter. They had been many places and seen many things; but their stories meant little to Jack, because after a while they all sounded alike. Travelers tended to see what they saw at home. It soon seemed to him that the life of an innkeeper had little but labor in it, and that that labor was an endless round of the same, so he moved on.

Several villages later, he went to a storekeeper, for it seemed that the lights of the store and the beauty of the objects to be sold or their goodness or their usefulness was never-endingly different. And then too, there would be the people who came. Jack scrubbed the floors, and washed the tables and shelves and cases, and arranged the goods, and even sometimes waited on the customers. But before long, each day seemed like the day before, so he moved on.

He tried several more things: he worked with a farmer; he ran errands for a man of the law; he ground herbs and chemicals for an apothecary. And eventually he spent some time with a traveling company of players. But though the crops differed on the farm, the legal problems varied, diseases called forth many mixtures of medicines, and the small parts he played required costumes of widely separated periods and actions that fit the nature and time of story, he was never content. All too soon it seemed alike. And when the art was learned, it no longer seemed worth the doing.

In despair Jack began to think that what had begun so happily and so surely would end with a trip home and a life no better and no worse than those he had seen. But it would not content him, of that he was certain. And if he did not hurry, there would not even be a choice there for him. One year had gone, and the second was passing. What to do?

One day, at the edge of a village, before a house that seemed to belong to a small but tidy farm he saw a sign: ADVICE GIVEN AND RETURNED. A. BUTTER-WORTH, PROPRIETOR. Jack puzzled over the sign and finally decided to go in. He had nothing to lose.

Jack was warmly welcomed, given a meal, and then listened to as he explained his problem. A. Butter-worth nodded his head and said he needed to think a bit. In the meantime he offered to take Jack around the farm. So Jack saw the cows and asked how many quarts of milk they gave each day, and he saw chickens and asked about the eggs, and he saw fields of rye and barley and asked about the planting and the hoeing.

After dinner A. Butterworth began to tell stories. He told of wise men and great, poor men and merchants who had come to him for advice. He remembered them as friends, and Jack realized that these men who had come had been given good advice, but they had returned some-thing as well, a feeling of joy and peace and above all, wonder. If he had some of what A. Butterworth had, would that provide the content he sought?

Finally A. Butterworth turned again to Jack. "And now my boy, what of you?"

"Do you think--is it possible I might learn some of what you know?" Jack asked.

A. Butterworth nodded, "Yes, lad, of course," he answered, "but not yet. For anyone who seeks knowing must first find the ten-winged dragon."

It was the first time Jack had ever had to confront the possibility of dragons. And the idea did not appeal to him. Dragons were nonsense; and ten-winged dragons were utterly nonexistent. How could a sensible person think oth-erwise? Yet there it was--a sensible man, a wise man even, was proposing a search for a ten-winged dragon. Jack was tempted to laugh, but did not. Instead he asked,

"And where might such a thing be found?"

"Why that's up to you," said Mr. Butterworth. "The search is yours."

The next morning, after a restless night, Jack announced that he had decided to search for the dragon. It seemed foolish, but he had no other choice, he felt. He wandered for days, asking occasionally for ten-winged dragons and looking in all the likely places: deep pits, mountain canyons and half-explored caves. But none of these yielded any results.

Then one day Jack passed a field in which an inventor was toying with a heavier-than-air machine of a new variety. It had wheels and wings and a great fire in its innards that spouted flames and belched smoke. Jack watched for a long time. It is like a ten-winged dragon, he thought. He imagined himself flying the machine right up to the house of A. Butterworth, proprietor.

The next day he saw a wind-mill, tall and stately. The wind whirred its many blades around, and the water it drew from a stream spouted into the channels at the edge of a field like something truly alive. Jack stood and watched and said, "Well, here is a ten-winged water dragon."

Since he was running short of funds, he found a clockmaker who needed assistance, someone to clean the shop and wait on the trade. They were familiar duties by now, and the customers were very like the visitors at the inn or the people who bought in any shop. Jack soon saw that. But he amused himself sometimes by wondering what they would think if he asked them about ten-winged dragons. Sometimes, too, in the town, he saw everyday things that suddenly became, to his way of looking, ten-winged dragons.

Watching the clockmaker one day, and realizing that his two years were almost over, Jack was suddenly seized with an idea. He understood something of how the wheels and gears and screws of a clock worked. And he had learned a lot about shaping metal. Could he make a ten-winged dragon? He set to work in his spare time. First he decided how it would look. This was not easy, because by that time he had thought of dozens of ways a ten-winged dragon might look. But finally he chose one--fierce and yet with some fun in it. Slowly he molded and pounded pieces of pliable tin into the shape he had chosen. Then he put in a clockwork that made all ten wings move at once. The clockmaker, who had looked with wonder at Jack's occupation, now laughed with delight and offered Jack a permanent job with him. But Jack explained that now that he had made a ten-winged dragon, he must go back to his friend A. Butterworth.

Jack set off at a rapid pace. There were three days left before the two years were up. Yet as he moved along, he found himself less and less able to hurry. A cloud in the sky was a ten-winged dragon, and he had to stop and look. A bunch of children watching two young roosters fight were like people watching a Punch and Judy show at the village fair. And a stream flowing beneath a bridge seemed to have in it patterns enough to tell all of the past and all of the future. Its mysteries held him an hour or more.

It was two days by a straight road before Jack reached the home of A. Butterworth. There things looked the same, but not the same. The rooster on the weathervane all but winked in greeting, and the door knocker seemed to grin in spite of its stiff brass mold.

"Welcome, boy, you are back in good time," said A. Butterworth.

"Well, not exactly," said Jack. "Tomorrow's the day I should be back to my village, and I will never make it."

"Since you won't, you won't. Then there's no hurry. Now, what can you tell me about ten-winged dragons."

Jack began at the beginning. He told of every possible ten-winged dragon he had seen, and finally produced his own tin dragon. When the clockwork was wound and the wings began to flap, it was a sight to behold.

"You've done it," A. Butterworth said in delight. "You've found not one, but a dozen dragons, and you've gone one better, you've made your own. I couldn't ask for more."

"Well, since you can't make it home in time, stay around. I need to think about you a bit."

The idea pleased Jack. And for the next few days he helped A. Butterworth on his farm. They hoed potatoes together and found the most amazing sights to see. They milked the cows and found beauty in the hide of a cow and in her eyes, and homely comfort in her warmth. They hunted eggs and fed the chickens and saw again and again the movements of people in the feverish activity in the henhouse. They were pleasant days.

"You've worked on a farm before," said A. Butterworth the third day.

"Yes, of course," Jack said. "But it was all work." He stopped to think. "What makes this so different?" he asked.

"Ten-winged dragons," said his friend. "It helps to look for them. I guess you're ready for home, but don't stop your dragon search."

"But what about my life? I'll have no choice?"

"Does it matter so much now?"

"No." said Jack slowly. "No, it doesn't."

So Jack went home. The village elders heard his tale and pondered and pondered. The story was a mystery and a wonder. And when they saw the mechanical dragon, the obvious thing seemed to be to put Jack in charge of a toy store. He was delighted. He loved making toys, inventing new wonders, but he did more than that. His shop was a place where dreams were made, where old ideas became new, and new ideas acquired firm foundations. The children came, not just to spend their pennies, or to see that their parents and grandparents bought, but to play, to talk, to see things they never would have seen anywhere else. And they left to look for things they had never known existed.

It was said that the village people sometimes wondered when their children began to look for ten-winged dragons or for nine-colored rainbows or even for mile-high haystacks. But it did not seem to do them any harm and in fact there was a new charm to them that made their elders begin to wonder about ten-winged dragons themselves.

In later years the town prospered, as never before. People came, of course, to buy Jack's toys, for their fame ranged far. But it was more than that. There was a wonder and a gaiety about the town. And children who went away took a spice with them that made others long to see the place from which such young ones had come. Yet, all would have agreed that it was not the prosperity that mattered, it was the sense of adventure that made each day special. Many people thought all the credit belonged to Jack, and there was some truth in that. But he said, when he heard someone say it, "It's all of us, not any one, you've all made what we have." And there was truth in that, too. At least for those who had sense enough to look for dragons.

What has all this to do with the role of the children's editor? Certainly I do not want to even pretend that A. Butterworth in his wisdom and dignity is the epitome of every editor, or any editor. Nor is Jack either editor or author. Yet, no matter how much I dislike drawing morals (and I do), and no matter how much I dislike tearing allegories and symbols out of the context of a story, of finding them where they were never meant to be, this story does illustrate in the best way I can imagine the real role I see for the editor, the role that lies behind the usual image that the outside world sees. It is often an unconscious role, one performed as a part of each day without thinking of it as the primary role. And yet, in the best analysis, that is what it is.

Well, let us begin with the author and with Jack. Jack did not become an author. I hope you noted that. But his needs at the beginning of the story were like the needs of a great many beginning authors and some fairly experienced authors, too. Jack was bright, he had lots of ability and he was ambitious. He was not going to be content with the common run of things. He wanted something more and he was determined to find it. Most authors begin their writing careers with hope and determination. And some begin with talent, as well. Those who get on well generally have all three.

But sometimes, as with Jack, that hope and determination and also that talent is undirected. Authors at every stage of their career--from novices to very experienced professionals--can be much the same. Their interests are broad--as the interests of good authors, especially authors of fiction, must be. They have lots of ideas. They move in many directions, writing first one thing and then another. But sometimes the subject they choose is too broad. Sometimes it is too small. Sometimes it is in a direction that seems to work but does not, and sometimes it does not work from the beginning but they do not know it. They are too close to see. And if sometimes they are satisfied at first with what they have written when they should not be, their lack of appropriate focus or whatever will some day rise to haunt them. Unpublished writers sometimes have great faith in markets. If they can just find the right markets, they feel, in some magical way they will immediately be able to sell as much as they care to write. Others look for other kinds of magic. Jack was concerned with markets in his own way. He kept looking at various types of occupations, convinced that if he found just the right slot, he would be instantly transported into a world of work where there was no boredom, no routine, and a monied future. This is what some authors want, too.

Jack was also concerned with the style of what he did. If it had to do with people, he thought, it would always be interesting. Or if it had to do with the out-of-doors on a farm it might be good. Or if he were constantly surrounded by handsome goods in a store, he would be happy. But none of this was true. Putting on different faces and different costumes did not work. In the same way, authors sometimes think success comes from imitating the right successful author, or finding just exactly the right form in which to cast a book. And so they work at this, trying to find an external pattern that will make all the difference, only to discover, as Jack did, that this does not seem to get them where they want to be either.

The next step is to look at the worlds of ideas around. Jack tried this, too. He worked for a druggist, thinking to learn about chemicals; he ran errands for a lawyer and might have learned something of the law; and certainly traveling with the players should have given him some worthwhile ideas about life and the world. In much the same way, authors wanting success and sure publication search for ideas that have not been written about, new life styles that make good backgrounds for fiction; they read encyclopedias and a few nonfiction works on a subject and think they have done enough to qualify them to write on some new subject for children. It will succeed because it has not been done. But this eventually leads too often to the same blind end.

All this comes about because they, and Jack, have not yet discovered that all superficial things eventually become dull, and that seeking an immediate end tends to lead to a short end. In their need to find a focus--to find a slot for themselves--they have allowed themselves to see only the outside of things. They have never gone beneath the surface of anything to find what it may hold for them. Most of all they have not searched inside themselves for answers.

At this point, enter A. Butterworth, the editor's editor, the paragon of wisdom who appears only in stories but who makes a good image for us here. Of course, A. Butterworth did not think of himself as an editor. In fact, he was not one. Which makes him easier for an editor to talk about.

Eventually the author with talent sends a manuscript to an editor who for one reason or another sees that talent. It may be subject, characters, plot, setting or writing style that appeals. But something attracts the editor's interest. And here, A. Butterworth and Jack have something to say.

What was A. Butterworth like and how did he treat Jack? The story does not tell us all. But we can imagine some things. First, since he was a man who was used to giving advice, presumably he would try first to find out the scope of advice that was wanted and would be taken. After all, why waste good advice on someone who is not going to use the advice once given? In other words, advice givers like A. Butterworth need to assess the abilities and real interests of those who ostensibly seek advice.

Editors do not read all the manuscripts that come to them. Someone else sorts what comes, generally, and sends the impossible back. But even so, most editors read enormous quantities of material of varying quality. And they want to choose the manuscript that will make the best possible book. Most manuscripts are not perfect, whether they come from published or unpublished authors. The story the author has in his head--the book he intends to write--is perfect. It is generally the translation to paper that is imperfect. Or there may even be a flaw in the heady vision of what the book is. In any case the author is too close to see what he has or has not done. A lot of manuscripts show promise of one sort or another. The trick is to find authors who will understand and use advice in the best possible

way, in order that what has been done may become better.
The ones an editor chooses are sometimes surprising.
There is sometimes more to be gained, although at the
same time there is more risk involved, from encouraging
the author who has tried hard to achieve a difficult thing
and failed, than from encouraging an author who has done
the obvious successfully. The second reveals a person for
whom the superficial may be enough. The first may conceal a person who has the intelligence and capacity to grow
to meet the dream that has been attempted but not reached,
the person who is reaching into himself for the truly special. The editor looks for not cleverness or cuteness, but
for concern, for true humor, for compassion, and for an
indication of the ability to write.

A. Butterworth has an advantage here over the ordinary editor. He had Jack right there. He could talk to
him and find out a good deal of what made him run. The
editor must often judge just by the manuscript the author
has produced. Of course the editor does not have to give
more than a hint of encouragement either, or an enticing
portion of advice to see if the taste appeals. At any rate,
the editor, like A. Butterworth, in contemplating the future
of any manuscript that is not perfect (not that any book is
ever perfect), is evaluating more than surface effects. A.
Butterworth was not looking at just the jobs Jack had held.
He was looking at Jack. And the editor is not looking just
at a manuscript, but for the author behind the manuscript,
for the abilities, the problems, and the realities that lie
below the surface of the author. With a new author those
days are totally unfathomed. With a known author the
depths have been sounded in places, but never everywhere.

Once A. Butterworth had assessed Jack's native abilities and presumably found him to be a bright lad, he set
about giving him advice, but it was cryptic. He told him
to look for ten-winged dragons. It was a bit of advice that
forced Jack to create something out of his own inner self
and gave him a focus for doing so.

Editors are like this, at least most of them like to
be when they can. Some people think editors spend their
lives dotting "i'"s and changing "which" to "that" before restrictive clauses. They do do that sort of thing, but they
do a lot more, too. On any manuscript, whether from a
new author or an author who has published fifty books, when
it has something good going for it but does not quite make

it, dotted "i'"s and "which" and "that" in the right places
will not make the difference. It takes something more. It
takes an author looking deeper into himself, finding things
there that enrich what he has done, that give his work
depth and scope and focus and additional levels of meaning.
No editor can put words into the typewriter of an author and
do for any book all that should be done, not when the problems lie in basic thinking, as they most often do.

An editor can show, sometimes, how ideas can be
handled. Editors can even rewrite some parts of a manuscript to show how effects can be achieved. But the thinking
and the final words ultimately must be the author's. And
the editor, either by conversation or letter, must so stimulate the author's thought processes that the desired effect
will be achieved. This kind of advice is not nuts and bolts
advice, but questions, suggestions and hints designed to
make the author re-examine what he has done. And the
desired result is not to create the book the editor has in
mind, but to fulfill the book the author wants to write.
Sometimes the editor succeeds, and sometimes the editor
fails. One would like to think that the right approach always arises in the mind and presto--creativity has been
achieved for the author and humanity. But it does not always work that way. Sometimes it does. But then again,
upon receiving advice--sometimes far too humanly and im-
perfectly given--the author may spout with anger, fume with
the horror of being misunderstood, sputter in a lack of
comprehension. Yet even so, these lesser reactions can
bring out the desired results. Out of sheer spite the author
may accomplish what he knows he can accomplish. Which
is, of course, just what the editor wanted to have happen
anyway.

Like many authors, Jack was baffled by the advice
he was given. But because any encouragement looked good
at that point, he went off on what seemed to be a foolish
quest. No editor wants an author to follow advice blindly.
A. Butterworth would have been unhappy, I think, if Jack
had brought back only his mechanical dragon. That was a
great thing, but all the other dragons he had found were
equally important, and in some ways more important. All
editors hope that the authors to whom they give advice will
convert whatever they are told or asked to do into their
own terms. Because a book comes out of experiences,
both remembered and un-remembered, carefully stored in
the unconscious of the author, and because those

experiences have been shaped and focused by the unique
mind of that author, only that person can bring a creative
unity out of whatever chaotic jumble of stored impressions
gave a story birth. Yet the questions, insights, and constructive appraisals of an editor can sometimes stir just the
right response somewhere, so that on first thought or twentieth, somehow the author sees where it is he has failed to
convey to someone else all of the good things he knows are
in his mind. The author, at that point, may for the first
time see clearly, himself, just what it is he is doing in his
book. And the book may suddenly change completely. Or
it may simply be refined in certain ways, honed sharper to
tell its tale more clearly.

A. Butterworth, when Jack came back to him, was
obviously delighted with what Jack had done. But he was
not in a hurry, as Jack was, to call his learning finished.
He did not send Jack on his way immediately, convinced that
he had conquered the world. Just so, it is the editor's job
to help an author see his future, not in terms of the books
he will write, the subjects he will choose. Those decisions
belong largely to the author. But the editor can help an
author see directions and see how technique and insights
can be used in many different ways. No author is a finished
author after a first book, or even a tenth book. There are
always more things to write about.

A. Butterworth's sign said, "Advice given and returned." In order to give good advice, he must have been
a man who could learn from all he touched, as well as a
man who could help those who came to him. The advice he
gave was a return on insights he had gained just from knowing people and from seeing how other advice given had
turned out. Editors, too, grow and learn. Each author
needs something different from an editor, calls on different
knowledge and different perceptions. In the midst of such
diversity, no editor can give good advice without having
learned from other editors, from many authors, from all
the people encountered. The relationship between an author
and editor can be a deep and long lasting one. It is based
on a creative understanding that has little to do with everyday life. It is possible to know exactly how someone else's
mind works without knowing if that person takes sugar in
his coffee, enjoys music, or even how much education he
has. The understanding lies deeper than that. The editor
knows the true mental and spiritual capacity of the author
and tries to make him use those to the full. And out of

such a relationship an author can create better books, sometimes, than would otherwise be possible. The editor is a
second mind, helping the primary mind when necessary to
focus a particular set of ideas in a way that is unique to
that mind.

This is not to say that editors are responsible for
the quality and content of any author's work. What an author does is wholly his own. But an editor can be a catalyst between chaos and creativity, a catalyst that makes it
possible for the author to see his ideas and write about
them more clearly than he could do on his own.

Editors, of course, do more. They do all these
things that people think of them as doing--the mechanical
parts of editing. And they also act in a judgmental way,
keeping always their own ideas of quality, of what a really
fine book is; in the center of their minds is a standard of
publication to strive for, even if it may seldom be reached.
And all of this, too, is a way of bringing creativity out of
chaos. So are the problems of reaching prospective pur-
chasers. But without a good book to begin with, why try?

And so the ten-winged dragons of editing--the fortunate moments of real joy--are the creative insights editors
sometimes obtain into people who write, the sudden realiza-
tions about a manuscript that may help an author reach his
audience with greater effectiveness, the meetings of minds
that help make books truly alive, for a wider audience of
readers. The excitement of publishing is discovering the
new: new authors, new illustrators, new ideas, new forms
of writing and patterns of expression, new art forms that
carry new messages and old to a new generation.

A. Butterworth and Jack Boggs had their rewards.
And so do editors--in the delight of seeing what others can
do and in sometimes helping to make these things possible.

PART II

CANADIAN COMPOSITE

INTRODUCTION

by Samuel Rothstein

Canada is almost pre-eminently suitable, as both setting and subject for an international conference, because we
incorporate to quite a remarkable degree, so many of the
features, interests, and alas, the problems to be found
elsewhere. To begin with, Canada manages somehow to be
simultaneously both a developed and a developing country.
We can claim the high standard of living associated with
economic maturity, but in our need to move that economy
away from over-reliance on raw material, and in our difficulties about achieving economic independence, we are kin-
dred spirits to many countries in the third world. Secondly,
like so many other countries represented at this Pacific
Rim Conference, we have had to contend with the constraints
and complexes, psychological complexes, imposed by colonial
tradition. Indeed, if there is any pride of place to be sought
in such matters, we Canadians can boast that our province
of Newfoundland was Britain's oldest colony, and our city of
Victoria is her most enduring. And while the influence of
Britain and France, Canada's original colonial powers, no
longer dominates our culture as it used to, we must still
contend with the overshadowing effect of living next door to
the greatest western power of the twentieth century. So
we can well appreciate the difficulties which other countries
face in learning to form and nurture a distinctive culture,
and have much to learn from them.

On the other hand, if the Pacific Rim countries represented at this conference are interested in cultural borrowing, they certainly have come to just the right place.
As is evidenced by the fact that Canada is, by far, the
largest book importing country in the world, we are skilled
and experienced in seeking out and utilizing the best in
thought, scholarship and aesthetic creativity from abroad.
Canadians sometimes deprecate themselves as "local yokels, "

but make no mistake about it, we are the real cosmopolitans.
It is a claim which can easily be verified in another way
by any day's excursion in any large Canadian city.   Canada
is officially bilingual, but it is actually polylingual.   Chinese, Ukrainian, Italian, Portuguese, Hungarian, German,
Punjabi are living languages in Canada, alongside English
and French.   Indeed the latest reports indicate that something like thirty per cent of the children in Vancouver schools
have English as a second language.   The school children,
I may say, are not the only ones in this category.   At the
University of British Columbia, English 100 and 200 are
prescribed courses for all students, and on being asked to
account for this, former President Norman MacKenzie said
it was because he thought it so advantageous for our students
to know another language in addition to their own.   And our
present President, Dr. Kenny, is supposed to have said,
on being asked how many students there were at the University of British Columbia, "Oh, about fifteen per cent."

To end on more serious and more truthful matters,
while the language and cultures which our immigrants have
brought with them add new and colorful international flavors
to our Canadian melange--you notice I did not say "mosaic,"
for once--another motif for multi-culturalism is being ren-
dered more prominent by the new visibility and vigor acquired by the literature and art of our native peoples, and
a new appreciation too.   Some while ago I had the pleasure
of hearing the director of the Museum of Anthropology introducing a showing of British Columbian Indian carvings
and paintings at the Vancouver Art Gallery, and that director
is not given to exaggeration.   He referred to that art as
one of the great achievements, not in Canadian or North
American art history, but in world art history.   And he
meant it, and it was true.

In this efflorescence of indigenous cultures Canada
links hands once again with half the countries of the Pacific
Rim.   So I suggest to you that Canada may well be regarded as a kind of microcosm of the patterns and poten-
tialities, of the pitfalls and progressions to be found in many
countries round this Pacific Rim.   As such, we could logi-
cally and comfortably associate ourselves, as hosts, to our
counterparts.   More important, as microcosm too, we can
now turn to examining ourselves, knowing that we do so in
the greater clarity, rigor and objectivity that comes from
seeing ourselves in broad internationalist perspective.

Chapter 1

THE HOME OF WE-SAKE-CHA

by Anne Anderson

At this time I speak for the whole of the Indian nation, because all Indians are one, we are all brothers and
sisters; and we also call you folks white brothers and white
sisters, of course. My mother often said, "Never be
ashamed of your race," and my mother was really proud of
her race, and in those days, long ago, it was very hard to
be an Indian. We were never given a chance, we were
never given praise, it was very hard for us to live, and
walk, and hold our heads high, and yet my mother and
grandfather made us do these things. We were a large
family of ten children and we lived in the town of St. Al-
bert, just a few miles north of the city of Edmonton.

When I first started to teach, I wanted to teach
adults, but I could not find a book in Cree anywhere. I
decided that I would have to have my own book right away
and I wrote around to many Indian areas to find out if there
was such a book that I could base my work on. But there
was nothing, so I started to write one book, and the first
thing I knew there were other books demanded and it just
went along and there has never been a dull moment since I
started to write.

Cree is a phonetic language and we use only fifteen
letters of the alphabet, and when I went to school, to an
elementary school, we were taught phonetics and it helped
me along, because all you do is learn the sounds of the
fifteen letters of the twenty-six letters of the alphabet. And
therefore you sound your words and you write them down as
they are sounded. I have been visited by many people from
Canada, from the United States and Europe, and many people
have sent for my books. I have been visited by professors
and retired classicists and they all wanted to know how I

recorded an unwritten language. Some had been written
down by the white race, but never was it written properly.
We Indian people have what we call an "Indian throat," and
we can pronounce many sounds, or procure many sounds
that others can not. As I went on with my writing, I found
that there was no dictionary, and what in the world was I
going to do? Most of my students were of the white race,
and they all wanted a dictionary, so hurriedly one time I
took an old Winston dictionary, and I turned the whole thing
into Cree, at least the words that were available in Cree.
After all, we have never had words like "traffic jam" or
"women's lib" or a number of others. But these words are
needed now and I get sheets of material from Ottawa saying,
"Will you please transcribe these words?"--and it is pretty
hard.

But perhaps those of you who are teachers are not
aware that the children can not pronounce all the letters of
the Roman alphabet. I get so angry in Edmonton sometimes
when I get a phone call and a teacher says, "Well what's
wrong with Indian children, they appear retarded?" This is
because they can not pronounce letters of the alphabet.
Well they can not because they have never heard them. We
use only fifteen letters of the alphabet, and the words are
phonetic and there are not sounds for all the letters of the
alphabet. And if a teacher does not know this, is it any
wonder that she thinks these children are retarded? And
some never will know all the letters. I have been "he" to
my husband all my life because he could never say "she."
We do not have the letters "sh" written together. We use
them written separately in sounds, therefore a "she" is
actually a sort of bad person in the Cree language. "She"
means, well, say, "a bitch." I can remember going to my
aunt's place one time on a reservation because my mother
was determined that we speak her language. And Aunty said
to me in Cree, "How are your little brothers and sisters?"
I had one little sick sister, and I said, "She is not too
well." And Aunty just grabbed her mouth and said, "Oh,
you must never, never use that word." So we do not say
"she." My husband will say, "he went to town"--it is me,
he's talking about. It does not matter, you know; I am still
a human being and I am still going along fine. Nobody ever
criticized. We spoke the language as unwritten, and we said
it in any old which way and we were happy, humorous people. You know, we can laugh if we are dying, or we can
laugh when we are starving, while our white brother, he
looks pretty sick when he is starving or dying. But I think

it is up to the teachers to be aware that the children, the Indian children, cannot pronounce all those letters of the alphabet, because this is where we have to start now, with the small child.

We native people wish that everybody would listen to us. Ten years ago, when I got started, we were not being listened to. The Indian was just a forgotten race, content out there somewhere in the woods and partly starving, because everything was taken away. He could not hunt, he could not do this, he could not do that, he had to abide by laws that he could not understand. Probably, he never went to school. It was very very hard for the native person. So, therefore I knew I could help and when I first made my dictionary, people just went crazy for it and I have sold several thousands of copies. However, I had to learn myself, because I could not turn to anyone for help. I tried, mind you; I went to the elder chiefs, but they said, "You are doing a wonderful job, you just go ahead," and that was because they lacked education. Today most of my people are professional people, if that is the correct word. But they learn very fast because they know grammar. Many times, native people who have worked in Ottawa for years will come to me and they will say, "Mrs. Anderson, please explain what a pronoun is and what a noun is." We did not have to learn grammar, we just learned as we heard, and we said it as we heard it; there was no need of writing the language.

Today there are still some who say, "Why do you write the language, it's against our way of life?" But I am an optimist. I look forward, because I feel that we cannot be here and hunting buffalo--where are our buffalo today? They are gone, and where are our moose? They will disappear the same way if we do not watch. So we must try to educate our younger children, because the elders are too set in their ways, we can not change them. They want to be Indian, and I think this is beautiful, too, because they can show us a few of the primitive ways of life. The true language is the primitive Cree language, the pure Cree, and this is what I try to retain in my books. Today Indian children speak an English-ized or French-ized Cree, and this is what I do not want in my books. I use the old words, which are so beautiful to hear, words that are very explicit, mind you. Perhaps a word will have twenty letters in it, while in English the word will have only four or five letters. But those words are explicit or explanatory words,

and you know what you are talking about. And so this is
what I found as I went along; I found many things, I was
educating myself. And as I stand here with my traditional
dress, I just feel as if I own the whole world, I guess; I
even feel as if I own all of British Columbia, this beautiful
green country.

I feel I am a child of Mother Earth. Mother Earth
was always our mother to the Indian people, and she provided for us lakes and streams, and food, and herbal remedies and berries, and that is all that mattered. We did
not have to go and get a doctor, we doctored ourselves with
herbal remedies, and we were good strong hardy people.
I can truthfully say that I have never been sick. My mother
always had her medicine pot on the back of the stove, cook-
ing, boiling up some kind of stuff, whatever it was, herbs
of every description. I am proud of my Indianness, and I
am very pleased to be included here because I think it is
time we people, we of the Indian race, speak, and I hope
that you will listen to us. Because we have a few things
that we could teach you too.

Now to talk about books and stories. I was appalled
when I saw all the beautiful books here, books everywhere,
of every description. But poor us, the native people, we
do not have too much material. We have, as you say,
"grammar" books, and that is about it. But we will have;
give us time. However, we Indian people love legends,
and the parents or the elders would sit and talk to their
grandchildren and tell exciting legends. We have one
legendary figure known as We-sake-cha. He is a trickster,
mind you, and he is loved by all his people, all the people
of the forest, birds, animals or whatever. But he lives on
his trickery; he is a really naughty old man at times. He
is sly, he is lazy, he sleeps, he takes time, he never does
anything for himself--but this is the way the story goes.
We have many short stories for children.

One fine autumn day the geese were gathering at the
lake, preparing for their long flight south. We-sake-cha
heard them, and wished he too could fly away. Now We-
sake-cha had the power to turn into an animal or goose,
or bird, or anything he desired. But he first thought that
he had better ask his little brothers, as he called them.
He ran down to the lake and he saw many geese all talking
about their flight. We-sake-cha arrived at the lake and
the geese were terribly frightened. They tried to fly and

We-sake-cha had the power to say, "You are going to sit still and you are going to listen to me." And the geese sat and they listened. And when he got down to the edge of the lake he said, "My little brothers," and he held his hand up, "don't be frightened." He said, "I would like to ask a question." The geese were very anxious to know what he had to say, so in turn they asked, "What is it, big brother?" "I would like to turn into a goose, and fly away south with you, if you don't mind my tagging along. You are all such kind friends, I know you would be wonderful company." Before We-sake-cha finished the question the geese all hollered, "Oh no! No, it would be too difficult!" "Yes, it is difficult," others were saying, "you are so big, and your voice so loud that the hunters would be sure to get you, and we would be in danger. Oh, please don't come, big brother," they all said, "it is dangerous." They were not eager to have him tag along.

The geese did their best to discourage him but We-sake-cha is a stubborn one, and suddenly the geese found themselves in the midst of loud honking and sure enough, there, swimming towards them, was a huge big ugly goose, diving and honking and having the best time of his life. The hunters, way out yonder, heard, and were surprised to hear such a honk of a goose. "What kind of a goose is that out there?" And they saw that there was a group of geese, a flock of geese out in the middle of the lake. Immediately they got into their boat and headed for the flock. The geese were terrified when they saw the boat so near. They started toward the shore, some flying and others diving, and the hunters could not believe their eyes, when suddenly before them they saw this monstrous goose, and he was still having the best time, diving and splashing about. He did not even notice the hunters coming by. But when We-sake-cha saw them, he was so frightened that he started to run instead of flying, and quickly the hunters saw a man run into the forest. Of course We-sake-cha had dived, and then he got to the edge of the lake and was back to his own self. And he ran into the woods. The hunters were not surprised for they said, "Oh, it's We-sake-cha again, he must have turned himself into a goose."

And sure enough, this is exactly what had happened. Do you suppose he will try to be a goose again? Thank you, my brothers and sisters.

Chapter 2

JOURNEYING WITH GLOOSCAP

by Kathleen Hill

I come from one of the smallest of Canada's pro-
vinces, and though small is, in this case, beautiful, still it
must be confessed, we Nova Scotians are "peninsular,"
which is just one degree away from "insular." And, like
most of our kind, we are apt to feel a little too pleased
with our exclusiveness and, at the same time, underneath,
not too sure of ourselves. A conference such as this,
which exposes our psyches all of a sudden to a great many
new people and new ideas, is therefore, unsettling. All
this week I have felt my mind expanding, my ego shrinking,
and my foundations tottering, and at last I even found myself expanding my literary conscience, in connection with
the Glooscap stories.

Ought I to have exploited our Indian people, I asked
myself, by retelling these tales from my own view-point,
and thus perhaps debasing them? I wondered how the Indians
themselves thought about it. So I asked our friends, Anne
Anderson and Princess Ame-Shun, and after some thought
both answered, "No, if anything we are grateful to you for
preserving them: they might all have been lost, if our non-
Indian scholars had not taken the trouble to write them
down." But I was not satisfied; perhaps they were just being kind. I know how I feel when someone borrows a loved
possession, does not even ask my permission, and then
breaks or loses it.

I began to go back to the beginning and remember
how it all happened. It was fifteen years ago, and the
great Indian legend boom had not really begun, nor had much
been heard from the native peoples about equal status. I
had been earning my living in other fields, when one day,
a CBC producer phoned to ask if I would read an old book

of Micmac legends, compiled by a man named Rand, to see if I could adapt some of them for children's television programs. I read the book quickly, and the strangeness of it, the Indianness of the tales, excited me. I wanted to do them, so I chose for a sample script the easiest one, Nukme and the Ice King, one that was compact, with a distinct hero and a clear story line; and on the strength of it was hired to do a thirteen-week series. I was delighted, but then came the morning after. For when I faced the job of adapting twelve more, I found stories which, to my eyes, were not stories at all; many were incidents, others were a rambling series of them, disconnected, crude in style, I had to add here, subtract there, combine when I could, delineate characters and invent dialogue--above all, give them a beginning, a middle and an end.

Now I assure you, that though feeling compelled to make these changes for my audience of modern, mainly non-Indian children, I do not think I ever felt any lack of respect for the material. I certainly did not look down on it as inferior literature, only as stories unsuitable for my purpose. Indeed, there were many passages in the Rand legends which stood out, gemlike, from the surrounding clutter, beautiful, poetic and pure. This unevenness puzzled me even then, but I simply assumed, in my hurry, that it was the peculiarly Indian way of telling legends. Now, looking back, I see that I was quite wrong, for when I began the second series of TV legends, the first thirteen having gone over well, I happened upon another collection of Algonquin legends. This second lot had been compiled by Charles Leyland of Boston, directly from the Penobscots and Passamaquodys of New England, and though many of the tales were generally the same as Rand's, in feeling and style they were very different. Why?

It might have been because the two compilers were different men and told them differently, but each claimed to have taken them unchanged from the lips of Indian storytellers. And Indian story-tellers themselves declared that their legends were part of a single song or poem, handed down orally from generation to generation. In that case, they should not have differed so. Rand's were pedestrian, Leyland's were slyly humorous, lilting and poetic. And then at last, here in Vancouver, fifteen years later, it dawned on me. The Indian story-tellers too, had been retelling the legends, filling in bits when memory failed, adding an incident here, a character there, substituting, combining, eliminating, adapting, just as I had.

"Bluenose" was herself again, her conscience clear. I had not debased the stories; I had only, like the Indians before me, retold them, in the best way I could. I hurried to tell Princess Ame-Shun my solution, and she not only agreed, she clinched it. "Of course," she said, matter-of-factly, "some Indians tell stories better than others." As simple as that. So all my soul-searching, sparked by the intellectual stimulation of this conference, had, it seemed, been quite unnecessary. On the other hand, though my publisher, Dodd Mead, has suggested that I do another Glooscap book, I think I will not. From here on I shall leave Glooscap to his own people.

Chapter 3

SOMETHING OF MYSELF

by Ruth Nichols

I shall talk about my experience as a Canadian writer, and also about the process of being a working writer day by day--since it has always surprised me how vague people's ideas are about what a writer actually <u>does</u> with his time.

Robert Fulford (editor and critic), recently wrote a delightful article in which he ascribed to writers in general the dark conviction that the whole world is against them. He remarked that if one gathered all the most prominent editors and publishers around a writer and had them chant in chorus: "We love you! We need you! We want to <u>help</u> you!" the writer would go home and announce to his wife that now at last he knows the <u>real</u> truth--they all secretly hate him.

Fulford is, of course, talking about something real, and that is the danger that someone engaged entirely in solitary mental work will become separated from reality-- or at least from the common ground that makes it possible for us to function in the world. But I hope that writers are not really quite such pathetic creatures. I am deeply antagonistic to the romantic concept (which, although in a critical fashion, Fulford's article still reflects) of the artist as a sort of Promethean infant--a being whose talent exempts him from normal social rules and justifies any exaction from other people. I think that when any talent is present in an unusual degree it creates the danger of overbalancing the artist and making him, in fact, less evenly developed and mature than the average adult. But I do not regard this imbalance as either a special mark of favor or as an inevitable cross. It does mean that the artist will probably have to make a special effort toward moral development and

189

the attainment of personal maturity, quite aside from the development of his talent.

However, we are straying into deep waters here, so let us return to my original point, which is that I as a Canadian writer do feel loved and wanted. I am filled, in fact, with surprise and gratitude at the response my work has received. Canadians are very generous toward their own. This is partly because, thank God, a certain nationalism has replaced the cultural self-abnegation that characterized us twenty years ago.

Nationalism does, however, also involve the negative possibility that we may overestimate the work of Canadian artists. We must not let it lead us into overestimating the second-rate, for a cultural context in which this can happen can vitiate the artist's devotion to the standard which, beyond himself, he most warmly acknowledges: the criterion of true excellence, on which alone a genuinely national culture can be founded. In terms of my own work, I am therefore torn between gratitude at the generosity of my countrymen and a feeling that my own work to date has been overpraised. I certainly hope and intend to achieve excellence, but I am many years of hard work away from doing so.

Another thing that creates difficulties in the pursuit of excellence is the reputation of being remarkable "for one's age." This I am, with the hopeful appearance of my first grey hairs, beginning to outgrow. The mentality of the child prodigy differs so crucially from that of the adult artist that many prodigies fail, even physically fail, to make the transition that becomes unavoidable by the age of twenty-five. One has heard so often of a talent that withers away at about that time, as Branwell Brontë's did; or of a Keats, a Marie Bashkirtseff, a Thomas Chatterton, who were unable--who perhaps did not even want--to live through the transition.

I began attempting to write for publication at a very early age; my first published book was written when I was eighteen. All my life I have been familiar with the wish to please, which is perhaps the deepest motive of the child prodigy, and with the complicated hostility that such a child receives from many adults. I therefore approached the ages of twenty-five and twenty-six well aware that it was going to be a difficult time. The experience fully justified my apprehension, for I had to face, explore and discard the

motives which had forced my premature development and
which had underlain all my work up to that time. Having
done this, I have had to forge a new identity as an adult
artist dedicated, whatever the limitation of my talents, to
an objective excellence. After three years of hard work I
believe the transition is accomplished, and that Song of the
Pearl, which will appear this fall, marks the debut of a
writer who is no longer either a child or (with all possible
respect) a teller of tales for children.

So when asked how I feel about being a Canadian
writer, I find myself unable to separate my generalizations
about this country from the whole personal context in which
I have become a writer. The natural beauty of Canada
means a great deal to me, though I am probably too pessimistic about human nature to raise a really liberal protest
when I see that beauty desecrated in the name of profit.
In the context of Canadian culture, I have been in the right
place at the right time. If you asked which means more
to me--the culture or the land--I would have to say the
land. To me it has been of tremendous importance to live,
as we all do in this country, so near the wilderness. What
is fantasy, after all, but the realm of the subconscious,
which none of us can completely ignore and from whose influence none of us can escape? The wilderness inhabits us.
In the proximity of wildness to cultivation, we in this country live out a great natural metaphor. The inescapability
of that physical fact has greatly fostered my own kind of
revelation.

The first illusion I find people have about me is that
my success, because it came young, came easily. In fact,
of course, I had kept writing through ten years of rejection-
slips before my first book was accepted; so by the time I
published A Walk out of the World I had spent half my life
as an apprentice.

The second illusion, which I am sure is less shared
by librarians than by the general public, is that having published three or four books, I am set up for life with a comfortable independence. "Oh, you have a book in print?"
they say. "How nice, now you can just sit back and relax."
Well, even if I did not find a lifetime of idleness a night-
marish prospect, it is no more possible for me than it is
for most Canadian writers. My average yearly earnings
from all my books might touch two thousand, five hundred
dollars. One can see one reason why literature has tradi-
tionally been the pastime of gentlemen.

And I am not sure it should be otherwise, except that it creates for the writer the problem of how he is to live. As a woman without dependents I have found this problem less agonizing than most, yet I have found it difficult enough. The hardest issue has been one of self-respect. The Women's Lib movement has rightly pointed out how important to one's self-worth is the ability to support oneself; but for me to do that--granted that literature in this country does not offer the artist a living wage--would exhaust the time and energy needed for my primary work. I am fortunate that the existence of a very happy marriage and an intensely supportive husband have made it physically and morally possible for me to choose the leisure I need. But to do this without loss of self-respect has demanded a further effort of growth, since it involved rejecting a social standard I found I had deeply internalized.

For the actual process of writing I therefore need what I have been fortunate enough to find, a protected environment--even, as far as possible, a routine and boring environment. This is partly an effort to correct the effects of a too-great sensitivity; but also I have the liveliest respect for the dictum of Gigi's aunt: "Are you bored? Well then be a little bored: it helps one make decisions." For me, everyday life has to offer enough inadequacies to jolt the imagination into compensatory action. I think many writers function this way, and that this is one reason for the self-generated problems which so exasperate the onlookers in a writer's life. Marcel Proust's asthma, and the years of invalidism which alone made possible the writing of Remembrance of Things Past, is perhaps the most celebrated example of this mechanism.

Since my fantasy books are basically explorations into the subconscious, I often take a significant dream as my starting-point. This is true both of The Marrow of the World and of Song of the Pearl. I keep a nightly record of my dreams in a series of notebooks which now stretch back several years. I also read texts on English grammar and style, in an effort to find my own idiom and wean myself from the Tolkienesque language which my critics have so rightly deplored. I read little fiction, since I prefer to spend my time on historical or anecdotal literature which I can transmute for my own use--Henry James at the dinner-table, overhearing a fragment of conversation which in due course he transformed into The Spoils of Poynton, was using a technique I try to imitate. Among the few novelists I reread regularly are Jane Austen, George Eliot, and Proust, whose concept of the redemption of everyday life in the transfigured light of memory lies very close to my own aims as a writer--a fact which will perhaps be intelligible as yet only to those of you who have read Ceremony of Innocence.

Music also helps in the writing process in ways it is hard to define. My own relationship to music is that of a listener, not a performer, and my taste is almost exclusively for music of the Middle Ages and Renaissance. I like early music partly because it is complex and finished, but also because it makes none of that demand on the emotions that I, for one, find so exhausting in products of the romantic era. And in music, more freshly than in any other medium, we can recover the voices of the past. It still fills me with a naive delight to be able to hear Caruso singing on a morning long before my birth, or to hear the songs Henry VIII composed with the touching amateurishness which was (as far as I can discover) the only lovable thing about him.

An excellent memory is another aid in the writing process. I usually have projects vaguely in mind relating to different historical periods, and being able to recover relevant information from the right mental pigeon-hole is much more convenient than a filing-system, so I try to train my memory.

The presence of a good editor is also essential in the production of a successful book. In the Mary-and-Martha relationship between writer and editor, I suspect it is the editor who sometimes has cause to feel unloved, for he is open not only to the writer's questions, confidences and pleas for money, but also to bitter reproaches whenever anything goes wrong. To be a good editor requires special gifts not only of taste but also of temperament, for it is the editor who maintains that delicate balance between business-sense and compassionate human relationship from which an author benefits so greatly. An author flourishes best under, and should keep moving until he finds, an editor who is also a friend. Having been so fortunate, he must be willing to trust his editor as the custodian of his business interests; to respect him in his editorial function as the ideal, articulate reader whose criticisms must be met; and to respect him also as a friend, for many editors subordinate themselves so nobly to the Artistic Temperament that we sometimes forget they are people too.

It is obvious that I hold no brief for the stereotype of the evil editor who oppresses the noble, obscure young artist. An author works for the market, and if he refuses the advice of those who will help him develop his talents in ways acceptable in the market-place, then he will remain unpublished. And that, except in the rare cases where one's integrity is <u>really</u> on the line, is too drastic a price to pay.

As Dashiell Hammett put it, writing a book is something like a trance: only when you awake do you discover whether what you have written has any merit at all. The editor's verdict is important in the many instances where the writer is too full of emotion, of what he <u>meant</u> to say, to judge whether he has in fact succeeded in <u>saying</u> it. My own editor over the years has been Margaret McElderry, first at Harcourt Brace and then at Atheneum; and it must be obvious that I have many reasons to be grateful to her.

Above all, the main element in the creation of a book is time. You cannot rush it, though you must try, precisely in order to understand the inadequacy of your efforts. I write at least two failed books for every one I publish. A good writer's humility is guaranteed, not only by the failures which will continue to strew his path as long as he practices his craft, but by the fact that he can give nothing less than himself, and for this he must know himself. One needs time to get to know one's private myth-system, and to watch these symbols grow and deepen under the impact of daily existence.

I am beginning to realize that, in exchange for the dubious delights of precocity, life offers the maturing artist the chance to experience and reflect long rhythms which are imperceptible to the young. Because these rhythms concerned him so deeply, Proust was over forty before he could begin to express his vision of Time Lost and Time Regained; and as I sense my own similarity of purpose--though whether I have a similar ability time alone will tell--I suspect my work is years away from its most significant beginning.

Chapter 4

PICTURE BOOKS AS AN ART FORM

by Elizabeth Cleaver

I begin with a great sense of inadequacy, because I realize how difficult it is to talk about pictures and because words cannot substitute for sensory experience and perceptual awareness. Accepting this limitation, I would like to share what I experience when I am working on a picture book, my struggles and delights, and to recount a little bit of my childhood experiences.

For the past years I have been on a journey traveling inward, and consciously searching for and discovering what meaning stories, myths and legends have for me. This is a great struggle and search, and it takes all my energy. If I look back at my childhood I can find two things that had a great influence on me. I always remember with excitement my first alphabet book with figure illustrations, which my father and I would read together before I fell asleep. To make the illustrations more interesting he recreated the hand shadows--rabbits, dogs, birds--on my wall. This possessed such a magic attraction that shadows, and shadow puppets, still have that same appeal for me. Another great influence was cut-out books; I could be left alone for a whole afternoon cutting paper and being transposed into another world. Cut-out books are associated in my mind with play and happiness. It is strange the way our childhood experiences can influence our lives and become the stuff out of which our work will emerge. I have always enjoyed cutting paper, and I still cut paper to create my collage pictures, from the textured papers that I paint, through various ways, without a brush. Collage is a contemporary way of making pictures by pasting, cutting and tearing paper, developing and discovering unexpected configurations.

Art is a process, during which it is possible to

195

search and discover meaning. As a visual artist, I find it a necessity to make art, and I find the picture-book form an ideal way to express my ideas. I love picture-books and one of the greatest pleasures in creating them is the way I change and grow and travel on to many new levels of existence. My work is the result of my ideas as an artist, and is subject to change as my experience changes. By making picture-books I am involved not just with pictures but with words and ideas as well, and I find out in the process what is important to myself. Also, by creating picture-books I can create a world and live twice, once when I have an experience or an idea, and then again when I re-create it. Through picture-books I can talk to myself, and I can also talk to others. Creating picture-books demands great discipline; the search for images also involves playing around with a number of possibilities and here I find solitude is necessary. My conversation is with the picture I am working on. Through collage it is possible to try out endless numbers of combinations and find the best possible solution, and this is why I find it such a creative medium to work in. It is not planned completely, but in part discovered and revealed.

Every book represents a new world I have to enter, with a unique set of problems to confront. After receiving a manuscript I read it many times, for days, weeks, and even months, until my mind begins to form the images spontaneously. To receive and realize new ideas takes a lot of energy; to be able to form mental pictures requires a special kind of devotion, tranquility and self-confidence. It is necessary for me to be inspired by the piece of literature, the idea I am working with, and to believe in it; to have a great feeling and love for it.

The unpleasant struggles I have to face as an artist are financial ones. If it were not for my family's help in many ways, I could not continue. It is really impossible to live from conferences and from royalties. Several Canadian publishers do not believe in giving artists advances on royalties while they are working on a book. I have received grants, but in the past two years the assistance I have asked for from the Canada Council for various book projects has been refused. Yes, it is very discouraging at times, but I will find a way. I love creating picture-books, and I hope I will be able to create the myths, the legends that are important to me.

Chapter 5

THE CANADIAN AUTHOR FOR CHILDREN
STILL LOST IN THE BARREN LANDS

by Claude Aubry

I will discuss briefly only two topics, myself and
me--oh, I am sorry, though; I meant myself as an author,
and me as part of a group, still quite unrecognized, the
Canadian Authors for Children.   Each time I address groups
of children at school, one question that always comes up
during the question period is--"Why have you become a
writer?" or, "What made you come to write?"   Mr. Southall
invoked the severity of his upbringing as the main cause
that brought him to write.   In my case, my parents were
severe too; never through punishment, though, but through
over-protection.   I was born in a small village, lost in the
Laurentian mountains, but what my parents did not realize
was that once past the threshold of the house, nature was
there, offering dozens of courses and teachers.   The bulls
and the cows were performing in the fields, unperturbed by
our eyes opened like silver dollars and glaring at them
through protective fences.   The dogs, however, disgusted
me, because they were so obviously and unscrupulously concentrated in their pleasure that you would have thought it
was the only important thing in life.   I admired the cats
for their discretion, although I thought they could have had
their little thing without loud screams in the night.   And
for a long time my parents continued to protect me, still
thinking that I knew nothing of what one was not supposed
to know of life at that age.

The rural school was two miles away from the village, so we had to walk through the fields, forests and all
kinds of things to get to school in the morning.   And two
miles again, in the afternoon, to get back home.   How many
days have I lost, or thought I lost, missing school?   During
those days I always tell kids that they were more intelligent

before starting school than they are after they have finished school. During those days I just walked endlessly in the fields, pretending I was starting a trip around the world, lying under a tree, amused by the rays of the sun fighting their glorious way through the leaves; or by the moving and changing monsters, the clouds in the sky; or lying along a little creek, following the games of the small fish, staring for hours at the water, running away, swiftly and for ever. And where? I was so intrigued, and wanted so much to know where this water ended its trip.

Or I stared at big somber boulders, imagining with a great deal of fright that certainly a ferocious Indian would spring out suddenly from one of these, and make me a prisoner, and bring me far away from my parents; or kill me and scalp me with his tomahawk. In our village, they used to tell us that when a woman had a child, it was the Indians who brought the child, and beat the woman, so that is why she was in bed. So, each time that my mother had a child, I hated the Indians so much, because I said, "They beat my mother." So you see, the terrible, terrible and so unfair images that we got of these fantastic people at a certain time in the history of this country. That is why I wrote Agouhanna, to bring back to our people the human side of the Indian nation in Canada.

In winter, when there were endless days of snow-storms and when the teacher had disappeared with one of the farmer boys (it happened you know), we were taught in the station, in the railway station, by the railway station-master, who had a certain education, probably up to grade eight, and had children of our age; and he taught us between trains. When trains came, making the little station tremble under a hell of a smoke and noises, we left our slates and chalks, and ran out to the platform to help the stationmaster roll his big mail wagon. We had great fun.

The results of such an educational program in my life are easy to guess. When I was sent to Montreal to further my education, I had nothing to learn then; I do not know why they sent me. I was then in grade three, and I was eleven years old. But at the age of thirteen I was introduced to Virgil's Aeneid. Imagine; I was bathed in Latin at that time, two years after coming from the woods; and this beautiful poetry fell on me like a sparkle that lit a flame in me that is still burning and will, I hope, burn for the rest of my life. I became a writer from that moment.

Another question often asked is, "What brought you to write for children?" Well, after all you have heard, obviously I should never have written for children. It is strange that there is no sex in my books. The freshness, the poetry, the fancy of childhood, this is what brought me really to write for children. I wanted to come back to all that I had when a boy, and had kept hidden, very deep within myself. To write for them forces me to stick to sincerity, fairness, simplicity, and justice. And this alone in our confused and rotten world is sheer poetry and fantasy.

Now I have come to the second topic, myself as an author in Canada. Who is a Canadian author for children in Canada? It is a patient, tenacious, persistent and some-what naive being. You have two very good examples in Ruth Nichols and Elizabeth Cleaver. Two artists, two writers of high quality--I will say of an international high quality--and they have said a word, very discreetly, about their difficulties, and it is very moving. And this is what the rest of this essay is on; how it is to be a writer in Canada.

I think still that too many Canadians think that the authors and artists live from the morning dew, or the snow in the winter. Last year, at the Loughborough conference in Toronto, I was in a highly pessimistic mood, and here is what I said at that time: The author in Canada has to be a patient, tenacious, persistent, somewhat naive being. For when an author has written a book for children a publisher has to be found, and this is not easy, even if the book is good and promising. Then, supposing that finally the work is published, in most cases it will gather dust in the publisher's warehouse, or the publisher will bring out a few thousand copies, and after this laudable effort the book will become declared out of print, and forgotten. The whole process is still a mystery to me, taking into account a few exceptions. Most of the time the publishers do not seem to be proud of what they bring out for children. The majority of Canadian bookstores seem to be indifferent to the Canadian book production for children. Libraries, school and public, do buy some Canadian books, now more and more I would say, and of course they cannot and should not buy Canadian because it is Canadian; we should buy because of quality. But we should not leave aside a quality book because it is Canadian, and this is the difference.

Often when I speak to classes of children, they ask me about my books but the school library does not have them. That is all right, that is personal, that is my own struggle. But now, some of our books can be favorably compared with the best in the world. But still too many people ignore their existence.

Now I am going to quote here Ruth Nichols, who said some time last year, "Children's literature is still the orphan of the publishing industry in Canada." And I will quote Irma McDonough, editor of In Review: "It is clear that the publication of Canadian juveniles does not have priority in any publisher's list at any time in our country." It is a pretty sad state of affairs. And she added, "The heartening thing is that we have the writers and the artists to fill the requirements, if we only give them the chance; for a writer does not grow unpublished."

To add to all this, Canadian readers are constituted into two groups, along with two official languages in Canada, French and English. This has advantages, but it creates difficulties as far as authors are concerned. Within each group, the Canadian author, in general, has then a very limited clientele. Too few authors of one language are translated into the other. There should be more of this, so that one group would come to know the other one better. And finally, the Canadian author for children has to compete on his own ground with mass-productions from the United States, England, France and other countries. We do need importations, but we are assaulted by mass-productions saturating our market with books of a poor quality. These countries can produce a book in hundreds of thousands, which is absolutely impossible here. So there are great difficulties in Canada for authors and the publishers.

This is where our governments should help. There is no other alternative, for there is a price to be paid if we want to keep our own literature for children. And only the governments can help to pay this bill, until our litera-ture can live on its own. It is a matter of wanting to keep our Canadian identity or not. I would like to quote Dr. Bain, who says, earlier in this volume, that "much of the future of the world is in the hands of writers for children." Well, if the Canadian author for children is not better en-couraged, if the publication of children's books in Canada remains a low priority, our literature for children will die, for it is still in its infancy. Then our children would have nothing of our history, of our geography, of our folk-lore, of our traditions and of our way of life; they will not have fiction created by Canadian imaginative minds. Our children will then ignore what we are, and what we were, what is Canada, and what made it. And then, they will not feel Canadian any more, and then Canada will have lost its personality, its soul, its identity.

I have made these statements before in public, as recently as last year, as a matter of fact. But now I am prepared to dilute somewhat my pessimism of last year. Since then there have appeared definite and encouraging signs that our literature for children shall eventually live, and progress to become well-established and finally recognized. At first there seemed but a few soldiers to defend our cause: we had Sheila Egoff, we had Irma McDonough--fortunately we still have them--Irene Aubrey, Alvine Belisle, Jean St. Pierre, Janet Lunn, to name some of them. Now we seem to have a small army, and I am impressed by the keen interest in children's literature, and at last in our Canadian one.

Some periodicals are making our works better known, such as In Review, published by the Provincial Library in Ontario, and the more recent one, Canadian Children's Literature, published at the University of Guelph. Some provincial governments are now giving grants for the publishing of books for children. The Canadian government has finally awakened to Canadian literature for children, with the recent creation of a Canada Council award for children's literature in the same amount as literature for adults, a five thousand dollar prize for an English work, and five thousand dollars for a French work for children. I am very, very pleased about these awards, even if I never get one myself. Another sign of progress is the actual number of children's books now being published. As a member of the French Award Committee, I had to read thirty books in French for children, published last year in Canada. Now this is not taking into account the English publications, so this means that it has been quite a good year for us. And I hope that this trend will continue.

Finally, the presence here in Canada of people from so many different countries presents a chance for them to come to know our literature and for us to come to know theirs. This should bring better understanding not only between these various countries, but also between the various elements of Canada that make her so rich. As Dr. Bain said, some of the reading children of today will be the leaders of the world of tomorrow.

Chapter 6

RING-AROUND-A-ROSES OF
FRENCH-CANADIAN BOOK MARKETING

by Suzanne Martel

Friends of books all, we are united in the great
fraternity of the written word. Every time I look out my
window I think of Joyce Kilmer's line--"I think that I shall
never see a poem lovely as a tree." Have you ever thought
of a more frustrating thought for a writer? I mean, what
is the use of writing? Why not just go out and look at the
tree, or walk in the garden? And then suddenly I remember
that maybe we are writing for those who never think of
looking out, or who cannot look out, or who do not know
other trees, and would like to know about palm trees, or
eucalyptus or baobab, or however you pronounce the thing.
So this is what we write, why we write; so after all, what
is a book, but a door leading to a garden of thoughts?
Isn't that nice? That is my own quotation, and you can
keep it, I give it to you.

A few years ago my sister, Monique Corriveau, who
is a writer, and I put on a puppet show for a conference.
It was called La Ronde du Marche de Livre. After much
inquiring around, with help from many people, I have the
title translated: It is Ring-Around-a-Roses of French-
Canadian Book Marketing. And it is a true story, based
on fact. Do not lose track of the fact that this is a true
story. So I will put on the puppet show without puppets;
I will be all the people. There are five puppets. The first
one is Miss Penwise; she is a children's writer, she wrote
The Saga of the Little Blue Rabbits, about twenty pages, a
nice story. There is a Publisher; there is a Bookseller--
he is a bad man; there is a Mr. Manuscript, a fellow writer; there is Miss Public Relations--she is a fictitious
character, and we really need her, but she is not real
unfortunately; and there is the Public.

202

ACT I

(Suzanne Martel's asides are in parentheses)

[Setting--a party, where everyone meets and talks together]

Miss Penwise: I'm so excited, I've just received my first
royalty, a cheque for twenty cents! (It really happened to
me.) They had 850 at the first inventory, now they have
849, so I have one reader. What a delightful person he
must be. Is he among you? I wonder why he bought my
book? Was it to read it? To sit on it, to give as a gift?
Anyway it's a nice worry.

[In comes Mr. Manuscript, a fellow writer.]

Mr. Manuscript: Miss Penwise, I bought your book, I read
it.

Miss Penwise: It was you! [she kisses him] And how is
your own book that you've been writing for the last ten
years?

Mr. Manuscript: Well, it came out two years ago; it has
five hundred pages.

Miss Penwise: Oh, it came out? Well, I wasn't invited to
the launching out party!

Mr. Manuscript: Well, believe it or not, Miss Penwise,
neither was I. (And if you think that's funny, that happened
to me, no later than April last year. Two books of mine
were coming out at the same time and on the Sunday I
called a friend, a neighbor, and she said, "I will see you
next Wednesday at the launching party." And I said "What
launching party?" They had forgotten to invite me. So,
I had planned to go to my country house in the woods,
where I run away with my dogs once in a while and where
I write for fourteen hours a day for two weeks. So I said,
"All right, I'm going to the country." So I went--no phone,
sixty miles in the woods. I was there; and suddenly who
arrived but the publisher, in his car, and said, "You can't
do that to me." "Well," I said, "I understand that you
could have forgotten inviting me, it could have happened,
because it's so obvious, but what I can't forgive you is that
you didn't ask the name of any of my family or my friends,
or anybody, so that I don't want to go to your party, and

I'm not going." But unfortunately we had one of those freak snowstorms, like you have only in Montréal, so nobody went to the party. So my lesson was lost, but still you can see what things happen. I don't know if those things happen in other countries. I must make a survey.)

Miss Penwise: Well, I'd like to see your book, even to read it.

Mr. Manuscript: By a strange co-incidence I have it in my pocket. You can't find it in bookstores, let me offer you a copy. (You know, it's very expensive to be a writer.)

Miss Penwise: Well, we share the hard life of the writer. Does your book sell well?

Mr. Manuscript: Only my publisher knows, and I don't see him very often.

[Enter publisher; doesn't remember that Mr. Manuscript is his author]

Mr. Manuscript: Dear Mr. Publisher, is my book selling well?

Publisher: Oh, by the dozen my dear fellow, by the dozen.

Mr. Manuscript: Really?

Publisher: Oh yes, once in a while we receive a phone call from someone who buys a dozen, a Mr. Manuscript. (You may laugh, but that also happened to me. I call Les Editions du Jour, and they say, "Oh yes, we sell a dozen once in a while to a Mrs. Martel.)

[Exit Mr. Manuscript]

Miss Penwise: Well, I've received my royalties, I want to thank you very much.

Publisher: Oh, it was nothing.

Miss Penwise: How do you explain so few sales?

Mr. Publisher [haughtily]: Oh, is it my fault, madame, if your books don't sell? (Well, that's sure to get an author back into the woodwork for a few months and leave the

publisher alone. And that happens too, and it has happened
not only to me, but to most writers. Of course, I'm
speaking for everybody else but my own publisher now.)

[Exit Miss Penwise]

ACT II

[Enter Miss Public Relations, who used to work for a soap
company]

Miss Public Relations: Oh, Mr. Publisher, I have a proposition for you. ("Proposal," I think, eh? Which one is
it? Well, since Miss Public Relations is very prim and
proper, her proposal or proposition is very prim and
proper.)

Miss Public Relations: Let me sell your books for you. I
used to sell soap. Books look like soap, they have the
same shape. We'll make a lot of suds, we'll clean the
shelves, give a book away with each soap box. I have
ideas that are bright as bright. We'll bathe the customers
in literature, immerse them in words. We'll get the children to wash their teeth, we'll get them to read. We'll
brainwash the whole lot. We'll get slogans, spots on T.V.
No, no spots. We're soap, no spots. Publicity in magazines. I can see it already: BOOKS CONTAINING A NEW
AND IMPROVED FORMULA--PAGES WHITE AS SNOW--
BINDINGS THAT ARE SOFT FOR THE HANDS--and--AU-
THORS THAT ARE NINETY-NINE PER CENT PURE. I'll
do all that for ten per cent of your sales.

Mr. Publisher: Well, I regret that I have no money; books
don't sell, you know.

ACT III

[In a bookstore, enter a customer and the bookseller]

Public: Do you have The Saga of the Little Blue Rabbits?
I heard it talked about on T.V. I'm not sure of the name
of the writer. It's a Mrs. Penwise, I think.

Bookseller [brusquely]: (Because a bookseller when you ask
him for a children's book, especially a French-Canadian

one, doesn't like it, because that's a subspecies. I don't
know whether it is a poor relative or a relation; anyway,
it's a poor one. And usually, the children's books are
away in a corner. Remember that was in 1970, but the
situation is the same.) It's not out yet.

Public: Yes, it's been out for two years.

Bookseller: Then it's out of print.

[The phone rings and he goes behind the counter.]

[Miss Penwise enters.]

Public: Oh Miss Penwise, I've seen you on T.V., I was
trying to get your book, but they don't have it here. You
know, it's my niece's birthday, and I always get her a little
nothing. (I've heard that one too.)

Miss Penwise: By a strange coincidence I have one in my
purse. Let me sell it to you at cost. (It's very expensive
to be a writer.)

Public: Well, I won't ask you to autograph it in case she
wants to change it. (That has also happened.)

[Exit customer and Miss Penwise; she puts on dark sun-
glasses, in case somebody should recognize her--no luck
that someone would, but just the same...]

Miss Penwise: Do you have The Saga of the Little Blue
Rabbits?

Bookseller: What again, twice in the same day for a
French-Canadian book? It's amazing. No, we don't have
it, but we have a wonderful French book, or a Belgian
picture-book, or a new American translation.

Miss Penwise [Meanwhile browses around, and finds a copy
of her book. She dusts it off.]: You have one.

Bookseller: Ah, the jobber probably put it there.

Miss Penwise: Mr. Bookseller, do you have any more
Canadian children's books, especially French-Canadian ones?
(At that time, and it's still so, there was a rule that for
a bookstore to be accredited, the bookseller had to have

five hundred copies of French-Canadian books in his store.)

Miss Penwise: Do you have any more?

Bookseller: Well yes, I have four hundred and ninety-nine more in crates in the cellar.

Miss Penwise: Do they sell well?

Bookseller: Oh yes, when we have them, but you know, the publishers don't send them, and the public doesn't ask for them.

ACT IV

[Two years later and the royalties have come in. This time two books have been returned, so the inventory is at eight hundred and fifty-one books. Miss Penwise rushes to see the publisher, and we embark on the Ring-Around-a-Roses of the Canadian literature market.]

Miss Penwise: Mr. Publisher, how is my book doing?

Publisher: It does not sell well, Miss Penwise, it does not sell well. Why doesn't it sell, Mr. Bookseller, why doesn't it sell?

Bookseller: Because the public does not ask for it, Mr. Publisher, because the public does not ask for it. Dear Public, why don't you ask for it?

Public: Is there a book, Miss Penwise?

Miss Penwise: Yes, there is a book, dear Public, I wrote it. Mr. Publisher, what's going on with my book? (And so on, and so on. And that's the sad drama of French Canadian books.)

* * *

Now we come to the fairy tale part. In the old days, when I was a little girl, at the end of the year we used to get prizes. They were beautiful red-bound volumes with gilt edges and the dullest stories inside for reading on summer days. But now suddenly, around the 1960s, it was decided somewhere that prizes should be abolished, because it was bad for children to compete, and it was bad for them to know that hard work should be rewarded. So no more prizes.

Because of that decision, the publishers did not sell the hundreds and thousands of books they used to sell every year, and which encouraged them to try, once in a while, to publish a worthwhile book. So in 1961 there were twenty-one French Canadian books published for children. In 1963, there were fifteen. In Expo year in 1967, there were six. In 1969, in all of Canada, two thousand books were published. Of these, one thousand and four hundred books were from the Province of Quebec, which shows you we could write. Of these, four were for children. And the following year, in 1970, there were two books for children. So our French-Canadian literature for children was dying. At the most important branch of the Public Library in Montréal, they had eighteen thousand volumes for children and of those, two hundred were French Canadian; not enough to fill two tiers. The librarians dusted them, re-arranged them, but they could not make them grow. So, our little princess, Littérature Jeunesse, became a Sleeping Beauty. It is a sad, sad story because books are the soul of a people, its identity, its image to the world. And we did not have that.

So one day in 1970, Paule Daveluy, who write Summer in Ville Marie, and I invited about twenty people to meet at my house, because I have a dining room table that is as large as a skating rink. Twenty people who did not know each other. All we had in common was our love of children's literature. And we wanted our children to have this essential element of culture: books in which they could find themselves in familiar surroundings, written by authors especially for them. So that day, quietly, without a cigar or anything, Communication Jeunesse was born.

Most of us in Québec grew up in France through our books. We remember Les Tuileries and so on. Probably it is the same for English-speaking people in Canada; you grew up on books from England or the United States. We grew up and got to be more familiar with French surroundings than our own. I know that in every book there was always a chateau and a parc. Now that I have been to Europe, I have found out that a chateau is a large house, and a parc is a garden, and I'm living in a chateau and never knew it.

So there we are, twenty of us, writers, publishers,

librarians, booksellers (they dropped out very fast, that is
too bad), educators and, to show how broadminded we were,
one critic. So we got a charter, we wrote rules, I in-
vested in a coffee-maker and twenty cups, but what we said
and what we did and what we decided was not half as important as what we talked about later on while we were drink-
ing coffee. We got to know and appreciate each other, to
feel the importance of our mission, to get a new sense of
the value of what we were doing. Because there was nothing
more depressing than writing books, and then having "a
dying fall" afterwards. We were revalorisé--does that
mean anything in English?--that is, we got a new sense of
our values. That takes a whole sentence and usually in
English it takes one word, and we take a whole sentence
to translate; this time it is the other way around. Now,
after a couple of years of getting together (it takes a while),
the government has learned of the urgent needs of the publishers and the writers. The publishers knew that they had
writers who had treasuries hidden in the cupboard, or their
heads. And the writers knew that they could send in a
manuscript and perhaps see it published before the end of
the century. So our Prince Charming, Communication
Jeunesse, gave the Sleeping Beauty, Littérature Enfantine,
the kiss to wake her up; they got married and they had
many children, called Volume I and Volume II and an Illustrated Album--and that is the end of my fairy tale.

     In 1974 (the latest official figures), there were forty
books published for children in Québec. In 1975, there
will be between forty and sixty. And not only that; there
are now beautiful books, with beautiful coloring, very well
printed. And so we are back in business, we are back on
the map, and we are just starting. Librarians had better
prepare for an onslaught. Their job is not finished, we
are going to fill those shelves. Now all we have left to
do is to wake up the booksellers, because our books are
still behind the counters. Mr. St. Germain, from the
Ministère des Affaires Culturelles, told me that there will
soon be a meeting of all the booksellers, and that the ministry will try to interest them, convince them, that it is to
their advantage to have children's books, and have them
near the door, not behind counters. Perhaps soon the new
writers will see their books in a bookstore.

     Now we have serious competition from Europe; you
have seen the beautiful French books. We do not want to
dispense with them, we still need them. But we, as

French-Canadian writers, would like a place in the sun too.
There is a certain snobbishness about French culture, you
know, but that is lessening because we are developing a national pride, and we must educate the public also--that's the
next step; and we have to educate the critics, too.   In
Montréal we have one critic--oh he is a gem.   When he is
forced, poor man, because it is his job, to read a children's book, the greatest praise he can muster is, "I was
not bored." He deplored the fact that in the last few years
there has been no politico-socio-cultural outlook in our
children's books.   He is very worried; he is looking for
himself in books and he cannot find himself in our children's
books.   So only the librarians are left.   They are about the
strongest-willed persons in the world.   They are surrounded
by books but they are working just like the ladies who sell
candy--you know, surrounded by chocolates but not eating
them.   Whenever we need a morale booster we go to the
library.   Where else will we find our books lovingly read,
and repaired, and upholstered--no, that is not the word,
rebound? Anyway they have been read and commented
upon, and the librarians know us.   We are persons, and
we have done something, and we go out of there feeling,
"I can do it, it is worth it."

So we will write for children, publishers will publish
children's books, librarians will guide their choice.   As
Dr. Bain said, and I think I will have his words inscribed
on my ceiling, "It is the writers of children's literature
who now have the potentially most powerful voice for the
future." We all go back to our work strengthened,
revalorisé, with a greater consciousness of the importance
of our endeavours.   What Communication Jeunesse has done
for our literature, the Pacific Rim will do for children's
literature around the world.   So we must all go and carry
the message back.

The government has now learned how essential its
help is, and the Canada Council and the Ministère des Affaires Culturelles have begun to help more and more--and
they plan, I think, to do even more in the future.   Publishers have met authors, and shown themselves to be human.
That was a surprise for many of us.   Now librarians will
put faces to books and will be able to quote from real live
authors.   And the writers themselves, well, you all know
writers have egos and as Ivan Southall says, "Writers have
egos, otherwise they would not be writers in the first
place." Egos are voracious beasts, but timid.   They need

to be fed, or the delicate flower that is inspiration will wilt. We will go back to the world in our head, to our world of paper, pencil, typewriters, knowing in all modesty that without us none of this would have been possible.

Chapter 7

AH, PUBLISHING!

by May Cutler

What I have to say may not seem very pleasant.
You have been hearing how great children's--Canadian children's--books are, and "aren't we all wonderful." Frankly,
I think the state of Canadian children's books is a national
disgrace. I could name you twenty individual American
publishers who in one year bring out more quality children's books than we do in ten. And they just bring them
out as a matter of course.

A sense of searching that is almost an industry has
developed in this country. It is associated with children's
books, yet has nothing to do with their production. There
are fancy librarians occupied with children's books, and I
am not talking about the ones who actually serve the children. There are conferences, there are book fairs, there
is money for traveling expenses, and for books about children's books, and for magazines about children's books,
but there is no money for the production of children's
books. I think that I probably have more right than most
people to say this, because I have been able to produce
books in Canada that could never have come into existence
without Tundra Books, and I have brought honors to Canadian children's books that they have never before received.
Our William Kurelek book was on the New York Times list
of the best illustrated books of the year. The following
year another Kurelek was on it. We were the first even
to have been noticed by Graphis in Switzerland, which
salutes the best in children's book illustration every few
years. We have a long string of awards, and there are
others we are good enough to win. William Kurelek's A
Prairie Boy's Summer was nominated for the National Book
Award in the United States, and then was removed because
he was a Canadian.

I think the three Kurelek books that we have published, A Prairie Boy's Summer, A Prairie Boy's Winter, and Lumberjack, have received something like fourteen major international awards. We have sold something like twenty thousand copies of the first of these, A Prairie Boy's Winter, in Canada. Houghton-Mifflin has sold nearly as many of all three in the United States. Collins in England has just published the first of them and will be doing the others. Flammarion in France is bringing them out, because I could not interest French-Canadian publishers, and they expect to sell a large number in Canada. I have two German publishers competing for them, but I do not particularly like their standards, so I do not know yet whether we will reach an agreement. We also have a Dutch publisher interested, as well as a Scandinavian. And all this activity is just over the Kurelek books.

A book much closer to my heart, because it cost me so much, is Ann Blades' Mary of Mile 18. It changed my attitude, I suppose. If I am very anti-nationalistic, and very resentful of many of my fellow publishers, and especially of the Canada Council, it is associated with the production of this one book. It moved me far out of nice Canadianism (which means doing everything sweetly and kindly), into doing what I believed was excellent. And I was determined to do it. Ann Blades had sent Mary of Mile 18 to most of the publishers in Canada before it came to Tundra Books. After all, we were barely in existence at the time, and one of the last one would normally think of. I was so delighted with the book that I felt I had to find a way to publish it. I applied to the Canada Council--this is an old story and I am sure many of you already know it-- for help, because it was a color book and very expensive. Their anonymous readers sent back a letter saying, "Isn't it a pity that there are so few children's books coming out in Canada, and that we can't do better than this?" So I was turned down, but I decided somehow or other to publish that book. I did, finally, and in the first year it sold only fourteen hundred copies. Last year it sold thirty-five thousand.

It is a very special book, and it is a book I am proud of because it is unique and unrepeatable. Even Ann Blades herself could never repeat it, because the whole tension and excitement came from her particular effort and love in one particular situation. She is not a school-trained artist, but by God, she conveyed what she felt. Of course, that is part of the charm of naive or primitive painting, the painting of untaught or self-taught artists. When it reaches her particular dimension, such as doing it for the children in her class, it comes through. That is the most important thing, not the fact that it was chosen as the Canadian Book of the Year for Children the following year.

However, that was terribly important to me at the time, and I do rather love Canadian children's librarians as a result. It is a specialized book and it is very hard for people to imagine what was involved in selecting it. It is not hard now: somebody looked at it the other day and said, "Oh, well, anybody can see that's a great book." And I said, "Yes, that's nice," since nobody could see it six years ago. Mary of Mile 18 is one book which I do believe will be around twenty, thirty, or forty years hence. Most of all because the children, who are the final arbiters, the last (often the last thought of, I am afraid, in all of these matters) to judge, love it. And it is moving outside the country too. Bodley Head is bringing out the English edition, and Jungbrunnen in Vienna is bringing out a German edition with an initial printing of eleven thousand copies this summer.

I could go on and tell you about Takashima's A Child in Prison Camp, which I am sure everybody on the west coast knows about. It too has gone into several languages: it has been published in Japanese, in a separate American edition, and it just came out this spring in Italian. A play with a cast of two hundred and fifty was produced from it in Tokyo last year. And it just goes on and on.

Probably none of these books would have been published without my efforts. Somebody might have recognized Ann Blades' Mary of Mile 18, but the Kurelek books would not have existed, for I was the first ever to ask Kurelek to do a book. He had been painting these marvelous pictures for years, and I had often thought he could do a wonderful book. I asked him, and he said he had always wanted to do a children's book. Here is a good example of why I am so resentful. I had Kurelek's A Prairie Boy's Summer for nearly two years before I could find the money to bring it out. Kurelek is a very special kind of guy, and he withheld the paintings from exhibition. They were worth money, and he was not as rich at that time as he is at the moment. His paintings have enormously increased in value within the last two or three years. But he withheld them from the market until I could publish the book, so we could have the launching together.

I now have in my office manuscripts that have been there for more than two years, and there is no money to publish them. I can bring out a novel for four or five thousand dollars. But I can not bring out a children's book for that amount. I am doing two this fall: the new Kurelek, Nativity in Canada, and a beautiful book on Quebec by the Japanese artist Muke Tanobe, who married a French-Canadian. He has produced beautiful paintings of the children of Quebec, Quebec family scenes, and so on. Each of these books involves an investment of over twenty thousand dollars. Now how many of these can one afford to do a year?

Let me give you some idea of an attempt to find cheaper ways of producing children's books. You can not produce beautiful picture-books cheaply, that is for sure. For five years I have had the manuscript and drawings of a story about a dachshund, done by Philip Stratford, who is a professor at the University of Montreal. A few other things with drawings have come in, so we decided to produce some mini-books as a new departure. They are tiny, tiny books which will be priced quite inexpensively. But I did not even have the money for these, because we just can not overinvest. At least with Kurelek books I know the money will eventually come back, because they sell well, but the other things are very dicey.

One amusing anecdote will give you an idea of the difficulties of waiting until you have money and so on. A young girl by the name of Marla Stephenson, living in Victoria, sent in a charming story about a toad, and I thought it went rather well with the story of the dog, and the two other ones, so I kept it. Usually, if you keep something of an author's or an artist's, after a month or two they will write you a note and ask what is happening. You write back and ask them if you can keep it longer, or you send it back, or whatever. But she never wrote, and somehow we never got around to writing her. Eventually I decided, well we are going to publish this. So we wrote to her, and got no answer. We telegrammed and got no answer; we tried to phone her, and there was nobody by that name living on that street in Victoria. Then I phoned the police department in Victoria and they went out to the house but nobody had ever heard of her, and the house had been sold twice in the two years that had passed. We were really wondering what

we were going to do--publish a book without even informing
the author? So, being an old newspaper woman, I thought,
oh well, newspapers always rescue people in times of difficulty. I wrote the Victoria Colonist, and they were about
to publish the letter when it turned out that a young man
who worked there knew her. He saw the letter and said,
"Oh I know her, she's moved. I don't know the town, it's
about two hundred miles inland, and she's doing some pot-
tery." And he was able to get hold of her address. This
is the sort of problem you run up against, and you can see
that I face it in one way, as a small publisher who can do
pretty much as I please. But the large publishers do not
even face a problem in this sense, because they just do not
agree to publish books that are going to lose money.

I think one of the most unpleasant things we have
been faced with has been the new nationalism that has developed here, with its emphasis on Canadian-owned publishing houses, and what that did to such publishers as the Oxford University Press of Canada. So far as I know, it was
the only publishing company in the country that had a consistent and regular program of children's book publishing.
We not only have nationalism to contend with, we have
provincialism. You have to operate in the right province to
get provincial grants. That an author might come from
there does not matter. You are very unlucky if you want
to publish books in some place like Prince Edward Island,
which has no form of subsidy at all. But you are quite
lucky if you are in Ontario or British Columbia, or Alberta,
as I understand it. In Quebec you are not very lucky, as
far as I know, in spite of some of the efforts. There is
not very much money available for the publication of children's books, and I think that French-Canadian children's
books are as bad as, if not worse than, the English-Cana-
dian ones.

Now, how bad are Canadian children's books? Very
bad. If you go to the Frankfurt Book Fair, and do not just
hang around the Canadian booth, but go and see what is going
on--or more importantly, go to the Bologna Book Fair,
which is the children's book fair in the world, where nearly
all the great publishers of children's books congregate--you
will see what I mean. You probably will find between forty
and fifty really great publishers of children's books. They
stand out; they are almost a little self-recognition club
based on the kind of work they do, because Bologna, like
Frankfurt, is just as full of junk as any other book fair.

They have a special sense of excellence, of originality, of
creativity, and I was very proud to have been accepted into
that particular group. Several of them are publishing our
books, such as Jungbrunnen in Austria, which is doing
Mary of Mile 18. And I am working with Jonathan Cape on
an English edition of a Swiss book that we think is a gem.
We understand each other, but it is very hard to convey
this to you when the terms of reference are the really piti-
fully small collection of Canadian children's books that are
even worth talking about. Of course, children's books are
lovely to deal with and to feel happy about. But there is
such a thing as originality and excellence. It is very hard
to come by, and not many people in this country are ready
or willing to stick their necks out very far for it.

        I understand that some marvelous people have nego-
tiated for children's book prizes from the Canada Council.
I do not think that the Canada Council has deigned to honor
these with the Governor General's award title, which does
not matter to me, given what I think of the way the Governor
General's awards are handled. But it does indicate why we
have so few really quality children's books in Canada.
There is contempt among the literary establishment for
them. Oh, it is all right when a member of the literary
establishment does a children's book. We can accept a
Dennis Lee or a Mordecai Richler. But when Mary Jane
produces something extraordinary, that is something else.
I also find it interesting that these awards should be only
for one book in English and one book in French. Only recently in the New York Times the National Book Award for
children's literature was criticized for being impossible to
give. The article said that there really should be two
awards, one for a picture-book, and one for a book that,
as a story, would be a good story no matter who illustrated
it. They said it was like comparing apples and oranges--
how can you decide which is the better of the two? Maybe
these great negotiators will keep at it. I think they upped
the award from two to five thousand; let's hope they keep
at it and let us have an award for picture-books.

        These awards will produce more authors. Whether
they will produce more children's books is dubious, because
there have to be publishers to produce children's books.
And it is not a profitable business in Canada. You can hit
the jackpot with one quality book now and then, but you can
not develop a whole collection of quality children's books on
this haphazard basis. To give you an idea of the dilemma

that one faces, three years ago I was wondering where I
was going to get the money to publish Ann Blades' second
book, A Boy of Taché. No matter how I calculated, there
was going to be a four thousand dollar deficit! It had
nothing to do with overhead, it was just for printing and
color separations and so on. I remember that particular
afternoon so well. It was a summer afternoon and here I
was struggling with this and feeling very depressed. Then
a phone call came from a woman informing me that various
educational branches of provincial governments had just given
her one hundred and seventy-five thousand dollars to collect
children's poetry across the country, and wouldn't I like to
publish it? Now, there is nothing the matter with collecting
children's poetry; in fact it is great. But you see the situation that I mentioned at the beginning. There is money
for absolutely everything except the actual production of
books. She was very resentful that I was somewhat cool
about it. She felt that she must be something great if she
had been given this windfall, and who was I to be less than
excited about it? This is an example of what Tundra Books
has put up with for the last year or two.

I do not pretend that I do anything to make anyone on
the Canada Council like me. In fact, I do not want them to
like me, because I think one of the weaknesses of the whole
Canadian literary set-up is that everything is based on who
likes whom. It should be based on the quality of the work
one is doing, and nothing else. I do not make phone calls
to them. I have no sweetness and light. I make applica-
tions as formal as possible, because I feel it should be
done in exactly the same way that anybody who knows no
one at the Council would do it, and there should be no special way of going about it. It is up to them to know what
is going on, and to act accordingly. Of course, that approach does not work.

Just let me cite a few recent examples of what is
going on. You must realize that while I am encountering
the difficulties of finding a few thousand dollars here and
there to publish children's books, I am seeing hundreds of
thousands of dollars absolutely thrown away on trying to
export books to England and the United States. These are
fiascos, and so is the amount of money wasted on the Frankfurt Book Fair. It does not sell a book. You do not go
to these kinds of fairs to buy books from national groups.
It is like going into a museum to buy. Mary of Mile 18
sat in Frankfurt year after year, and nobody was the least

bit interested. Publishers have to have their own booths at
fairs or the fairs are not worth anything, because there is
no contact. I went over to Frankfurt, and during the few
days of that single visit I negotiated a whole series of
rights.

There is a psychology involved in this, and I was
aware of it at the Montreal book fair. That was another
of our big expenses, certainly unjustified. I think it cost
something like four hundred thousand dollars. Last year
at Montreal there was a whole string of national exhibitions.
The Greek government had an exhibition, and the Iranian
government had an exhibition, but there was nobody there
to negotiate rights or to look at books. This year it is
even worse, from the lists that I have seen in advance.
Very few individual publishers are coming, except for the
Americans, who were rather browbeaten into it, and a few
of the English publishers who were given the hint that it
was not too tactful not to come. I understand that the
British government has given some money to help them.
But other individual publishers--the Japanese, the Germans,
and various others who were there last year--are not coming back because there was nobody to sell to. It was no
business fair. There may be a future for it as a French-
language North American fair. I think there was much
more interest between publishers from France and the
French-language publishers of Quebec than between anyone
else. But this kind of thing costs a fortune.

While this sort of spending is going on, what can
you do? About three years ago we applied to the Canada
Council for ten thousand dollars to develop a series of
books on Canadian ethnic groups. That would have paid
for an editor and the necessary correspondence and long-
distance calls. The books themselves were to be written
and illustrated by people from the particular ethnic groups,
and quality books--our kind of book--would have been the
result. Two years ago, Tundra Books was the only publisher in the country which had produced any book whatso-
ever on an ethnic group with the exception of books on
Indians and Eskimos. I did not even think of it in terms
of ethnic groups, but it just happened that the radio program Identities decided to feature Canadian children's books
on ethnic groups. The person putting the program together
had a whole string of our books--Jewish, Japanese, Ukrainian, and I think Mary of Mile 18 was in it, because it is
about a Mennonite group. The head of the program said

that it should not be done just on the books of one publisher, and the researcher had to say there was no other publisher that had done that kind of book. You can see we knew what we were doing in that area. But let me get back to our application for money for a series. It went to the writing and publishing section of the Canada Council, was shipped over to Explorations, from there to the multicultural section, then back to Explorations. After a year and a half of this merry-go-round, it was turned down.

More recently, about four months ago, I had a rather impressive group visit my office, and I was very flattered that they had done so. The group consisted of the great French-Canadian singer Gilles Vigneault, John Glassco, and Elizabeth Cleaver. They had a project for one of Gilles Vigneault's lullabies, with Glassco doing the English translation, and Cleaver the illustrations. I thought it was a great project. Elizabeth said she would like an advance to help her with it, and I had to say that Tundra does not pay advances because we have to invest so much in our books beforehand. We do pay standard royalties afterwards, but we just do not have the money to make advances. So she applied to the Canada Council for a very small sum to see her through the few months--I think it was two thousand dollars. Her proposal was turned down.

This is the kind of thing that is going on, while hundreds of thousands of dollars are being spent in other ways. There is a whole industry, or anyhow a bureaucracy, associated with children's books, and it is like a group of ants swarming over a very few grains of sugar. And it is a frustrating thing, and how do I keep my sanity in this? Well, some would argue that maybe I do not, but I try to keep out of it, I try not to participate. It is easiest that way. I am very lucky in that I have a happy office and a very happy home life. Out of this I can carry on my outside wars, and I will bring out my one or two books a year, and here and there other publishers will bring out a good children's book. This is the basic situation.

Chapter 8

CHILDREN'S BOOKS AND MULTICULTURALISM IN CANADA

by Lubow Kuz

Over a hundred years ago the Fathers of Confederation thought mainly in terms of English-French relations. However, it has been a consistent policy of Canadian governments since Confederation in 1867 to encourage and even to subsidize immigration and settlement in order to develop our vast and rich natural resources as well as the economy. As a result many people from many lands, but predominantly from Europe, have come to this country and acquired citizenship. For several generations this non-British, non-French element has been steadily increasing in numbers and in proportion. This element is referred to as the third element, the third group, the third dimension, the third force, or simply the "ethnic groups." Whatever the name, these Canadians are a fact of Canadian society and life just as are the British and French. Michael Novak, in a recent issue of A New America, made an interesting observation on the U.S.A.:

> Among the nations of this planet the United States is in a fortunate position. Our peoples reach out to virtually every other culture, with bonds of family memory and shared tradition. An event can hardly happen at any place upon this planet without profoundly effecting some part of the American population, a revolt in Cambodia, a tidal wave in Pakistan, terrorism in the middle east, civil war in Ireland, invasion on Cyprus, revolution in Ethiopia, insurrection in the Dominican Republic, each such event is for some Americans a family event. And each touches some part of the American people with sympathy, sorrow, outrage or concern. We are, in fact, but not in

221

consciousness, the most multicultural people on this earth. [1]

If this statement is applicable to the United States of America, which historically is a melting pot, how much more so it should apply to Canada. In search of national unity, however, a century ago, and even only a generation ago, pluralism was seen as a threat. It was feared that immigrants from some countries might not be adaptable to the Anglo-Canadian tradition. Equally, they were expected to shift their emotional, intellectual, familial and behavioral norms into the dominant culture pattern very quickly. These norms have been imposed unconsciously rather than consciously, and few Anglo-Canadians seemed to recognize the hurdles that they asked others to jump. Success has always been respected, but economic success did not always mean equivalent success in status, prestige and cultural respect. Many immigrants came to feel great gratitude towards Canada and its social system, but anger towards and resentment of WASP pretenses. Along with this went lack of trust and belief in their own self worth.

In 1968 French-Canadian culture received official status, and the government pledged itself to support and encourage its development. In December, 1968, at the Thinkers' Conference on Cultural Rights in Toronto, [2] Senator Paul Zukyk argued that the concept of a bilingual multicultural Canadian nation is realistic, and the very essence of a dynamic Canada. The theme of a bilingual multicultural nation echoed through a number of subsequent major conferences such as the Ontario Heritage Congress of June 1972, and other major ethnic congresses also concerned themselves with this aspect of the Bilingualism and Biculturalism Commission's mandate. The publication in 1970 of the Royal Commission's Final Report on the cultural contribution of other ethnic groups, Book Four, [3] recognized the compatibility of a bilingual yet multicultural nation. The Commissioners realized the basic difficulty of distinguishing clearly between an individual's cultural contribution, resulting from his membership in a cultural group, and his contribution resulting from deliberate integration with one of the two official linguistic communities.

The federal government tabled its response to Book Four in the House of Commons on October 8th, 1971. It said in part:

... we believe that cultural pluralism is the very
essence of Canadian identity. Every ethnic group
has the right to preserve and develop its own culture and values within the Canadian context. To
say we have two official languages is not to say
we have two official cultures, and no particular
culture is more "official" than another. A policy
of multiculturalism must be a policy for all Canadians.

... The government accepts and endorses the
recommendations and spirit of Book IV of the
Royal Commission on Bilingualism and Biculturalism. It believes the time is overdue for the people of Canada to become more aware of the rich
tradition of the many cultures we have in Canada.

... The government while responding positively
to the commission's recommendations, wishes to
go beyond them to the spirit of the Book IV to
ensure that Canada's cultural diversity continues.

... In implementing a policy of multiculturalism within a bilingual framework, the government
will provide support in four ways.
   First, resources permitting, the government
will seek to assist all Canadian cultural groups
that have demonstrated a desire and effort to continue to develop a capacity to grow and contribute
to Canada, and a clear need for assistance, the
small and weak groups no less than the strong and
highly organized.
   Second, the government will assist members of
all cultural groups to overcome cultural barriers
to full participation in Canadian society.
   Third, the government will promote creative
encounters and interchange among all Canadian
cultural groups in the interest of national unity.
   Fourth, the government will continue to assist
immigrants to acquire at least one of Canada's official languages in order to become full participants in Canadian society. [4]

   Again and again it has been stated that a mentally
healthy person, a productive adult, is one with a positive
self-concept. How is the ideal self reached? In children
the ideal self is a combination of the most valued assets

found in their immediate environment and cultural matrixes. At the risk of over-simplification I will ask: how can children of a non-Anglo background, and even more so, a recent immigrant, develop a positive self-concept surrounded by the North American mass culture, reading about British, American or at best Anglo-Canadian heroes, setting standards for themselves reflecting a British or American culture, when these are often in conflict with their own real selves?

The lack of a multicultural policy in Canada has recently become most noticeable in the school system. Following is an excerpt from a paper, The Bias of Culture, by the Multicultural Committee of the Board of Education for the City of Toronto. It deals with cultural identity:

> Given the specific bias of culture which forms the base of a school system, it must follow that the individual schools of the system transmit a specific and dominant message to the young personality for whom that base and the heritage it represents is alien. The message is simply that the cultural base which previously provided that personality with its identity, and all the necessary assurances of its validity is inexplicably no longer valid. During the beginning stages of his or her new school career the student is unable to participate in any meaningful way in the host culture represented in the life and character of the school environment. Simultaneously the lack of meaning and value of the old culture becomes a source of discouragement. Trapped between a life in which participation appears overwhelmingly impossible, and that in which participation no longer appears valid, the immigrant student is relegated to an amorphous and marginal existence between two worlds which our mutually discreet culture represents. But life in that narrow corridor between two cultures is untenable in the human condition, and the drive to achieve identity is indomitable. The student's own original culture and the new host culture conflict and place him or her at the centre of competition for his or her cultural allegiance. Three possibilities exist for the student in this situation. First he or she may remain in the corridor simply as the result of the necessity to avoid the stress and consequences of affirming one allegiance over the other. Second, he or she may elect to align

himself with the culture of the school and become
caught in a dual process of seeking acceptance in
one and rejecting the other. Third, he or she
may maintain the allegiance with the family and
its culture, along with the rejection of the culture
of the school. What is obvious about these possibilities is that from the student's position none of
them is educationally, emotionally, socially or
culturally viable. Each possesses consequences,
serious impact, the effect of which may remain
with the student throughout his or her entire life. [5]

Although the report related to school environments
and programs, its conclusions are quite applicable to children's books, which form the basis of a child's early education. They apply to the cultural content of the early and
later books that surround a child and especially to those
which introduce a child to reading. Unfortunately, in most
of my contacts I have noted that when referring to the question of multiculturalism, people think exclusively of easing
the integration of the new Canadian into the Canadian way
of life, most often the Anglo-Canadian way of life. School
programs are set up to ease immigrant children into this
culture. English classes are organized, booklets are published geared to the children of ESL (English as a second
language) classes, and poor readers. This, however, is
only one aspect of multiculturalism.

I am also concerned with the Canadian-born children,
perhaps third- or fourth-generation Canadians, whose ethnic
cultural backgrounds are neither Anglo nor Franco nor native. These are my children, these are descendants of immigrants from the early 1900s. With which group will these
children identify? Practically from the day they are old
enough to read they will be taught to relate to the British
Isles and the United States as part of their acculturation,
while reference to any other nation will be shown as alien.
It will thus be, for example, very important and very Canadian for children to relate to the economic state of Britain
and the United States, or to the state of health of some
noted British or American figure, while their concern for
developments in the country of their culture base is un-
Canadian. So indicates the report on multiculturalism by
the Toronto Board of Education.

Furthermore, in history textbooks, in history picture
books, contributions of the non-English, non-French

minorities to the development of Canada are scant, if not
non-existent. This state of affairs raises a question in the
child's mind as to the nature of his own culture. The fact
is that those generally derogatory or condescending comments tend to inculcate in a child's mind the concept of being part of an inferior culture. For example, a picture
history book such as O Canada! by Isabel Barclay[6] mentions
immigrants of non-Anglo and non-Franco backgrounds only
by way of saying that they arrived and settled. A Picture History of Canada, by Owen and Toye[7] has one sentence: "...
people came from Britain, Scandinavia, Finland, Russia,
Poland, Germany, Austria, the Ukraine, and Italy." A
Picture History of Canada, by Kathleen Moore and Jessie
McEwan,[8] has no mention of ethnic settlers. None of the
above has any pictures of non-Anglo or non-Franco or non-
native Canadians.

Next, I would like to read from a survey of intermediate history books. Thirty-five history books were examined by Darlene Zolenyi.[9] I will read just a few of the
terms used to describe settlers of non-Anglo background:
"men in sheepskin coats; stalwart peasants; born on the
soil; half a dozen children; problem; strong cheap labour;
poorly dressed; miserable; illiterate; uneducated; ignorant;
jeered at; sneered at; proud; extreme nationalistic notions;
endless hordes; happy; strange customs and costumes; halt-
ing English."

Following are the descriptive terms used to describe
British and American immigrants: excellent settlers; color
and variety; dominant group; most desirable settlers; politically active; law abiding; hardworking; longstanding. And
this is taken from thirty-five Canadian history books.

There has been much discussion about whether the
maintenance of a strong non-Anglo or non-Franco culture in
the home, and especially the maintenance of the original
language, was not harmful to the child growing up in an
Anglo-Canadian society. Many studies recently have shown
that children with English as their second language are
more likely to be placed in a vocational program, a trade
school, as opposed to an arts and science program at the
high school level. In October of 1971 a report on program
placement bore out quite different results. The children
were divided into four groups: Canadian-born students
whose mother tongue was English, Canadian-born students
whose mother tongue was not English, foreign-born students

whose mother tongue was English, foreign-born students
whose mother tongue was not English. Surprisingly, they
found that the children least likely to be placed in vocational or trade schools, and children most likely to succeed
in an arts and science program at the high school level,
were Canadian-born children whose mother tongue was not
English. They drew the conclusion that perhaps these children, brought up with a strong-rooted culture, had a better
self-concept, a greater sense of security and, therefore, a
greater energy for reaching their ambition.

When I first began the preparation of this paper I
went to a few Toronto children's libraries for assistance.
When I asked to see some books with a multicultural aspect
I was invariably referred to the translated fairy tales. The
collections were generally good, but these are not what I
consider true multicultural books. They are fantasies, taking place in a make-believe world, and their cultural content depends on the translator. We are all familiar with
the contention that children's books reflect the culture of
the author; this also holds true for the culture of the translator. The illustrator is especially important. Every culture has its own art form, and to me it seems not enough
just to represent visible aspects of, say, German, Italian
or Chinese culture in the pictures; rather they should be
representative of the art form of a nation. Many of the
folk tales have been retold and rewritten so often that children do not even realize that these are not English folk
tales and credit is often not given in the text or on a title-
page.

When I explained to the libraries that I was not looking for folk tales, I was led to the section on other lands
and other peoples. Although the books in these sections do
give children a knowledge of their backgrounds (I am not
criticizing these books, they are necessary to teach children
about other cultures, about their own and their parents' land
of birth), these are not genuine aspects of multiculturalism,
either. Surely we are not trying to tell children that their
culture belongs in another land and not in Canada. Finally,
when I explained that I wanted stories set preferably in
Canada, or in the United States or Britain, but with characters who were not of English background, or where at least
one character would be of an ethno-cultural background, the
search became tough. Such books are few and far between
and the odds of a child borrowing such a book from the library were not great. One editor, who does not wish to be

identified, told me, "We are publishing mostly wishy-washy books for children in Canada that identify with no particular group, and no particular child identifies with them." This editor felt that Canadian children's publications would have to change in the near future.

In one particular library in a section of Toronto which is culturally of varied background, but with few recent immigrants, I reviewed two hundred recently published picture-books. I found, first of all, that there were very few Canadian publications. Secondly, of the two hundred, only one hundred and thirty-three contained any proper names at all. Of the one hundred and thirty-three, only thirty-five used at least one that was not common in English or French, or that visibly made the children ethnic. Of these thirty-five, twenty-nine were set in other than English-speaking countries. This means that out of two hundred books only six were set in an English-speaking country and used names other than John, Mary, Paul, etc. To continue talking of names, a book called Let's Have a Party[10] did have very interesting ideas: how to make Polish cards, how to make Ukrainian Easter eggs, how to make Chinese ornaments, etc. But the children in the book are called: David, Rosie, Josie, Kate, Kim, David, John, Julie, Janet, Katharine, Anne, and William. Although I do not have any statistics, I did notice that when people did have different names the different names were usually accompanied by an accent, or at least their parents had an accent--they were recent immigrants, but often their cousins had English names. In a few cases the child goes to visit grandmother who keeps certain quaint and beautiful traditions, or makes different breads, suggesting that the parents have integrated so well that they do not do this any longer. Of course, another kind of book can be found. An illustrator at this conference offered to illustrate a true multi-cultural story. The setting would be most neutral and universal--McDonalds Restaurant! There would be various children, all of whom would be dressed in obvious national dress. To make the point even stronger, each child could be obviously eating the other child's national or ethnic food, and they could dance together a polka, or another folk dance. An exaggeration perhaps, but not that far removed from what some of the stories are. Not only do they try so hard that they come across as phony, but they are also very poor literature. Then we wonder why children do not want to read them. Two types of books are almost entirely missing; biographies and auto-biographies of ethno-Canadians, who have toiled for, and

contributed so much to this land. There are also very few
stories or accounts of the seasonal traditions or celebrations
of various ethno-cultures.

Authors with ethnic backgrounds would be more likely
to know and understand the hardships of growing up in a
different culture and to portray that culture honestly. Again,
according to the Canadian Consultative Council on Multiculturalism, the better one understands the ancestral language,
the deeper will be the understanding of a group culture, and
the stronger will be the creative base for the talent that
exists. For culture, as Book One of the report on the
Royal Commission on Bilingualism and Biculturalism points
out, is a way of living, thinking and feeling. It is a driving
force animating a significant group of individuals, united by
a common tongue, and sharing the same customs, habits
and experiences. Without a knowledge of the language it is
not possible to penetrate the way of living, thinking or feeling of a particular group. An example is found in the paintings of William Kurelek, which so poignantly express the
joys, the sorrows, and the struggles of the Ukrainian spirit
in the difficult Canadian environment. No one unfamiliar
with this culture and psyche, which presupposes a knowledge of the language, can do the Canadian-Ukrainian experience justice. And without this experience, without taking
into account the experience of all the peoples who developed
Canada, what can the Canadian experience, and by implication, the Canadian identity, be? It has been said (incor-
rectly, I feel) that it takes at least two generations of speaking English to become fluent enough to write in it. Perhaps
this statement should be discussed with Peter Newman,
editor of Maclean's Magazine, a first-generation Canadian
of Hungarian descent.

Here the government could play a role in funding or
commissioning authors of various ethnic backgrounds to write
stories, biographies, historical fiction that would represent
our multicultural country. Authors should be encouraged to
use ethnic names for their characters; they should realize
that not all Canadians have identical traditions and reflect
this in books. Children of ethnic backgrounds in books
should not always be obviously recent immigrants, and yet
it could be made obvious that they are, say, bilingual.
Most importantly, illustrations in children's books must be
representative of the various cultures in Canada. This is
relatively simple when different races are involved, but
when you get into a European-based cultural group this

becomes more difficult without stereotyping. The culture
has to be brought out in the surrounding landscape, the
architectural spirit, etc.

The importance of multilingual public libraries can
not be overstressed. According to my research, the libraries of Metro Toronto are attempting to supply their
branches with books in thirteen different languages. Not
all public library systems, however, agree to the necessity
of books in other languages. This brings me to a whole
new area. I turn to librarians who encourage children's
reading. Where are your multicultural books placed? In
some libraries there is a special section called, "Juvenile -
Fiction - Ethnic." What is the message in such a section?
These books surely could be placed with their respective
genres and children would feel less conspicuous, less singled
out when they seek a book in their own language, and there
is the chance that an English-speaking child might come
across one and realize that there are other bona-fide languages in Canada besides English.

In conclusion, I would like to say that non-immigrant
Canadians should realize that the support and development of
each culture is in their own interest. There are at least
two reasons for this. The first is that they and their society can benefit from the enrichment of their own culture by
assimilating aspects of other cultures. The English language, for example, would never have attained its magnifi-
cence if our forefathers had resisted infusions from other
languages. The second is that it reduces the likelihood of
a widespread feeling of alienation among immigrants and
their children. People who feel alienated from the society
they live in are much more likely than those who feel at
home to behave anti-socially, and this is especially true of
young people. No one, except those few who seek the destruction of our society, would want our educational system
to contribute towards widespread feelings of alienation and
attendant anti-social behavior. Unless we take into account
the cultural backgrounds of our immigrants we will be pro-
moting widespread hostility. Morally, legally and prag-
matically, in the interests of non-immigrants and immigrants, we are bound, therefore, to adopt a thoroughly
multicultural approach towards public education, both through
the formal educational systems and through books.

Notes

1. Novak, Michael. A New America (Box 48, Bayville, New York 11079).

2. Thinkers' Conference on Cultural Rights, 1968. Resolutions, Papers and Deliberations. Ottawa: Canadian Cultural Rights Committee, 1969.

3. Canada. Royal Commission on Bilingualism and Biculturalism. Book IV. "The Cultural Contribution of Other Ethnic Groups." Ottawa, Queen's Printer, 1970.

4. Canada. House of Commons Debates. October 8th, 1971. pp. 8546, 8580-81.

5. Toronto. Board of Education. Multicultural Committee. "The Bias of Culture."

6. Barclay, Isabel. O Canada! Illustrated by Cecile Gagnon. Toronto: Pagurian Press, 1974, p. 96.

7. Owen, Ivan and Toye, William. A Picture History of Canada. Illustrated by Clarke Hutton. Toronto: Oxford, 1968, p. 64.

8. Moore, Kathleen and McEwan, Jessie. A Picture History of Canada. Illustrated by famous artists. Toronto: Nelson, n.d. o.p.

9. Zolenyi, Darlene. "Survey of Intermediate History Books." (Unpublished.)

10. Roffey, Maureen. Let's Have a Party. London, Toronto: Bodley Head, 1972.

ENVOI

by Roy Stokes

When the Lord Mayor's Show has passed and the streets are rapidly emptying, a very humble vehicle comes along--its duty is regarded as essential. I am now in that same position. My function is that of gathering up what is past, there is nothing new to say.

I want to look back a little, and perhaps make suggestions as to what lies ahead for us. We are determined that this effort shall not finish here, but that it should provide a springboard for the action which, as we are becoming increasingly aware, is important in a number of directions.

Just before the Second World War Charles Morgan, a very fashionable novelist of the period, and a dramatic critic of considerable note, wrote a play called <u>The Flashing Stream</u>. In that play the central character, a brilliant woman mathematician was joining a naval research station. I recall the actress, Margaret Rawlings, saying:

> It's all new to-night. Soon I shall know every scar on the leather of this chair. And the ink-stain on that desk. Whose desk is it?

The character was looking forward to a period of several months in an unaccustomed situation. I thought, as we all gathered, that we were in something of that situation, we were strange to each other. It must have been an atmosphere of considerable strangeness, particularly for those who had come from some considerable distances. You came to know the scratches and the inkblots on our characters so well and so quickly, and I think it was entirely due to that perception that we were able to function well from the start, and not reach the final evening thinking, "if only it were beginning now." It is apparent that we have

232

absorbed so much that we are exhausted. Above all, we have established contact with those countries where the situation relating to writing for children was not really well known to us. There has been an enormous amount of interest, and a lot of it has been the discovery of much that is being well done. But so soon as one begins to think of that, one thinks rapidly of the vast undone. We have so much more to do than we have as yet accomplished.

There are problems which we must face if any further progress is to be made. For one thing, those of us who inhabit the world of books need to pull ourselves up sharply from time to time, and to remember that children do not live solely to read. Reading is an incident in their lives, albeit an important incident in a child's development. Children are not reading machines, there are certain impediments to their reading pleasure, which we could dismiss with a shrug of our shoulders, as none of our business, because we are concerned only with their reading. Without some cooperation on our part, however, they have little chance of developing the reading potential which will add to their enjoyment and to their stature as human beings. It has been made all too obvious in the preceding papers, that poverty, hunger and lack of medical care must be overcome before children are presented with books, or even with a basic education. In the words of Carvallo de Núñez, "Children who lack food cannot enjoy fantasy." Although one hears the voices so often, from those who say, "Oh, what nonsense, I'd sooner read than eat any day," those voices always come from well fed, well nurtured bodies. They come from those who are going back to homes of security and strength. We can never hope that the work of our writers and artists can have the impact which it should in countries where poverty, above all else, is the basic human condition which needs to be remedied.

Those of us who can simplify some of our problems into bilingualism, even if we're not sure what the other language is within the bilingual bracket, know that the language problems of Singapore or the communication problems of the hundred and twenty languages of the Soviet Union, make the situation in Canada seem almost inexpressibly simple. Yet without an attack on language problems the fruits of the full flowering of writing for children can never be developed.

We are naturally concerned when we hear that in countries where reading ability has been taken for granted, reading skills begin to fail. Time and again in our

discussions we have discovered that the readers who needed
material for a particular stage of personal development did
not have the reading ability to master that appropriate material.   Consequently there follows the call to simplify and
oversimplify, to write the answers to the world's problems
in four-letter words on a postage stamp.   There are things
which play into the hands of this problem.   I wish to invoke
no old bogey, but nothing has concerned me more than the
fear of what can happen to growing populations when they
are exposed to what is currently offered as television fare
on this continent.   It is not simply that the time involved is
taken from something which might be a better pursuit.   We
cannot deny that we have a medium of great promise but,
to date, it is one of negligible fulfillment.   If we continue
for much longer to feed pap, not only to children but to
adults also, then the teeth will rot and decay.   We are
likely to have a generation which is incapable of critical
thinking because it is not, for much of the day, given material which requires critical thought; and when critical
thought decays, the way is open for all the worst excesses
of political demagogy and commercial exploitation.   The
program which the CBC put on a few weeks ago, entitled
The Great Canadian Culture Hunt, when it covered, on successive evenings, publishing and then television, was a terrible reminder of the depths to which even the CBC is prepared to acknowledge we have sunk.   One felt at the end of
the program on television that they were themselves admit-
ting that there was little left to be done, but to pull the
plugs out, let the lights fade, and all go on home.

There are some problems, apparently small in themselves, which are very widespread in their effect.   One to
which I must make reference is a basic issue so far as authorship is concerned and one which will torment us for
several years yet.   It is quite obvious that there is a growing body of fine writers and fine artists emerging in many
countries.   Publishers are seeking to be alert to recognize
this increasing competence and readers must be prepared to
lend an eye and an ear to the products of their talent.   But
an overriding problem still remains and grows larger every
day for the creative writer or artist.   The ever-increasing
cost of raw materials and of labor has resulted in the price
of books soaring to unbelievable heights and we have no
reason to believe that the topmost point has yet been reached.
Some simplistic minds argue that these heightened book
prices are good for the author, in that they automatically
increase royalties.   Statistically, of course, this is true.

But ten per cent, or whatever else it may be, of the book's increased cost is nowhere near enough to cope with the regular and steady increase in the cost of living. The artist therefore, cannot share proportionately in the prosperity of a developing country. In Canada, for example, those who pay lip service to the importance of books for children and young people can feel nothing but shame when Ruth Nichols has to admit to a total annual income from her writings of twenty-five hundred dollars a year. This is not adequate recompense for one whose first writings have enjoyed critical acclaim. Appreciative criticism is of enormous value to a young writer, but it does not spread very far on the breakfast toast. Similarly, Canada has greeted Elizabeth Cleaver as an artist with a glorious and expanding talent and we stand proudly on international occasions and listen to others joining with us in praise. Yet she, too, has to reveal that she cannot live on the proceeds of conferences and royalties alone.

There are those among us who know that we should blush that this can be so. As book prices rise they pass more and more out of the purchasing power of individuals and into the realm of institutional purchase. This is gratifying for the author or the artist in every sense other than the economic one. Since the author wishes to communicate a message or a sense of pleasure, it is gratifying to look at multiple copies of books in libraries, and to observe how many people have received the message, or have derived the pleasure. The message goes on and on, week after week, and month after month, the pleasure builds for generations. The administrative mind of the library, hardened by budget cuts and financial problems, takes pleasure in the accumulation of so much value for the price of one initial purchase. Re-binding can grant a second life to an exhausted child, which was once of pristine beauty and promise. The author, we are sometimes told, should feel pride that libraries have selected this work for the treatment, in preference to the others which have been rejected. Maybe the book sold originally for ten dollars, maybe the author received a whole crisp dollar bill in recompense; how inconsiderate of these authors to want to eat, while readers are enjoying their genius free of a direct charge.

I have supported the principle of public lending right throughout all the postwar years. I have supported it as a measure of the most elementary justice, because artists and writers deserve something better from the communities they

serve than a starving neglect. I have no doubt that it will
come, in some form or another, in every country which
tends towards a civilized and civilizing outlook. The length
of time which it takes governments to enact the necessary
legislation is profoundly regrettable, the opposition of the
library profession is irresponsible, but we must remain
confident that the dawn will break. In the meantime, we
who have been inspired by the work of authors and artists
should give whatever support we can to advance the day
when it is not necessary for them to starve in order to
serve us. Until that time comes, we shall continue to rely
on their artistic integrity, secure in the knowledge that they
will serve us better than we serve them. As Ruth Nichols
said, "I will continue to write for the joy of others, as
well as for myself."

I hope that our guests within this country will not
feel themselves to have been imposed upon, if I say that
we had one purely local objective in the planning of this
Conference. We wished to see Canadian writing, illustrating and publishing for children against the background of
other countries. It has been apparent throughout that every
country, every region of every country gives evidence of its
own distinctive flavor. Nevertheless, like a good country
stew, the individual characteristics lose themselves in the
whole. The conference has shown that it is possible to
think and speak about writing for children irrespective of
national or linguistic boundaries. There is a commonwealth
of children, a universality among them, which gives us hope
for the multi-cultural communities which are likely to become more numerous throughout the world. It is unrealistic
not to allow oneself to dream that the children on this tiny
world could make a more successful attempt to live in a
spirit of mutual trust, justice and love than the adult world
has done. Somewhere along the road from childhood to age,
imagination slackens, doubt and suspicion increase. A vision of themselves and a deeper understanding and sympathy
for others will help children in the future to extend the
years of concern farther than we have done in our generations. But this means that each of us, working in our own
fields, in our own languages and in our own regions of the
world, must develop a critical awareness of what we are
doing, and above all of what we are failing to accomplish.

If we are to establish a chain of writing for children,
then each link must be as strong, and this includes being as
idiosyncratic as possible. There was a time when some

writers knew that their influence would spread no further
than the boundaries of their own language. Now language
skills are increasing, even if only slowly, but more and
more is being translated, and children will increasingly be
able to sample the best of world writing. The local problems which face us have, consequently, an international setting. In one sense there are no local problems any more.

In common with most countries, Canada has its difficulties. During the six years in which I have been in Canada one or two bristles from this country's hair shirt have
become very familiar. The most heartfelt cry, next to the
odyssey for the Canadian identity, has been: what is wrong
with Canadian publishing? It is highly probable that these
two questions have related answers. Many people have
found their true identity in their literature, their history,
their music, their art--and nowhere else. An understanding
of what a people stands for is a subject worthy of the highest realms of creative endeavor.

The subject of Canadian publishing is a large one,
but some questions regarding the book trade as a whole suggest themselves. I have always maintained that a School of
Librarianship has a duty to encourage people to ask the
right questions, rather than to provide any answers. This
is all that I plan to do now. It is naive to suggest that, as
yet, there are many Canadian writers who can command an
international audience. This is not necessarily due to the
quality of the writing; it is that somewhere along the route
the marketing system does not take them out of a purely
Canadian context. Yet we admit every time we discuss the
matter that a larger market is essential for a healthy book
economy.

It is difficult to see even a healthy home market
emerging with such an extraordinary poverty of bookshops in
Canada. Outlets there are, but bookshops are rare. If we
ignore the role which a good bookshop and a good bookseller
can play as an integral part of a book trade, we are liable
to be led into error. There is also an appalling dearth of
genuine reviewing journals. There are a few notices, but
very very few reviews. Above all there is an almost complete absence of the kind of reviewing which can reach the
audience which is terribly difficult to tap--the parents,
whose constant attitude towards reading and books is an
essential part of a child's intellectual development.

If I felt that Canadian publishers had one problem above all, it is that their marketing skills are nostalgically antiquated. Let me take just one example, and I choose deliberately not a writer for children. There is, in my estimation, one novelist now living in Canada who is, by an immeasurable distance, ahead of any other. A writer who was utterly unknown to me when I left England and is, to the best of my knowledge, not available in England. For three or four years after I came to Canada I asked almost everyone I met: who are the current Canadian writers that I should know? It was a long time before I was introduced to Gabrielle Roy, a novelist who deserves to have the world-wide acclaim which has been accorded, and so rightly accorded, to a somewhat similar author, Willa Cather.

Gabrielle Roy has done all that an author can, but it remains a mystery why she has not been promoted to a larger reading public. One is tempted to believe that Canadian publishing has inherited a death wish or a desire not to succeed. There are many publishing problems which I know are not exclusively Canadian. They are issues of considerable complexity, and many people, in many different fields of children's literature--authors, publishers, readers, parents--have been advised, in a variety of ways, to stop worrying about it, to let nature take its course. We are sometimes told it does not matter very much anyway, adopting the phrase "... you're wasting your time." The eternal gospel of despair.

I am asking that we should not forget the smallness of the world in which we live. The multicultural and multilingual problems of Singapore are, of course, a problem for the Singaporeans. Carvallo de Núñez speaks of children living in one of the remote villages of Peru; nobody has ever put a book into their hands, and if they did, they couldn't read it. This is a problem for Peru, as it is for all the other countries where similar situations exist. But we must never attempt to deny that these examples are the responsibility of us all. For over three hundred years we have listened to, but not heeded, the voice of John Donne: "any man's death diminishes me, because I am involved in Mankind." Throughout this venture we have all offered our hands in gestures of greeting and of friendship. Now we set out to return to our respective places around the rim of this Pacific. If we keep our arms extended we need not part, because our ring can be complete. If our authors keep on writing our voices can be heard through them, and nation

will continue to speak unto nation. Our children and their
children need not remain in the ignorance of each other
which has clouded our recent years.

In my early years in library education, in the immediate post-war years, I conducted a regular survey with my
students. I used to ask how many of them, assuming that
the age for retirement remained constant, would still be
active in librarianship beyond the year two thousand. This
was done to counteract the feeling that any ideas which we
were discussing were not applicable to the nineteen fifties.
I used to explain that we were preparing for the work which
they would be doing in the prime of their years, somewhere
around the year two thousand and one. There was no call
for us to bridle our imagination by present limitations or
conditions. We were the guardians of the hope of the future.

In the course of time, maybe around the year two
thousand and twenty-five, men and women will be deliberat-
ing on matters of world importance. They will be making
decisions which will determine whether mankind is prepared
to grant the wish which we were told the grade-one children
in the Soviet Union voice every day: "... let there be
peace." The children will be those who are depicted in a
haunting photograph in a book from China, the children in
the hills of Peru, the hot villages of Mexico, and the language complex of Singapore, from New Zealand and Australia, from far south in the Pacific to Japan in the north.
All these children will make up the world which we relin-
quish to them.

The minds of those in whose hands the great decisions will be placed will be influenced during their most
formative years by the books which we write, illustrate,
publish, buy, disseminate and read to children. We can,
if we wish, say that it is unimportant or, that the problems
are too difficult. Or we can resolve to conduct ourselves
in the spirit of the closing words of Tennyson's <u>Ulysses</u>:

> ... Come, my friends,
> 'Tis not too late to seek a newer world.
> Push off, and sitting well in order smite
> The sounding furrows; for my purpose holds
> To sail beyond the sunset, and the baths
> Of all the western stars, until I die.
> It may be that the gulfs will wash us down:
> It may be we shall touch the Happy Isles,

And see the great Achilles, whom we knew.
Tho' much is taken, much abides; and tho'
We are not now that strength which in old days
Moved earth and heaven; that which we are, we
    are;
One equal temper of heroic hearts,
Made weak by time and fate, but strong in will
To strive, to seek, to find, and not to yield.

CONTRIBUTORS

ANNE ANDERSON is a writer and teacher of Cree and produces all the books in Cree that are used in schools and universities. She teaches Cree at Grant McEwan College and in night classes. She is owner and manager of Cree Productions in Edmonton which prints and distributes her publications as well as displaying her art work and herbal remedies. She is also widely recognized as a teller of Cree legends.

CLAUDE AUBRY grew up in the Laurentians and attended university in Montreal. He is Director of the Ottawa Public Library and of the Eastern Ontario Regional Library System. Two of his books for children, Les Iles du Roi Maha Maha II (The King of the Thousand Islands), and Le Loup de Noël (The Christmas Wolf), won the Canadian Children's Book of the Year Award for French-Canadian books in 1962 and 1965. His most recent book, Agouhanna, is also available in French and English.

DAVID A. BAIN is an educational psychologist in the Faculty of Education, The University of British Columbia. He received his M.A. from the University of Toronto in Child Psychology and his Ph.D. from the University of Maryland in Human Development. Dr. Bain is co-founder and Chairman of the B.C. Council for Human Development and was Co-Chairman of the Futurology and Education Conference at Simon Fraser University in 1973. He is the author of many articles in educational journals.

EDWARD BLISHEN has worked in England as a journalist, school teacher and university lecturer, and is now a full-time writer and part-time broadcaster. He has edited many books for children, written adult novels and wrote, with Leon Garfield, The God Beneath the Sea (winner of the 1970 Carnegie Medal), and The Golden Shadow, both of which are modern interpretations of Greek mythology.

241

GRAHAM BOOTH was born in London but grew up in Victoria, British Columbia. He was graduated from UCLA and received his master's degree in Fine Arts from the University of Southern California. Mr. Booth--author, designer, and active lecturer on the illustration of children's books-- has appeared on numerous panels concerned with children's literature and has received many awards for his work. He is the illustrator of the Mark Taylor "Henry Books" and his Spring Peepers, with text by Judy Hawes, received Honorable Mention in the Children's Science Book Award 1975. He teaches art at Fullerton Junior College, California.

CARLOTA CARVALLO DE NÚÑEZ is an artist and writer in Peru. She has written many children's stories, plays and songs, and has won awards for both her painting and her writing.

ELIZABETH CLEAVER was born in Montreal and studied art there. Her illustrations for The Wind Has Wings won the first Canadian Association of Children's Librarians Award for illustrations in 1971, and two Indian legends she illustrated, How Summer Came to Canada and The Mountain Goats of Temlaham won honorable mention for the same award. Her illustrations also won honorable mention from the Hans Christian Andersen Jury and in 1974 her Hungarian legend (published in English and French), The Miraculous Hind, won the Canadian Children's Book of the Year Award. Currently she is interested in combining printmaking and shadow puppets.

MAY CUTLER is the founder and President of Tundra Books of Montreal. Since her first publications in 1967, many Tundra books have won awards and prizes, including Takashima's A Child in Prison Camp, Blades' Mary of Mile 18 and Kurelek's A Prairie Boy's Winter, and her own book The Last Noble Savage. Mrs. Cutler was born in Montreal and holds an M.A. degree from McGill University and an M.A. in journalism from Columbia University. She has worked as a teacher and journalist.

TONI DE GEREZ lives in Guanajuato, Mexico. She is an author, critic and lecturer in children's literature. She has collected folklore for children under the title 2-Rabbit, 7-Wind Poems from Ancient Mexico, Retold from Nahuatl Texts.

SHEILA A. EGOFF is a professor at the School of

Librarianship, University of British Columbia, where her
specialties are Literature for Children and Young People
and Public Library Services for Children and Young People.
She is the author of The Republic of Childhood: A Critical
Guide to Canadian Children's Literature and editor (with Ash-
ley and Stubbs) of Only Connect: Readings in Children's
Literature.

LEON GARFIELD worked as a biochemist until his success
as an author allowed him to devote himself to writing full-
time. His first published book, Jack Holborn, won the
Boy's Clubs of America Junior Book Award. His second,
Devil-in-the-Fog, won the Manchester Guardian Award for
Children's Fiction in 1967. His third, Smith, won the Arts
Council prize of 1969--Best for Older Children published
1966-68. Both Smith and Devil-in-the-Fog have been serialized on television. In 1970 he and Edward Blishen won the
Carnegie Medal for their book on Greek myths, The God Beneath the Sea. This note does not include all of Leon Garfield's books for children and his latest one, Mirror, Mirror, was published in 1976.

KAY HILL has written extensively for radio and television.
Her book, And Tomorrow the Stars, a biography of John
Cabot, won the Canadian Children's Book of the Year Award
in 1969. Glooscap and His Magic is one of her books of
Indian legends. She presently lives in Ketch Harbour, Nova
Scotia.

MOMOKO ISHII has had a varied career in Japan, all concerned with children and their books. She is a writer, a
translator and in addition runs a children's library. She
introduced to Japanese children such books as Winnie-the-
Pooh and The Tale of Peter Rabbit. Her own most famous
book is Nonchan Kumo Ni Noru (Nonchan Riding on a Cloud).

MARGARET JOHNSTON is head of Boys and Girls Services
for the Toronto Public Libraries. She was born in Hamilton, Ontario and received her Arts degree and degree in
Librarianship from the University of Toronto. In the Toronto
Public Library she held various positions as a Children's
Librarian and as a Branch Head and became Head of the
Children's Department in 1970. She is well known on both
the national and international scene in children's literature
and children's librarianship through her work as a consult-
ant, on committees (the Newbery-Caldecott Award Committee) and through her articles in various journals.

JEAN E. KARL is Vice-President and Director of the Children's Book Department, Atheneum Publishing. Atheneum has a strong record of award-winning children's books. She is the author of From Childhood to Childhood, (a book about children's books) and her science fiction book for children will be published this Spring. As the publisher and editor of thirteen books by Christie Harris, she has a strong link with Canada.

LUBOW KUZ was born in Germany, of Ukrainian descent, and came to Canada in 1950. As a trained psychologist her special field is Developmental Psycho-Linguistics and in working with young children she became especially interested in multi-culturalism in Canada.

ELSIE LOCKE has worked as a librarian and a writer in New Zealand. She has written two children's historical novels, The Runaway Settlers and The End of the Harbour, and many historical and fictional articles for the New Zealand School Journal.

SUZANNE MARTEL has gained great popularity as a writer of science fiction for children. Her two best known books are Titralak and Surréal 3000, which has been translated into English as The City Underground. She has an overall interest in and knowledge of children's literature in Quebec and in 1972 was Présidente de la Rencontre de Communication-Jeunesse.

MIRIAM MORTON is an author, a translator and book editor and has also worked as a social worker and a nursery school teacher. She is the editor and translator of many works from Russian literature, including A Harvest of Russian Children's Literature (1967), The Moon Is Like a Silver Sickle: A Celebration of Poetry by Soviet Children (1972), and Twenty-Two Tales for Young Children by Leo Tolstoy (1969). Her own works include: The Arts and the Soviet Child: The Esthetic Education of Children in the U.S.S.R. (1972) and Pleasures and Palaces: The After-School Activities of Soviet Children (for young people) 1972. She has also translated from the French Colette Vivier's The House of the Four Winds (1969). Miriam Morton writes: "The central motivation for my work is to make available to American young readers translations from the outstanding humanistic literature published in Russia and in France. A second motivation is to reveal the basic elements in Soviet child and youth culture in my writings for young readers and for American educators."

RUTH NICHOLS was born in Toronto and educated in Ontario and British Columbia. She studied Religious Studies at the University of British Columbia and wrote her first fantasy A Walk out of the World when she was 18. She won the Canadian Children's Book of the Year Award in 1973 for her second book, The Marrow of the World.

VILASINI PERUMBULAVIL is Coordinator of Children's Services, National Library of Singapore. She was born in Singapore and graduated from the University of Malaya in History, and with a Diploma in Education. She received her Diploma in Librarianship from the New Zealand Library School (Wellington). She has written many articles on children's reading and children's librarianship, particularly as these apply in Singapore and Asia.

SAMUEL ROTHSTEIN is a professor at the School of Librarianship, The University of British Columbia and the School's founder and first Director. He is internationally known in library circles as a speaker and as the author of numerous articles and essays in librarianship. He is a graduate of The University of British Columbia with an M.A. in French and of the University of Illinois with a Ph.D. in Librarianship. In 1971 he was honored by York University with the degree of Doctor of Letters.

IVAN SOUTHALL has worked as a free-lance author in Australia since 1948. He has written many adult and children's books. Three of his children's books have won the Australian Children's Book of the Year Award: Ash Road (1966), To the Wild Sky (1968) and Bread and Honey (1971). He was also awarded the British Carnegie Medal for Josh in 1971. He says that he "enjoys writing for children more than any other activity."

ROY STOKES is Professor and Director, School of Librarianship, University of British Columbia. He is the author of The Function of Bibliography and has revised the last two editions of Esdaile's Manual of Bibliography.